# speak
## Natur

GW00691684

What is popularly known as Nature Cure, explains the immutable, inviolable Laws of Life which govern human health in every respect.

This book shows how health can be maintained and improved by supplying the basic physical and mental needs in proper proportion. The internal insanitation is the basic cause of all diseases ranging from the common cold to the dreaded cancer.

Disease is, in reality, a diminution in the health level and cure lies in the restoration of health, in the removal of the cause(s). The Science of Nature Cure charts the sane, safe and hygienic way of regaining health.

Wisdom decrees that those who have regained health this sensible way should continue to retain it by living in tune with the Laws of Life.

The present condensation of the book is by S. Swaminathan.

*Acharya Lakshmana Sarma (1879-1965) is known the world over as the Father of Nature Cure in India. His deep knowledge of Oriental philosophy, combined with his mastery of the Sanskrit language, enabled him to supply the missing links in the System of Nature Cure, as it was at that time prevalent, and thereby enrich it. Thus, he provided a firm and scientific basis for the principles and practices of Nature Cure.*

*S. Swaminathan, a practising Nature Cure expert in New Delhi, is one of the foremost disciples of the Acharya. Before his initiation into Nature Cure by the Acharya, he had his initiation into Yoga and Philosophy by Sri Pranava Brahmendra Ananda Saraswati.*

# Your Health Guide Series

# Speaking of
# NATURE CURE

## K. LAKSHMANA SARMA
## &
## S. SWAMINATHAN

**NEW DAWN PRESS, INC.**
UK • USA • INDIA

NEW DAWN PRESS GROUP

Published by New Dawn Press Group
New Dawn Press, Inc., 244 South Randall Rd # 90, Elgin, IL 60123
e-mail: sales@newdawnpress.com

New Dawn Press, 2 Tintern Close, Slough, Berkshire, SL1-2TB, UK
e-mail: ndpuk@mail.newdawnpress.com

New Dawn Press (An Imprint of Sterling Publishers (P) Ltd.)
A-59, Okhla Industrial Area, Phase-II, New Delhi-110020
e-mail: sales@sterlingpublishers.com
ghai@nde.vsnl.net.in

*Speaking of Nature Cure*
© 1993, The Nature Cure Publishing House, Pudukkottai
ISBN 1 84557 028 6

PRINTED IN INDIA

# Preface

The Science of Natural Hygiene is not a technical subject, the property of any exclusive body of professionals for exploitation of the people for profit, but a Liberating Science which seeks to restore to them the independence and blessings they have lost due to their ignorance of it. It will be seen in this book that independence from drugs and doctors, and even from professional Nature Doctors, is of profound value for Health and Happiness.

Nor is this a dry study. It is by itself a Liberal Education, which gives a normal and intellectual satisfaction that cannot be had anywhere except in the ethico-religious philosophy of our ancient sacred lore, called the *Upanishads* or the *Vedantas*. In fact, it will be found by the reader that this Hygienic Philosophy is an integral part of that philosophy and is pervaded by its fundamental truths.

Those who study the subject in depth and practise it in their daily lives can become self-reliant. The author wants that everyone should be his/her own doctor.

Nature Cure is a science by practising which the sick become healthy, and healthy become healthier. It is for all. Its approach is wholly constructive. It does not employ any poisons, either of vegetable, animal or mineral origin.

Let everyone care for his/her body, mind and spirit as intended by Nature.

*S. Swaminathan*

# By the Editor

The *magnum opus* of Acharaya Lakshmana Sarma is presented here in a condensed form, practically in his own words. I have given the most careful attention to it, to ensure that all the main features of the book are retained in this edition.

However, those who want to have a comprehensive study of the subject may study the original work published by the Nature Cure Publishing House, Ganeshnagar, Pudukkottai, Pin-622001 (India). They may, with advantage, also go through the monthly journal *The Life Natural* published from Ganeshnagar, Pudukkottai. Each volume of the journal is a mine of information for those who want to master Nature Cure.

The Acharya wanted everyone to be his own doctor. And the Editor hopes that this condensed edition would help further in achieving this objective.

142 Jamrudpur,
Opp. LSR College,                              S. Swaminathan
New Delhi-110 048

# CONTENTS

# ONE

# Divine Science of Health

Health is man's greatest wealth, which means that he who has health must cherish it with care, lest he should lose it. To this end he must have adequate knowledge of how to live for health.

Health is not merely the absence of disease; it is a *positive* quality of the living body, of which fitness for one's work and happiness are distinguishing marks. Indeed, as we shall see later, health alone is real, and not disease, which is only a symptom of a fall in one's health level.

## Curing Disease the Right Way

The cure of disease is not a distinct science but is an integral part of what may be called The Life Natural or Natural Hygiene. That is to say, it regards the cure of disease as one of the concomitants of the recovery of lost health, and not something independent of it. Efforts to cure disease which are not aimed at health-recovery, are therefore quackery even though practised by 'experts' — that is, by men who are licensed by the State. That this is so will appear from the following confession by Sir James Barr, Vice-President of the British Medical Association: *"The treatment of disease is not a science, not even a refined art, but a thriving industry."* And this remains true and will always be true.

In God's creation there is a mysterious relation between ends and means. This means that for achieving any particular end one must employ the appropriate means; otherwise, the end that is reached will not be what we desire. That is why it is said that *the end does not justify the means*. What this means is that improper means must not be employed.

Applying this principle to the quest of health, we have to understand that we must proceed in accordance with the teachings of this True Science of Health, wherein the giver of health is recognised as God Himself. It is for this reason that we designate this science as 'The Divine Science of Health'.

## Law of Cause and Effect

Human health and happiness, as everything else in the world, is governed by the Laws of Nature, which are inviolable, inexorable, irrevocable. One of these is the *Law of Cause and Effect.* As you sow, so shall you reap. Those who live in tune with the Laws of Life keep their body and mind clean and maintain health. Hygienic living is the cause, health is the effect. Conversely, unhygienic living is the cause, disease is the effect. Unhygienic means do not bring health, but loss of health.

## The Ultimate Effect of Medical Ministrations

Unfortunately, in modern days the average man takes his health for granted, that is, he assumes that for him health is an inexhaustible possession, which will not be lost by any amount of self-indulgence, in violation of the Laws of Hygiene. He has also an inexhaustible faith in the "ability" of medicos to restore him to health as often as he loses it. Actually, because these men do *not* employ hygienic means, they confer only a *semblance* of health; true health cannot be won through their ministrations, because the means used by them are wholly *unhygienic.*

The final effect of medical ministrations is to land the patient in the third and last stage of disease, in which the bodily substances — blood, flesh, nerves and the organs — become degenerate; from this state of degeneracy arise diseases affecting the heart, lungs or brain, of the body as a whole; the much dreaded cancer is just one of them.

## Medical Failures: Recovery through Natural Methods

There are always quite a large number of *medical failures;* these are patients who have been reduced to a state of utter hopelessness, being sufferers from doctor-made diseases, mostly chronic, and often of a fatal tendency, for which the medicos have admittedly no cure. A very few of them come to hear and accept the message of hope given by this Divine Science and are redeemed from their hopeless state and given a new lease of life and health. Many of these redeemed souls become faithful followers of the Life Natural and thus *stay cured* and enjoy a high degree of positive health for the rest of their lives. Also they are their own doctors. So today Nature Cure happens to be the system of last resort.

## Why Drug Treatment Should not be.Resorted

In brief, the practice of medicine is based on a policy of violence to life and the living body, tending towards the ruin of Health, while that of Hygiene proceeds on the principle of non-violence, which is in *harmony* with the Laws of Life. This means that the two are poles apart — that each is opposed to the other, and that they would cancel out each other if combined.

Real, that is *radical*, cure can come only by removal of the cause of disease which is the sum-total of past unhygienic conduct and persistence in it. Therefore, to escape from the cumulative effects of following the wrong path, the patient must stop living unhygienically and begin to live in the right way, thereby making amends for his past mistakes. Continuing to rely on doctors is therefore a suicidal policy. That way the cause is never removed. In the words of Dr. Weir-Mitchell: *"At the back of disease lies a cause and the cause no drug can reach."* Drugs, vaccines and serums do not remove the cause of disease; they only aggravate the ill health that is there, and thus sow the seeds of more and more diseases.

## God The Indwelling Healer

There is a mysterious Power inside the living body which is ever actively safeguarding life and health and even curing diseases in a radical way by restoring lost health, provided there is no foolish intermeddling. In the West, hygienists call this Indwelling Power 'Nature'. But from our sacred lore we learn that Nature is just the Divine Power that creates, sustains, destroys and recreates the universe. She is immanent in all creatures and maintains them in health so long as they do not seriously transgress Her Laws, which are Laws of God, because *She is not separate from God.* So it must be understood that this blessed science is a Divine Science and that God Himself is the Indewelling Healer in all creatures and also the Teacher of this True Science.

## Unity of all True Knowledge

Some readers may argue that it is improper to bring in the name of God here. Our reply is that we believe not only in God, but also in the fundamental unity and inseparability of all true knowledge, and it comes naturally to us to trace to God all the blessings that we enjoy in life. Among these blessings is right knowledge by which we live to some good purpose. We concede to others the right to accept only that which appeals to *them* as true and to reject all else. That does not prevent us from teaching the science as we understand it. But whoever wishes to follow this system must at least accept that there is, in the living body, a mysterious Power, *not known to science,* which hygienists and even some doctors call Nature's Healing Power, *Vis Medicatrix Naturae.* We shall deal with the unity of all true knowledge later. Those who believe in God, *whatever the religion they follow,* will find no difficulty in accepting the teaching given here, because we shall steer clear of all sectarianism, as far as possible; not only Hindus, but also Buddhists, Muslims, Christians, Parsis and others will find that this teaching is in harmony with their own religions.

## Become Self reliant

The Life Natural is both preventive and curative, the prevention being effected by building up better health. Allopathic preventives are different; they prevent disease by *giving* disease, which is wrong as will be shown later.

The best policy for the health lover to follow is to become and remain independent of *all* doctors — not only those that practise violence but also of those that profess to practise non-violence. That means that every follower should aim at being his own doctor, subject, of course, to guidance by Divine Grace. Guided by Grace one should do all that needs to be done and avoid doing whatever ought not to be done. As for the return of lost health, one must rely on God alone. Reliance on God, according to Bhagavan Ramana Maharshi, is true self-reliance, because God is no other than one's Real Self. That such independence is alone blessed was neatly expressed by Bhagavan Manu, the earliest Law Giver, in the following lines:

Dependence on others is misery;
Dependence on oneself is happiness

## Natural Hygiene—A Domestic Science

It should be understood that this hygiene is the only true science of *Rejuvenation*. In favourable conditions it restores and prolongs youth.

For practising this system with success it is not necessary to master the intricate details of anatomy, physiology, pathology, toxicology and pharmacology. A single textbook by a highly cultured and experienced master is enough for guidance. Hence it is our wish and prayer that this science be studied and practised, by the Grace of God, as a Domestic Science, by every one in his own home. There should be no dependence even on one that professes to be a Nature Cureist or Hydienist. It is difficult to find a professional of such profound intelligence and of such noble character as would be worthy of implicit trust. Also there are principles involved in this science which would be unintelligible to the vast majority of people. In particular, I may here mention Vital Economy, a principle of the greatest importance in the practice of this science. But this principle seems to be insufficiently understood by a great number of professors of Nature Cure. The follower must therefore aim at perfect independence and qualify himself for it by devout study and practical experience, always relying on God for guidance. This will be explained later.

# Druglessness

# TWO

Nature cure is based on the transcendantal truths of Metaphysics as taught in our ancient Vedantic lore. Other systems are based on a more or less complete ignorance of those truths. Hence there is an irreconcilable difference — a mutual antagonism between this science and all the other sciences. For one to become a real follower of this science, it is necessary to renounce one's faith in, and allegiance to, every other system in which he may have had faith before.

It should be clearly understood that what is bad for the healthy is also bad for the sick. No one claims that drugs are good for the healthy. Extensive observations have proved, if proof were necessary, that drugs are ruinous to health in the long run, and that drugged patients with the passage of time become less and less curable. Hence, all forms of drugging must be given up, first. Then alone one can take to Nature Cure, whether simply for health culture, or for cure of disease. It is also necessary that the renunciation of the other systems and the acceptance of this science should be once for all.

Drugs are unassimilable foreign matter, poisonous in their very nature though in different degrees. Sometimes they are immediately fatal. Always, they are ruinous to health. And this is true, in whatever way drugs find entrance into the body. They may get in through contamination of food from metallic cooking vessels, through contact with metals in occupation, or by medication. The giving of a drug by a licensed poisoner does not change its real nature. Hence, drugging should be totally renounced. Even the so-called medical prophylactics, which medicos say are preventive of future disease, must be renounced. This will be dealt with later.

## Law of Dual Effects

Drugging is of two kinds, based on the principles of drug-selection and dosage. There was formerly only one system of drugging, now called allopathy. In this system drugs were always chosen empirically, by 'trial and error'. An apparent and temporary benefit was accepted as proof of the effectiveness of the drug. Only the immediate effects were considered, the remote ones were as far as possible ignored.

There is a Law of Nature regarding effects called the Law of Dual Effects, which was first stated clearly by Dr. Lindlahr. It says that every cause has as a rule two effects, an immediate and a remote one. The former is transient. The latter is more or less permanent, and is always the opposite of the immediate effect. The real effect is the remote effect, and not the immediate one. If the immediate effect seems good, the remote effect is evil. Also, if the immediate effect is seemingly evil or unpleasant the remote or real effect will be both good and pleasant. Applying this test to allopathic medicine, it is impossible to escape the conclusion that allopathic medication is bad. We shall deal with this point a little later.

## Homoeopathy Based on Wrong Assumption

A new method of drugging was invented not very long ago by Hahnemann, to which he gave the name of homoeopathy, because in it the drugs used were 'similar' to the disease, being those that would give the disease to a healthy person. He it was that gave the old system the name of 'allopathy'. As 'pathy' means disease, the name is quite appropriate.

Hahnemann prepared his drugs in very attenuated doses by a method called 'potentisation'. In each dose the drug was in so small a quantity that its presence cannot be traced by chemical analysis.

The whole of homoeopathy is based on the wrong assumption made by Hahnemann, that "Nature is a *poor* healer". Nature cure would be impossible but for the fact that Nature is not only a very powerful healer, but actually She is the *only* healer there is. There is no other.

* Because of this meaning of 'pathy' it is wrong to call Nature Cure 'Naturopathy' as many do. It is Naturotherapy.

7

Homoeopathy is like allopathy in being based on the distinction between doctor and patient. Hence it is not going to help in solving the health problem of the masses.

## Progression of Disease

Diseases are not many. There is only one disease all through life, from birth to death. But this one disease appears again and again out of an inward abnormal condition, and reappears from out of it but with a progressive change in its outward features and symptoms, in the degree of its seriousness and in the difficulty of its cure. This progressive change falls into three distinct stages. In the first stage the disease is of the kind called acute. It is transient. There is a considerable degree of health and vitality. Hence it is possible to cure it by removing the cause, the internal condition. Such a cure is possible only in a natural way; it is not at all possible by drugging, nor by any other method which does not consist in making amends for past mistakes and in reforming one's mode of life afterwards. Usually an acute disease is suppressed by medical violence, whereby it is driven in, to merge into its cause, the abnormal condition. In this process the abnormality of that condition is greatly increased, and hence worse and more difficult disease forms arise out of it, leading the patient to the second stage. Now the diseases are apparently milder; but they are more deep-rooted and obstinate. These are called chronic diseases. The same mode of antivital treatment being followed, the third stage is reached, of destructive diseases. Medicos call them degenerative diseases. For a long time there has been a steady increase in the incidence of these diseases. When this stage is reached, death is near at hand. But every hour is full of pain, and death does not come soon enough. This long view of disease progression gives us a clear perspective of the true nature and effects of allopathic practice.

## Retrogression of Disease

Nature cure alone can cause a reversal of this progress from health to incurable disease and premature death after a period of intolerable suffering. Even after the destructive stage is reached, it is possible for the victim of allopathic stupidity to be led back to health, if only he discards the medicos and takes refuge in Nature. Now the progress is backwards, towards health, and hence it is called Retrogression of Disease. At first the patient goes from the destructive to the non-fatal chronic stage, and later from this to the acute stage, and finally to health.

## Even 'external use' of drugs is bad

Every allopathic 'cure' is a case of falling to a lower level of health. Every natural cure is a means of rising to a higher level of health. Thus it will appear that the wise policy is to adjure unnaturalness at once and take refuge in Nature Cure.

Drugging is equally against Nature, whether drugs are used externally or internally, as even drugs used externally do penetrate into the body and get lodged in some vital organs or tissues. If they did not penetrate at all, they would not "produce the intended effects". Dr Lindlahr has given ample proof in his book on *Iridiagnosis* to show that these drugs find lodgement inside and cause the diseases noted against them in toxicology. If and when the drugs are expelled by a course of Nature Cure, the diseases also vanish by themselves. These facts, he points out, are fully corroborated by observations of the iris of the eye according to the Science of Iridology. Also scars are formed when an external sore or wound is healed by the use of drugs. No scars are formed when the healing is effected in a natural way. Hence it stands to reason that Mother Nature strongly disapproves of the external use of drugs also.

## Surgical Interferences

Surgery – due to inability of the medicos to give any relief by medication – is as a rule improper. It is a violent interference with the Order of Nature. In particular, the removal of organs or parts of the body, such as the appendix, the tonsils and so on, is positively criminal. The removal of the teeth which is now a routine procedure on the plea that the teeth are the foci of infection and are thus causing disease of other parts, is a serious mistake. Sick teeth can be restored to health and made serviceable as before.

Nature is a far more skilful surgeon than the medicos. She knows how to detach and remove a decayed part. For example, even in the case of gangrene, where a part of the body begins to rot, Nature effects a separation of the rotting part without affecting the adjoining healthy tissue. Where boneless portions are thus got rid of, they may grow up again as before.

The experience of Nature Curists in a great number and variety of cases has proved that surgical interference is as a rule unneces-

9

sary, and is too hastily resorted to by surgeons, who are altogether ignorant of the right way of giving relief. This is amply corroborated even by some eminent members of the profession itself. Dr Sir William Arbuthnot Lane, who was in his day the first among surgeons, said that the very existence of surgery as a branch of the medical system is a confession of the failure of drugs to prevent the conditions for which surgery is resorted to as a remedy. In particular, it is a grave crime of the medical profession, that they cut out and remove whole organs such as the tonsils or the appendix. While it cannot be stated as an unqualified rule that no surgical operation should be allowed, it is a fact proved by experience that these excisions of parts of the body are unnecessary – that it is almost always possible to save the organs from the surgeon's knife by a natural course of cure. This has been amply proved by many doctors among whom we may mention Dr. Lindlahr, Dr. B.P. Allinson and Dr. L.N. Chowdhury. In very few cases indeed does it happen that an operation is urgently required. Hence it is proper as a rule to try natural methods for saving the organs and to postpone the operations meanwhile.

## Dr. Allinson on Allopathy

Medical theory and practice have been roundly condemned by a few honest and intelligent members of the profession itself. This is sought to be countered by the plea that medical science has made great progress in recent times, and that therefore those pronouncements are out of date. Dr. Allinson of England has expressed the truth about allopathy in these words: "This is a system by which persons hope to sin against the laws which govern them and to avoid the penalty by taking nauseous drugs. It is an attempt to cheat Nature." This would suffice to show that medical science has not given up the false and vicious principles on which its practice is based. Among the authorities in this country who came to believe in Nature Cure may be mentioned Dr L.N. Chowdhury who died in old age around 1940. Concerning the premature death of his own wife, he said: "In our ignorance we killed her." He afterwards became a staunch advocate of Nature Cure.

In conclusion we say that allopathic treatment consists in fighting disease. This policy is absurd because 'disease' is only an alias for a fall in one's health-leval, which can be set right only by measures that will raise it. In hygienic practice, diseases are not fought against. This fighting is quackery, which Hygienic Science condemns.

# THREE

# The Philosophy of Nature Cure

Is there an entity called 'Life' existing as an independent reality? What is 'Nature'? Is there someone who is her Lord and Master? Allopathy holds that life has no independent reality, that it is just a transitory and erratic product of food combustion. Naturally it also denies Nature and God. Our firm conviction is that Life, Nature and God are all real *in their own right*. The human personality does exist, but it derives its reality from God alone.

Because of disregard of the teachings of the Enlightened Ones, and prevalence of materialistic pseudo philosophy, followers of our science get confused. The teachings of the Holy Ones, which arise from their own authentic experience of the profound Truth that underlies phenomena, are for us credible evidence, and not the babblings of men who do not know the truth of their own selves.

## Ponder over these questions

Let the reader think about these questions: What is the difference between the human or animal body before and after death and wherefore is there this difference? By whom or by whose power is this body, a load for four men, lifted and carried about with ease, and enabled to do hard work?

So long as the body lives, the microbes are powerless to do serious harm to it. But in the dead body they are able to prey upon the blood and flesh and reduce it to a mass of putrefaction very soon.

The numerous distinct organs of the body function of their own accord, without effort, or even knowledge, on our part. And they function very well in spite of handicaps, and the body lives for a considerable time.

## Life the Power Behind all Functions

So we may tentatively conclude that the body lives, protected by some mysterious Power and that when this Power abandons the body, then it is destroyed by the action of the microbes.

Then consider this phenomenon: an invisible speck of matter, coming into a dependent existence in the mother's womb, becomes endowed with a head and limbs, and in the tenth month comes out as a complete baby. By whose power does this happen?

There is also this question: How do the food essences become incorporated into the living body? Surely, there is some power that builds the body and incorporates these essences into it.

Also consider the enormous complexity of the bodily structure, and the great variety of its tissues. All these work together in co-ordination, making life possible.

The processes called disease are initiated, carried out and finally wound up, all at appropriate times. Who does all this?

Disease of an acute nature is an effort of Nature — and as a rule no help from us is needed beyond merely abstaining from eating. What does this signify?

It is found by experience that going through the prescribed methods of treating the sick is of no avail unless there is sufficient *vital* response. From this also we conclude that Life exists.

It is said by medicos that vital power comes from food. The absurdity of this belief which is patent to all that have practical experience of our system is another reason for the conviction that Life is real.

It is an undeniable fact that one who expends his vital power economically attains all the blessings of a happy life. He that does not do so is miserable most of the time. This confirms us in our conviction that Life is real.

## The Conscious Being Behind Life

But Life is unconscious, like earth or stone. How can it carry out all the varied and intricate functions of the living body, which it does, without a Conscious Being to direct and regulate its functioning? The notion that the activities going on in this world can go on without direction by a Conscious Being is a *gross superstition*. Since Life exists, there must exist also the power called Nature, the Mother of the Cosmos. And if she exists, surely there exists also someone who is her Lord and Master. It is He that is called God, self-dependent, supreme over Nature. That He *is* is beyond dispute. Let there be dispute, if it cannot be helped, about His true Nature and other relevant or irrelevant questions.

## How Maya Deludes Man

Dull-witted people who claim to be scientists entertain false notions due to the Divine Power of Illusion, called *Maya*, the cause of human ignorance. 'Nature' is Her other name. It is through Her action that man becomes deluded, more or less. And of all the men the most deluded are the imbeciles, the third-rate scientists who are devoid of the true scientific spirit, which is reflected in humility and freedom from dogmatism.

It is this Maya that creates the false interpretations of the evidence of the senses. Deluded by it these men and others misunderstand themselves and the outside world.

## Subtler than the Subtlest

The Self and the mind are far subtler entities than the subtlest things known to science. But these are subsumed as properties or attributes of gross and insentient things, the physical bodies. The former are far more enduring than the latter which come to nothingness very soon. Compared to the subtle the gross is unreal, and the subtle real. Thus said the Vedantins, and all truly cultured people accept this teaching.

## Power Behind the Mind

It cannot be said that the mind is the controlling and directing power of life because the mind, as a rule, knows nothing of the vital organs forming part of the body. The mind is really unfree, being subject to Nature. There must be someone of the nature of Consciousness, who is the lord of both. Wise people through their intimate experience of the Life Natural become fully convinced that there is a Supreme Deity, to whom even Nature is subject.

It is evident that the gross body lives by a power not ours. One must therefore take refuge at the feet of the Lord to whom that power belongs.

Whatever is inert can be moved or operated only by a sentient being; it cannot change its conditions by itself.

## Cosmos or Chaos

Here is a poser for those who deny the existence of a Supreme Being: is the universe a cosmos or a chaos? Scientists would rather admit that the world is a chaos than accept God even as a hypothesis. But if the world be a chaos then science loses its scope for its pursuit of truth. Hence the less bigoted scientists are willing to admit that the world is not a chaos, but a cosmos. That would necessarily lead to at least a hypothetical God. If this hypothesis be admitted, then further investigation would lead to its confirmation, and if a spiritual trend of mind sets in, then one automatically becomes a firm believer and devotee.

From this point of view, to the scientist God is Law and Order of the world. To the devotee, God is Grace. In the ancient sacred books this World Order was called Rita. Later it came to be called *Dharma*.

## Source of Bliss

There is another reason for believing in God as we do. There must be a Source of Bliss, from which all happiness flows. Happiness is enjoyed by all during sound sleep. In sound sleep the mind gets merged and lost in something, from which it returns on waking.

That something must be real, and must be conscious, or rather Consciousness itself. It cannot be unconscious, or unconsciousness. So say all the Buddhas, who are proficient in the Science of the Real Self.

In sound sleep the mind merges in that Real Self who is Bliss, and returns therefrom to the world, being refreshed and reinvigorated for the strains and stresses of life. This is the general rule; but there are exceptions to it. In any case, sleep is absolutely necessary for the continuance of life, a fact which no sane man denies. Only men who do not eat can get on without sleep. Whosoever eats must also sleep.

In sleep there are no objects of enjoyment. Hence the happiness of deep sleep is not mere pleasure, the outcome of mental contact with sense objects, but is the very Nature of that Great Self.

Enjoyment is therefore of two sorts; the natural and the artificial; the latter is the evanescent pleasure we derive from worldly objects; the former is the natural, uncaused, eternal Happiness of the Self, which arises from merely being alive.

It is that serene Happiness trickling through the dense sheath of ignorance into the mind which reconciles human beings to life in this world. Even the very miserable live on in the hope that some day they would be happy for some time at least before death.

"Only two persons remain immersed in Supreme Happiness, free from all worry; the unsophisticated little child and the holy one that has become one with One that is beyond the three qualities." So it is said in the *Shri Bhagavatam*. From this we shall know that there does exist a Bliss of the Real Self which is of the essence of His Nature. That bliss is pure; the happiness of the worldlywise which is only pleasure — is transient and leads to misery.

We believe that inside all creatures dwells One whose Nature is Reality-Consciousness-Bliss, by whom all creatures are prompted and enabled to live. Of this there can be no doubt.

## The Healing Power Within

God is the Indwelling Healer. To us is given the privilege of carrying out His commands, which comprise the teachings of the Life Natural. The fruit of good conduct lies in His hands alone. Though, following the custom of the world, we may talk and write as if we ourselves effect cures, it must be understood that this must not be taken seriously; for in our hearts we know that we possess neither the knowledge, nor the power, to effect cures, that the cure, the return of health, comes by His grace alone.

If it be objected that no one is able to see or know Maya, the answer is: It is the uniqueness of Maya that no one can see or know the truth about Her, except by Divine Grace, obtained by devotion to Him. God is not visible without because there He is veiled by His Own Maya. He would reveal Himself only to those who practise lifelong devotion and obedience to Him. The devotees who love Him and Him alone, see Him within them by the eye of illumina-

15

tion, and such are the Buddhas. The wise man accepts what these teachers say.

We do not seek to impose these beliefs on any one to whom they do not appeal. Everyone is free to believe what he thinks to be true. But the minimum of belief that a follower must have is this: There is some mysterious Power within us, which is intent on safeguarding our health and life as far as possible.

From all this we derive the knowledge that to deserve the Grace of God in the matter of health of anything else, we must seek to avoid violence to the *Order of Nature* which God has established.

## Gross, Subtle and Causal Bodies

From the Vedanta we also come to know that every creature is endowed with three bodies – a gross body, a subtle one and a causal one. The first is built from food. The second is made up of mind and life and cognate ingredients. The third is just Ignorance, which is the seed of the other two. Concealed by the darkness of this Ignorance, God dwells in the causal body as the Real Self.

Life is in the subtle body, along with the mind and the sense organs and the faculties of action. It is by the power of life that the mind and the gross body are joined together during one's life. Just as the electric current in light bulbs varies according to the degree of their receptivity, so too the life-force varies in the subtle bodies, according to their capacity to receive it. Not only that, the life-force in the gross bodies also varies according to the receptivity of these bodies. This variation is due to the degree of their encumbrance with foreign, toxic filth, which consists of uneliminated waste matter arising in the course of vital functioning in the disposal of excess food loads. Thus it happens that at any particular time the amount of available life-force in the physical body is always limited, a fact that to this day remains unknown to medicos as a class. But the available life-force can be economically spent, so that health may be maintained and enhanced. How this can be done is explained in the Chapter on Vital Economy, which is of profound importance for health and for cure of disease, so much so that we can say that he who is not fully enlightened on this important subject is unworthy to be either a teacher or a practitioner of this Divine Science. This is why we insist on everyone becoming his own doctor, if he can do so.

## Gandhiji on Allopathy

It must now be clear that diseases and their cure are the result of one's previous conduct. That being so, without making amends to Nature for one's hygienic sins, it is not possible to cure disease. The taking of drugs is NOT making amends for those sins. It was precisely for this reason that Mahatma Gandhi described allopathy as a Satanic science.

## Sattva, Rajas and Tamas

There are three grades of excellence and its opposite. Sattva, Rajas and Tamas. Food and medicine are also divisible according to these qualities. This will be propounded later.

Spiritual and other progress is by rising in this ladder of three grades. Degradation is by falling to a lower level. We shall not dwell further on this topic, but shall leave it to the reader to learn details from his own sacred books or spiritual gurus.

## How to Have Natural Happiness

One thing we must mention here. Man must not make pleasure – even happiness – the aim of his endeavours. Pleasure or happiness which comes as a byproduct of right living should be accepted as being quite enough. There must not be any greed for more than that. But in this way, by degrees, one will get more and more access to the Natural Happiness of the Indwelling Real Self, which will give one peace and contentment, which is the real essence of happiness.

On the other hand, he who pursues pleasures all the time suffers depletion of his vitality and becomes a victim of deep-rooted diseases, until he gives up his wrong ways and returns to Nature.

## Self-indulgence vs. Self-denial

*Self-indulgence is the great sin. Self-denial as required by the Law of God (or Nature) is the great virtue.*

Why should one not be self-indulgent? Why should one practise self-denial? The answer is that the former is a bad policy, while the latter is a wise policy. Indeed, by self-denial one becomes much happier than by self-indulgence.

The self-indulgent person miscalculates. In this world of relativity there are no certainties. Uncertainty governs all plans. The "cleverest" plans miscarry. We shall see this in the next chapter. *The Lancet* records an instance where a medical plan to do good to the people while at the same time doing violence to their personality in a way profitable to the medicos, miscarried and put them in an invidious position as enemies of the people. That they did not profit by this verdict of God on their sinful ambition makes their crime all the more unforgivable.

## This is Biology

What the sincere and earnest follower needs to know of biology has been given here. He need not go through the tangled woods of thorny trees, the big tomes on anatomy, physiology, pathology, bacteriology, etc., that have played havoc, confused medicos making them think they know all they need to know.

In the course of learning their crude art of treating the sick, they have lost their natural endowment of common sense.

# FOUR

# Prevention of Disease

Life is a mystery entirely beyond the scope of science. That is why medical men have failed to discover it and learn its secrets, in spite of 'scientific' vivisectional research. By philosophy and metaphysical studies something can be known about Life, sufficient for all practical purposes. Those who are ignorant of Life, or entertain a false notion of it are incapable of dealing with, or solving, the problem of health and immunity from disease.

In our hygienic studies we have found that health consists in the internal cleanliness of the living body. The fact that Nature, the handmaid of God, has provided a variety of organs that eliminate all kinds of morbid foreign matter shows that such cleanliness is an indispensable condition of health, which alone is, in our view, the cause of immunity from diseases of all kinds. So to be absolutely free from fear of future diseases, what is necessary is to maintain a high health level which means abundance of vitality. Measures which consist in making war on the human constitution — as stated by Dr. R.T. Trall, M.D., of the USA — are wrong, being capable of destroying health and even causing premature death.

## Sanitation – External and Internal

The chief means of preventing disease, especially zymotic diseases which are caused by the body being encumbered with foreign matter, which is toxic filth, is sanitation. This is of two kinds, external and internal.

External sanitation alone is within the scope of governmental action, through municipal corporations. Internal sanitation consists in the practice of Natural Living. This should be left to the individual. It belongs to private life. There is no such thing as 'public health'. The so-called public health is only the sum-total of private health of the great majority of people. Governments dominated by the allopathic system are utterly incompetent to deal with the problems of health. We have seen that this system is nothing but poison therapy. That part of it which deals with the prevention of disease is of the same nature, poisoning the bloodstream, the tissues and organs including the nervous system — the brain, the sympathetic nerve centres and the nerves that penetrate all parts of the body, regulating the functioning of all organs of the vital force.

## Vaccination and Inoculation

The practical methods adopted by the allopaths and imposed tyrannically on the people fall in two categories. One of them is vaccination, claiming to be a sure preventive of smallpox, which was discovered and propagated by one Jenner, an apothecary, not a well-qualified doctor. The other is inoculation for "conferring immunity" against other diseases, which was introduced by Louis Pasteur, a mere chemist, not a medical man.

## No Interference with the Order of Nature

The objection to all these immunization processes is that they interfere with the Order of Nature. One of the most sensible critics of politics, sociology and other departments of knowledge, Herbert Spencer, stated this objection as follows: "When once you interfere with the Order of Nature there is no knowing where the results will end."

But these interventions are perpetrated not once but hundreds of times, when you take into consideration not only vaccinations and revaccinations against smallpox, but also all the other interferences originated by Louis Pasteur.

## History of Smallpox Vaccination in England

An unbiased study of the history of small pox vaccination in England (from 1721 to 1946) – the only one available in all its details – shows that prior to 1800 there was not much incidence of smallpox in that country and what little incidence was there was due to external insanitation. As compulsory vaccinations and revaccinations were foisted on the people of England, there were repeated epidemics of smallpox, each more extensive and disastrous than its predecessor until 1871-72 when the most disastrous of all epidemics occurred, killing not less than 42,000 persons of all ages. The death-toll of children under five was 15,000. In 1881 there was still another epidemic.

Many people in England agitated against compulsory vaccination under the leadership of the National Anti-Vaccination League of

Great Britain. Leading citizens of England — Prof. A.R. Wallace, Prof. Crookshank, Councillor Asbury, Dr Hadwan, Dr Charles Creighton, Dr Winterburn, Sir James Paget and Dr William Scott Tebb, to mention only a few — put forth convincing data to support their stand that by vaccination the disease was not being eradicated but further spread. After the epidemic of 1871-72, the *Lancet* carried the following lament:

> Those who have been building hopes in their imagination of a great and beneficial system of *State Medicine* under which the causes of disease were to be controlled, must abate their hopefulness. It must be admitted that the existing system of vaccination has been sadly discredited.

Meanwhile, the City of Leicester stopped vaccinations and took to the practice of sanitation. The medicos, angered, prophesied disaster, but their prediction did not come true. On the other hand, the Leicester experiment succeeded completely.

Another great authority, Dr Charles Creighton, wrote an article in the ninth edition of the *Encyclopaedia Britannica* saying that smallpox being caused by insanitary conditions would suddenly vanish from the country when this cause was removed and sufficient improvement in sanitation achieved.

The continuing public agitation in England, backed by the opinions of eminent authorities against vaccination, compelled the British Government to appoint a Royal Commission on Vaccination in 1889. It took evidence for seven years, until 1896. The evidence was strongly against vaccination. It showed that vaccinations had caused numerous deaths and injuries, such as loss of eyesight. The Commission unanimously recommended that conscientious objectors should get exemption from vaccination for their children. The Conscience Clause was passed in 1898, but was not implemented on the right lines. Later in 1907 another amendment thereto made it possible for people to opt out of vaccination on conscientious grounds. Steadily, the number of people who sought vaccination went on decreasing. Simultaneously, standards of sanitation were improving and, finally, smallpox was eradicated from the country not through vaccination but by improvement of sanitation. In 1946, the Vaccination Law was repealed by the British Parliament.

## Complications of Smallpox Vaccination

Vested interests the world over, however, would like everyone to believe that smallpox had been eradicated from the world only through vaccinations and revaccinations, but it is not a fact.

There is enough evidence to show that smallpox vaccination, apart from not preventing smallpox, could actually cause many diseases like bronchitis, blindness, cancer, eczema, encephalitis, rickets, urticaria, etc.

## Petition to Parliament of India

Citing a lot of evidence against vaccination, twenty-four* eminent British doctors submitted a detailed petition, known as the Doctors' Petition, to the President and Members of the Parliament of India, immediately after the country attained independence and pleaded for repeal of the vaccination laws. Though there has been no incidence of smallpox in this country during the past few years and though the World Health Organisation itself is not in favour of compulsory vaccination any more, enactments both at the Central and at the State level still continue to be in force in India.

## Other Vaccinations and Inoculations

This brief narration of the futility of smallpox vaccination should serve as an eye-opener to those who blindly believe in different types of filth-medication and meekly submit themselves to it. Other kinds of vaccinations and inoculations (against measles, diphtheria, whooping cough, tetanus, polio, tuberculosis, etc.) still recommended by medicos the world over are equally ineffective. That every one of them produces its own complications is also a fact.

Bertrand P. Allinson, MRCS, LRCP; M. Beddow Bayly, MRCS, LRCP; Reginald Bowden, M.D.; Martha Cheland, B. Sc, MH; Ch.B, R. Fielding Ould, MD, MRCP; Cyril V. Pink, MRCS, LRCP; Dorothy Shepherd, MB, Ch. B; H. Tudor Edmunds, MB, MRCS, LRCP; Andrew Gold, MRCS, LRCP, LRFPS, J.H. Horseley, MBBS; Donald Morris, LRCP; H.W. Jordan, MB; H.Valentine Knaggs, MRCS, LRCP; Geo. McAlpine, MB, Ch. B.; Elizabeth McAlpine, MB, Ch.B.; J.A. Sykes, LMSSA; Ethel Unwin Vawdrey, LRCP, MRCS. LRFPS; H. Fergie Woods, MD, MRCS, LRCP; G.T. Wilkinson, LRCP, LRCSI; Edward Moore, MB, C.Ch., J.W. Swanberg, MB, B.Ch.; Gordon Latto, MB, Ch.B.; W. Harold Emslie, MB, Ch.B.; W. Ellis Morgan, MRCS, LRCP.

## Our Stand

The stand of the Nature Cureists on this point is clear. All types of vaccine, sera, etc., are only filth. And filth cannot produce health.

In addition to the improvement of external sanitation, let people be made health-conscious, in the real sense of the term, so that they could also keep their internal sanitation to the desired extent. Then and then alone can the world be disease-free.

The truth, however unpalatable to the vested interests, is that health and health alone provides natural immunity. And health can be built up by every individual *only* by living in tune with Nature's laws. Artificial immunisation procedures cannot be relied upon. They are harmful to human health.

Health has to be deserved and cannot be bought over the counter. And health is deserved by resort to hygienic living. This is the sane and safe policy everyone who wants to be healthy throughout his life should follow.

# Universal Basic Cause of Disease

Every health seeker has to study the Law of Cause and Effect in depth and must be guided, all through his life, by the correct understanding and interpretation of this Law, which is inviolable, inexorable. Anyone who has not cared to know this Law, out of ignorance, or seeks to interpret it wrongly, is bound to come to grief.

Germs are not the cause of disease, as is often assumed by most people. Germs are but scavengers recruited by the Life Power to clear the debris accumulated within the body by the individual through his wrong habits of living. To mistake the germs for the cause of disease is like mistaking fire-fighting engines for the cause of fire!

## Basic Cause of Disease

Let everyone understand the basic cause of disease. It is internal insanitation, which creates the toxaemic condition and perverts the body chemistry, that is responsible for all disease from the common cold to the dreaded cancer.

Everyone would like to know how this internal insanitation is caused. Here is the answer: Any wrong (unhygienic) habit of living will upset the internal balance and lead to internal insanitation.

Every unhygienic habit involves a wasteful action at either the body or the mental level, or perhaps both in many cases. As there cannot be an action without a corresponding expenditure of power, and as the power spent in every action –internal or external, physical or mental – is Vital Power, unhygienic habit entails waste – an avoidable waste – of Vital Power.

The power available at any given time in the body is limited. If some part of it is spent in wasteful activities connected with unhygienic living, essential activities will be starved of power.

Unhygienic habits lead to enervation. Enervation results in defective elimination. The waste matter that ought to be eliminated through the normal channels (e.g. the large intestines, the kidneys, the skin and the lungs) cannot be cleared and the body becomes internally insanitary. Cell and tissue waste, also get accumulated and the body becomes internally insanitary. With cell and tissue waste lying uneliminated in different parts of the body, the individual begins to realise that all is not well within.

*The universal basic cause of disease is toxaemia resulting from enervation due to the adoption of unhygienic habits of living. Once this is understood, prevention of disease, as also its cure, becomes easy.*

## What is 'Unhygienic Living'?

At this stage, it is necessary to understand the connotation of the term 'unhygienic living'. To cite a few instances —

(i)     adoption of wrong posture while sitting, working or walking;

(ii)    sleeping on a soft bed, a bed which tends to sag when a person lies on it;

(iii)   lack of physical activity or overactivity;

(iv)    sluggish breathing;

(v)     living or working in an unventilated place or place where there is air or noise pollution;

(vi)    living or working in a place which is dark, having no natural light;

(vii)   wearing tight clothes or clothes which cannot allow air to reach the skin (e.g., those made of synthetic fibre) or clothes which are incapable of absorbing the skin eliminants;

(viii)  eating without hunger, too many times a day, eating unnatural foods (either processed or manufactured foods) or stale, overcooked, fried foods, etc., or committing errors which could be classified as (a) wrong choice of foods, or (b) wrong modes of eating;

25

(ix)     taking drugs, sedatives, barbiturates, tranquillisers, etc.;

(x)      taking stimulants of different types, e.g., coffee, tea, cola drinks or alcoholic beverages, etc., or indulging in tobacco, cigarettes, beedis, hookah, cigars or snuff;

(xi)     taking in too much of water, gulping it, or drinking water when there is no physiological need for it;

(xii)    over-indulgence in sex or in other sensual cravings;

(xiii)   not paying enough attention to the proper development of mental health--and thus becoming a prey to one or more of the infirmities that go under the name of inferiority complex, fear, worry, phobias, anxiety, depression, irritability, etc.;

(xiv)    environmental maladjustment;

(xv)     adopting a wrong attitude towards work and doing it with a certain amount of aversion towards it; and

(xvi)    developing tension of some kind or the other.

The list above cannot, by its very nature, be exhaustive; it is only illustrative.

## Health is the Way

Drugs have no place in physiology; and the drug way is not the way to health. The sooner this is understood, the better it will be for mankind as a whole. All drugs – standard or spurious – are unhygienic and cannot restore the health of a patient. They would only bring down his health, cripple him – perhaps even kill him. By drugs, an acute disease is converted into a chronic one and a chronic one into a destructive one.

Health is the Way; there is no other way to health. Peace is the way; there is no other way to peace. Let this be understood by the health seeker. Let all his habits of living be health promoting.

If at any time a person is compelled to live in an unhygienic environment or he is forced to take to unhygienic habits he may develop an acute disease. And, in such a condition, let the basic cause of disease be understood, let him take to Nature's drugless methods of healing to recover his health.

26

In this book, an effort has been made to explain how even in modern days an individual could live in tune with Nature's laws and how by the adoption of a basic Philosophy of Life it is possible to avoid unhygienic habits. Tens of thousands of people the world over have taken to the Science of the Life Natural and are leading happy and healthy lives, without needing any medical aid whatever. They have realised that by adopting the Science of Nature Cure those who are ill can become well, and those who are well can become better.

# SIX

# The Fivefold Food

## Mode of Creation of Gross and Subtle Bodies

The practical methods of this science are determined in accordance with the mode of creation of the gross and subtle bodies of creatures, as taught in the Vedantas. It must be understood that creation is not something that took place at a remote time in the past, because it is going on even now. This is the substance of what we are taught in those sacred books: "From the Supreme Being was born the extremely subtle substance known as the 'Sky' (or Space) which is also called 'Ether'. From this Ether came Air. From Air was born Light, from Light, Water and from Water, Earth, from the Earth, plants, from the plants, food and from food the bodies of all the creatures came into being." What is meant is that all these five grades of substance stand in the relations suggested by this order of involution and evolution.

## Positive and Negative Foods

The plants, it must be noted, are the effects of the interaction of the earth with the other four elements of creation. So all the virtues of all the five reside in food that is wholesome. Such food is called *positive* food. Other foods are called *negative*.

## The Five Foods

Thus all bodies are made up of five kinds of matter. Hence health and longevity arise from the body being maintained in its proper relation to its original sources.

Contact with the earth is not direct but through food. But there is a direct contact with the other four. Therefore, there is no such thing as earth-cure, apart from food-cure. Food is one of the five sources of health and is therefore also the means of cure; without it the return of lost health would be impossible. By 'cure' we mean the return of health whereby 'disease' vanishes of itself. The use of earth as an aid to the cure is an item in the water-cure. Earth is used only as a medium for water.

The access of the extremely subtle force called Ether is very abundant in fasting; in dieting it is much less. If food be taken at wrong times or in excess, then the access to this power is cut off, and there is a weakening of the life-force and the disease becomes incurable. Of all the five, the sky-power is the highest and the most important, being the subtlest. The other four are next in value, in their natural order, as set forth above.

## Fasting and Positive Dieting

Like the two wings of a bird, both fasting and positive dieting are equally essential for the maintenance of health, and for its recovery when lost. But whereas the bird uses both wings simultaneously, the follower of nature cure has to use these two food-medicines alternately. This is to be remembered especially by one who has a deep-rooted, chronic kind of disease. Such diseases take a long time to get rid of, if reliance is placed wholly on the diet-cure, ignoring fasting. Hence the chronic sufferer must fast at intervals, as will be explained in its proper place.

Hence also it follows that wholesome positive food needs to be taken in medicinal doses, not in excess, as else it will do little or no good. *What is not food should never be taken as medicine.*

## No Inorganic Substances

No purely inorganic substances – such as metals or metallic compounds – is fit to be employed as medicine. It should be noted that word 'medicine' has been degraded by its use by medicos to denote *drugs,* which are poisons and deadly to life and subversive of health. So we must dissociate it from the false meaning given to it by the medicos, by the light we get from the Vedantas. *Drugs are not medicines, because they are poisons.*

All earthly salts, if taken habitually even in the slightest excess, will destroy health in course of time. *Hence common salt must be taken very sparingly,* if it cannot be renounced altogether.

Among plant products, the poisonous ones must be strictly eschewed, because they are not food.

## Food and Medicine

Food and medicine are two names for the same thing. Herein we must cherish the excellent teaching of Hippocrates of Athens, namely: *Let food be thy medicine and let medicine be thy food.* The former part of the sentence is for the sick, the latter for the healthy. To the sick, positive food is the true medicine not drugs which are inimical to health and life. To the healthy, medicinal food is the means of freedom from disease. Hippocrates was a hygienist who fully believed in Nature's practically unlimited power to sustain health and to restore it when lost. He condemned the use of poisonous drugs. The medicos wrongly call him the 'Father of Medicine', meaning thereby their own health-wrecking pseudoscience. Truly, he was a Teacher of the Hygienic Way, by which he cured his patients. So we must always remember that food and medicine are one and the same thing. This principle applies to all persons, well or ill.

## Ayurveda

This teaching is in harmony with that of the *Taittiriya Upanishad,* which says that Food is the Universal Medicine, because the creatures came into existence out of food which preceded them in the order of creation. For this reason the healers of the remote past did not consider drugs as medicine, as will be seen in the book called *'Ayurveda Sutram'* published some decades ago by the Mysore University. There fasting and better breathing, with herbal food-medicines, are prescribed for the sick.

The system known by that name, now practised by those who call themselves professors of Ayurveda, is a perversion of the art that originally prevailed, due to the use of mercury and other deadly drugs.

## Herbal Aids

The herbal aids to health recommended in that ancient book are Sattvic food-herbs, capable of healing all the three kinds of abnormality, called *doshas* – vital airs, bile and phlegm – mentioned in the books. Hence, in their use there is no need to search for specifics. All of them are good for all, as health sustaining. Therefore in our system, we do not recognise these three subdivisions of abnormality.

30

In *Taittiriya Upanishad* we have the sentence, "Food is called Annam, because it is eaten, and because it eats (the eater)." Also there is a Vedic text which says: "Food is death-giving, as well as life-sustaining." These two sentences warn us against misuse of food. Food that is misused becomes toxic filth and provokes disease. But if rightly used, it is the means of healthy bodily structures, and is thus a means of positive health and longevity. The *Upanishad* thus gives us the knowledge of the Unity of Food and Medicine. Those physicians who use non-food substances as medicine are quacks and should be boycotted by who care for health and a happy old age.

Thus, in our Divine Science we have this Fivefold Medicine, which is not distinct from Food, by remembering which we shall avoid mistakes that would cause suffering and disappointment.

# SEVEN

# Unity

Natural hygiene is unique among all the healing systems because of its exteme simplicity, which is due to the profound truth of Unity which it teaches. It is because of this teaching that it is easy for any intelligent man to practise it at home without dependence on any and every kind of doctor.

## Unity of Health and Disease

Diseases come and go, but underneath them all, and in between, Health endures continuously, more or less. Disease has no existence apart from health because it is only an outward, visible and tangible form of ill-health, which is only a diminution of Health. It may be called disease in its *latent* or seed form, the former being the *patent,* visible form of the diminished health.

All diseases become possible only on the basis of health; for health in some degree must be present as the *substratum* (or substance) of any and every disease. When health is completely lost, death ensues and then there is an end of disease also. Health is really indistinguishable from Life, and hence, so long as life continues, health also must exist, more or less. Health and disease are thus like the two sides of a single coin. Both health and disease subsist in Life; the positive essence of Life is health; the negative aspect of it is its diminution, that is, disease. For this reason we regard disease as inseparable from health, and therefore to be treated as a diminution of health, rather than as something existing independent of it. Thus is established the doctrine of Unity of Health and Disease, and this Unity is verified by the cure of all diseases alike by a single process of restoring health.

That disease is not an entity which means that it has no independent existence apart from Life's healthward efforts – has been realised by Dr. Carrel, who wrote in his book that disease is "the struggle of the body against a disturbing agent."

## Unity of Disease

Because disease or ill-health is only a diminution, or a lower degree of health, we must regard disease as rather unreal.

This is the proper policy to be followed, if we want a radical cure of disease, and not merely temporary and deceptive relief by suppression of any manifestation of ill-health. The practical significance of this teaching can be seen by means of the simile of light and darkness. Light is the substance, darkness is its diminution or apparent absence. Health is like light and disease is like darkness. Darkness is not got rid of by directly attacking it. It goes of its own accord when light is brought in, or increased sufficiently. In the same way, when health is raised sufficiently high, disease disappers.

Since no disease exists apart from Health, which is its substratum, it logically follows that all diseases are *one:* their apparent diversity is an illusion. All diseases alike are also one because they are Nature's efforts to raise the health to its previous high level. So disease processes of whatever kind are also vital processes just like health processes. Vital processes in a body not encumbered with toxic filth are called health. Those that take place in an encumbered body are called diseases. That is all the difference. Since diseases are vital processes, to fight them with drug poisons is criminal folly.

## Vital Effort Towards Health Continues

In this context an objection may be raised, that not all diseases are efforts for the return of health. Natural Hygienists are agreed that diseases of the first stage, namely, acute diseases, are Nature's efforts towards recovery of high-level health. But it is objected by some that diseases of the second stage, namely, chronic diseases are not so, that they are symptoms of greatly lowered health, due to Nature's frequent defeats at the hands of criminal medicine. This is substantially true. But we take the view that even in chronic cases Nature does not once and for all cease Her efforts for health but is only waiting for a favourable opportunity to make more vigorous efforts to achieve Her beneficial aim. In such cases Nature is making some efforts to eliminate the cause of ill-health, toxic filth. This effort becomes more vigorous and effective if and when the sinner, the patient, repents, returns to Nature after dismissing quacks who do not know the *real* cause of disease and, hence, who cannot help him recover his health. We may say that so long as a chance of cure exists, Nature continues Her beneficent efforts, however feeble.

## Three Stages of Disease

Diseases, as stated before, are of three kinds: *acute, chronic,* and *destructive,* according to the three stages of *Disease-progression,* which is what takes place when unnatural treatments are resorted to. It has also been explained that acute diseases are more or less superficial, shortlived and easy to cure, chiefly because they are themselves curative processes, and would lead up to health, if they be cared for in a hygienic way. This care is usually called 'cure' because it is in harmony with Nature's purpose. As a rule, all good effects are brought about by the union of Divine Grace and rightly directed human effort and as in truth what we do by way of caring for the sick — whether ourselves or others — is finally due to Divine Grace. The two factors, taken together, are called the cure of the disease, it being understood that such a cure is a *radical* cure, as explained before, whereas medical cures are as a rule just suppressions, which lead on to the next, the second stage and, finally, even to the third and last stage, which is *degeneracy,* in which destructive diseases inevitably arise. These are wrongly described by the medicos as degenerative diseases.

It must be understood that every suppression of Nature's efforts for health causes a fall in the health level, because Nature's purpose. the lightening of the encumbrances, is violently thwarted. Thus ill-health grows and health declines until the stage is reached when death is sure, unless warded off by a *timely* return to Nature.

## Retrogression of Disease

We have already seen that if and when the sinner-sufferer returns to Nature, this *Disease-progression* stops, and patient is led back to Health in the reverse direction. This healthward progress is called the retrogression of disease. In this progress back to Health the suppressed diseases of the past may and often do return, but in the *reverse* order. This is clear evidence that those diseases were not radically cured, but only suppressed earlier by the drug system.

34

## Latent and Patent Disease

Between one suppression and the next, disease remains in a latent, nameless and formless state, which is the connecting link between every two consecutive diseases. It is this latent disease that makes the subsequent disease possible, sometimes manifest as patent disease of a particular form, and at other times unmanifest, as latent disease, which persists throughout life in most cases. These names and forms of the one continuous disease are therefore illusory and misleading, the real part being the substratum of ill-health, which in its turn is not distinct from health. This view of the continuity and worsening of ill-health makes it clear that the medical way is the wrong way. In this way the cause is not removed; it can be done only by doing penance for one's past hygienic sins and then living hygienically ever after.

## Material and Efficient Cause of Disease

What is this cause? Indian logicians recognise that the cause is always twofold, consisting of a material and an efficient cause. This is to be understood by the analogy of the earthen pot which is an effect due to two causes, a material cause, namely, earth, and an efficient cause, the potter. In the present case, the material cause is the encumbering foreign matter, whose elimination is the disease-process, and the efficient cause is Nature (or God), using Life as the instrument. Life and its Operator have been studied in Chapter III.

How does foreign matter come into existence? The answer is, we *ourselves* are the cause of its presence inside the body. This has been explained in Chapter V.

Once a patient gets cured through Natural Hygiene, it is necessary for him to be a faithful and lifelong follower of this system because the same cause, if allowed to come into being, will produce the same effects.

Thus, *diseases are one, not only in their mode of causation, but also in their cure.* This will suffice to convince the follower of Nature Cure that these Unities are not only theoretically true, but also practically helpful.

## Helpful Hints

The following details about disease should also be known.

Acute diseases occur, as a rule, in the beginning, and chronic ones later, due to suppression of acute ones. But because of the persistent fouling of the blood-stream and the poisoning thereby of the nervous system, as well as the reckless drugging, chronic diseases are now occurring at an early age. Poliomyelitis is precipitated by inoculations, a disaster that did not exist before.

In the tropics there is more of acute diseases, while in the temperate and colder regions chronic ones are more common.

Often it happens that acute diseases have a background of chronic or destructive diseases in latency. They need to be treated with greater care so as to remove this background. Acute disease is characterised by a greater vigour of elimination, while in chronic ones the vigour of vital effort is much less. Hence, while the former respond to suitable treatment promptly, the latter do not do so. By this the two can be differentiated and correctly diagnosed.

Sometimes it happens that a patient of acute disease, who is reduced to a perilous state by medical incompetence, is afterwards rescued from the jaws of death by the natural way and lives to a great old age afterwards.

If acute diseases be radically cured, there is no chance of development of chronic or destructive ones, because by this real cure the encumbrances are reduced.

A patent disease, if suppressed, goes into latency, not if radically cured, for then health is re-established, and there is a perfect cessation of disease. Out of disease in latency fresh diseases can arise; but none can arise when the disease is radically cured. The right policy, therefore, is to follow the natural way. The reason is that in this way, life's eliminative efforts are powerfully helped. On the other hand, in allopathy this effort is always defeated.

Also in the natural way, as a rule the patients do not suffer so much as under medical care, or carelessness.

# EIGHT

# Mind and Health

Along with the five natural medicines described earlier, a sixth medicine is prescribed for keeping the mind in a state favourable for the observance of the laws of Hygiene, because the mind itself is the ultimate cause of health and disease. Diseases arise from defects of character that lie in the mind.

It must be understood, however, that defects of the mind do not as a rule directly cause disease of the body; bodily disease arises by the disobedience of the laws of Hygiene, which is due to defects of the mind.

There is an exception; if the body is heavily encumbered with foreign matter--which is provocative of disease--then mental tensions, like anger, fear and the like, may immediately set up a disease of the body. And this is so especially when the mental stress persists for some time. Hence mental states are of great importance for maintenance of health. The follower of Nature Cure must make an effort to keep his mind at peace, free from mental storms.

## Three Forms of Disease

Disease, it must be understood, may exist in any one of its three forms; the gross, visible form called *patent* disease, the subtle, *latent* form, which is simply low health or want of ease (dis-ease), and the *causal* form which exists as abnormality of the mind, which manifests as an uncontrollable craving for sense pleasures or otherwise.

The causal form of disease is in its turn due to a *primal* cause, namely, discontent, which is the consequence of privation of the Natural Happiness spoken of in Chapter III. An impure mind is so much the prey of worldly desires, that its access to the Divine Source of Happiness is more or less cut off. The devastating effect of desire may be so great as to cause loss of sleep, which is Nature's device to enable every creature to renew itself daily by a temporary Re-union with God, who dwells in the Heart. In natural living the mind in deep sleep goes into a state of union with its Source, namely God, and enjoys a profound happiness during that time; thereafter, being recharged with power to face the problem of life, it awakes to the world in the waking state. But restlessness of thought and action, sometimes amounting to a habit of sleeplessness, may result, and this sets up a state of mental disease, which in due course will manifest as an incurable bodily disease. One of the manifestations of this mental disease is an utter inability to control oneself in self-indulgence of any or all kinds. This means violation of all the laws of hygiene. When the indulgence is in sex relations, then the disease is called 'syphilis', though in Natural Hygiene we do not recognise it as syphilis, because in our view there is only one disease.

Men who are subject to inordinate desires transgress the Laws of Hygiene and reap the consequences, namely disease.

## Means of Mental Purity

Men who are relatively free from such desires obey those laws and are rewarded with good health and a long life with happiness and fitness for life's activities. Conduct that is regulated by right ideals is possible only with a pure mind, for actions are oriented from the mind. The body is a mere instrument of the mind.

Righteousness is the same for all, whether the aim is worldly well being or spiritual perfection; the difference is in the motive alone. There is no line of demarcation between conduct aimed at Health, and conduct aimed at Deliverance. Right conduct is necessary for all alike. Even for obtaining or recovering health, one must cultivate peace of mind as far as possible.

The means to attain mental purity and health are three-fold, namely, an intelligent faith in the soundness of the teachnigs of Natural Hygiene, self-surrender to God and fearlessness. If these are taken care of, and if the mode of conduct prescribed by this science is adhered to, the reward is almost certain. There is no need to practise any of the methods, such as auto-suggestion, that are advocated by self-styled psychologists. These are as a rule impracticable because the mind itself is in a perilous state, and hence cannot carry out their instructions.

## The Fundamental Truth

The fundamental truth that must be learnt and always remembered is that Divine Power alone confers health and thereby radically cures disease, but that one must cooperate with that Power by carrying out the practical part of the teaching which is penance for one's previous wrong conduct, details of which are set forth hereinafter. The follower must resolve to do his part, namely, the needful penance, and must stick to that resolve and carry it out faithfully and with perseverance. Doubts must not be entertained, nor must there be any laxity in the performance of the penance.

It must be understood that the follower has the right and duty to fulfil his part, namely to do all things enjoined by this science, but has little or no power to shape the result. This lies with God alone. It is not possible for man to make any bargains with Him. He must do all that he needs to do and leave it to God to bring about the results in His own time and in His own way.

## Mental Poise

To be able to carry out one's duties perfectly one should have a steady mind, free from fear, as well as from hope. Hope and fear are both weakening. They are two extremes; the mind is like a pendulum, it cannot remain at rest. The point of rest is where hope and fear neutralise each other. The mind must be kept at this middle point nearly all the time. If the mind strays to one end or the other, it must be brought back to the centre between the two extremes. By this means it will become possible for the follower to carry out the programme of conduct by which health can be recovered and maintained.

This much is for the purpose of ensuring that the practical teachings are carried out faithfully. Divine Grace does the rest; and, unless there are insuperable obstacles, the goal of Health will be reached.

It is also necessary for the follower to achieve a high level of mental health. This is a long-term policy, which needs the practice of religion, the goal of which is the spiritualization of the mind, until the state of Holiness is reached.

# What is Religion?

For one aspiring to reach the Goal of Religion, a great deal of help comes from the company of the Awakened Ones, or from the atmosphere that is there in their Presence. The Holy One is designated as the *Sat;* He is also called a *Jnani.* It is easier to reach the Goal by practising the methods of religion in such an atmosphere. This is called *Sat-sanga,* association with a Wise One.

A serious warning must be given here. Religions seem to be in violent conflict with one another, and the adherent of each religion tends to think that his religion alone is true. This is fanaticism, a disease of the religious mind, which must be avoided at all costs. The truth is that all religions are substantially true; they are all paths leading to the same goal.

Religions consist of two parts, namely, instructions about conduct leading to the goal and doctrines by which the prescribed conduct is sought to be sustained. But doctrines are likely to be too precise and dogmatic, leading to uncharitableness to those outside one's own communion.

The truth is that no doctrine can ever encompass the whole of the great Mystery that God is. But since the intellect demands some kind of doctrinal support, it is permissible to have beliefs. But these beliefs must be held lightly, as tentative hypotheses, and not as absolute truth; otherwise hatred of believers in other religions will arise and thus result in failure. *It is rightness of conduct that matters, not correctness of belief.* The practical behests of religions cannot be fulfilled by a bigoted mind. The bigot is lax in his religion, hoping to win Heaven by beating and killing the 'infidels'.

In all religions the essence is the same, namely, the practice of love of God, and goodwill to all creatures. None must be left out of this brotherhood of life. God does not belong to any one religion. Love means the gradual extinction of egoism and selfishness.

# Frugality in Eating

Most people suppose that one can progress in religion without reforming one's way of life. Such reform is the rebirth enjoined by all religions. Of this reform an important, but much neglected, part is reform in eating. All religions stress this need; but it is disregarded even by ascetics.

The man that eats like a pig cannot be a genuinely religious man. The earnestly religious man must practise self-discipline by means of self-denial to the needful extent. Hygienic living is as necessary for the religious man as for the worldly one.

Self-discipline includes control of one's cravings, which lead to self-indulgence through the sense organs. Of these the most important is said to be the sense of taste.

"No one can be said to have subjugated his senses, if he has not conquered the sense of taste, though he has conquered all the other four; if he has conquered the sense of taste, he has conquered all." Thus the *Bhagavata Purana* shows the great importance of self-control in the act of eating, so that one does not allow one's sense of taste to dominate one, but eats just the minimum of food. This is but proper, seeing that digestion is an act of the Divine Presence, as already stated. The impropriety of unrestrained eating has also been graphically described by Bhagavan Sri Ramana Maharishi in a Tamil verse, wherein the stomach accuses the soul of grossness in eating:

Oh iniquitous soul, you do not give me, your stomach, even one *nazhi* (24 minutes) of rest throughout the day; not even for one *nazhi* do you refrain from eating; never are you aware of the great suffering you inflict on me all the time, understand that hereafter I cannot bear to live with you.

From this we must see that unhygienic eating is a crime against the Divine Nature. Right eating is conducive to the health of mind and body alike. Fairness to the stomach is an integral part of Holiness. Without it one cannot be successful in the practice of Yoga, which is the name for strenuous effort to reach the Goal of Religion, which is integration with God in the Supreme Stage.

Yoga comprises a great variety of methods. Of these, four are prominent, namely, the Yoga of service to God by right action, that of devotion, culminating in Love of God, that of mind control through breath control and meditation and that of Quest of the Real by rejection of everything unreal. These are dealt with in the sacred books. By following one or more of these paths the follower attains the state of pure *Sattva,* and then easily reaches the goal. Meanwhile, the mind becomes purer and healthier free from the imperfections of worldliness.

Religion thus provides a non-violent means of eliminating the defects of the mind. The direct method, which means fighting the mind by means of repression, is as a rule doomed to failure, because this process rouses the mind's resistance, which is bad policy, because in such conflicts the mind becomes the victor; the would-be conqueror of the mind is defeated and discouraged. The process of mind conquest is by substituting higher ends for lower, worldly ones. This is a slow but sure path. As devotion to God deepens, attachments to worldly objects become worn out and are finally overcome and extinguished. By this process Holiness is achieved, which is True Health and Immortality.

The right mental state results in relaxation of mental stresses, and is thus an element of practical Vital Economy. As Kuhne said: *Nature Cure requires character.*

# NINE

# Food and Energy

Food scientists and the medical profession aver that our bodily energy comes from the food we eat. They "measure" the food values of different foodstuffs in calories and they have formulated a "calorie theory of food", which is meekly accepted as gospel truth by many people in the modern world.

We, of the Natural Hygiene School, have seen it in practice that the calorie theory of food is totally misconceived.

"Calorie" is a term taken from physics, signifying a unit of heat, it being assumed that food has to be burnt in the body to make energy available for use by its owner. As the physical energy released during the burning up of one calorie of heat is scientifically known, where inert bodies are concerned, it has been taken for granted that the same standard can be applied to the human body. And that is precisely where the fallacy of all this reasoning comes in, and where the "energy from food" theory breaks down.

## Human body not a Machine

The human body cannot be compared to a machine, which is a dead, inert object. A machine can be made to work or move on the requisite power being supplied from outside. The moment the power-supply is cut off or exhausted, or the moment the mechanical arrangement gets upset, the machine will come to a dead stop. The human being — a unity of body, mind and spirit — cannot be regarded as a mere machine. Food is not to be regarded as a fuel to run the body engine. Food serves certain definite purposes. On being digested, it supplies certain repair materials. The very digestive process is carried on by the Vital Force, which is not itself the product of food, air or water, or anything got from outside.

The human being has his Vital Reserve in the body, but he cannot get at the Reserve all at once. Its location inside is, and shall always be, a mystery to everyone. As C. Rajagopalachari put it in some other context;

> We know the pattern of the cloth
> But not the loom that weaves;
> We can, like children,
> Look at the dial of the watch
> But cannot open the case thereof.

Anyone trying to know the exact location of the Vital Reserve, or to know its quantum or quality through dissecting the human body, or through the so-called powerful scientific instruments, will fail, for it is superphysical and superchemical.

A yogi, or a realised saint, can visualize this Source, but to the ordinary individual, it shall always remain a mystery.

## How Energy Can be Conserved

We need not, however, worry over this. We may not be able to know all about the Vital Energy and the Vital Reserve, but it will be enough for us if we could follow the rules and regulations expounded by wise men of different climes and times, governing the effective expression of this energy in our day-to-day life. It would also be worthwhile to know – and this can be done without any difficulty–the conditions and circumstances under which this energy is wasted unnecessarily so that the health-seeker may conserve it.

Day by day, a fraction of this energy from the Vital Reserve is released, to be manifested through the different parts of the body, e.g. muscle, nerves, etc. The structural integrity of these muscles, nerves, etc. is to be maintained by the individual by supplying the basic needs of living-air, water, sunshine, food, excercise, sleep, relaxation, etc. at the physical level, each to the extent needed, neither more nor less. These basic needs, when supplied rightly and in the proper proportion, are utilised by the body; in other words, the Vital Energy acts upon all of them and utilises them for maintaining the structural integrity of different parts of the body.

If these basic needs are supplied sensibly, by living in tune with the Laws of Nature, the structural integrity of the different parts of the body is kept in ideal condition. With the muscles, nerves, etc., in good shape and form, the Vital Energy can manifest itself and the individual concerned can enjoy good health.

If, however, the supply of one or more of these basic needs is unbalanced, the structural integrity of the body suffers, resulting in weak muscles, nerves, etc. The weakness would depend upon the extent of the imbalance. The manifestation of energy would become more and more difficult. In other words, the person would become weaker and weaker.

## Food is a Tax on Vitality

As stated earlier, the very digestive process is carried on by the Vital Power, which is not itself the product of food, air or water or anything got from outside. Food cannot digest itself. It is digested by the Vital Force in order that the usable material, e.g. natural glucose, aminoacids, minerals, vitamins, etc. could be released from the food consumed. Where vitality is low, the assimilation of food is poor. After the assimilable parts are separated for being made use of by the vital organism, the undigested part is eliminated from the body by the very same Vital Force. Every activity inside the body should be attributed to the Power within.

Digestion is action, and so is elimination. In both the Vital Force is spent. It should be remembered that there cannot be an action without a corresponding expenditure of power.

Thus food is a tax on vitality and not the source of vitality as glibly assumed by many.

While the right type of food should be supplied to the organism in the quantities needed to meet a basic need of living, it would be foolish to think that food supplies any power to the body. Those who blindly believe in the calorie theory may go on feeding themselves and others even when there is no hunger thinking that they are supplying "energy" to the body through the food intake. Alas! they forget the simple truth that undigested food can only harm the body. Food not required by the system — and that is what food eaten without hunger is — or in excess of need, cannot benefit the body in any manner whatsoever.

## Refutation of the Calorie Theory

The calorie theory proclaims — irrespective of the condition of the body — that every individual 'needs' a certain minimum number of calories (heat-units) to keep himself going, that persons of different age groups and following different vocations require specified amounts of food capable of giving specified heat-units to the body. The calorie theory does not take into account the needs of the individual, nor his assimilative capacity. This reveals its hollowness.

The calorie theory, again, is the result of averages worked out on observations on men accustomed to conventional ways of living, which can, by no means, be regarded as healthy or hygienic. Such results can have no validity for a man who has made up his mind to live the hygienic way.

A high-calorie diet will always be an unbalanced diet. Those foods which are supposed to be rich in calories contain very little, or none, of the mineral salts, vitamins, trace elements, enzymes, etc., needed by the organism. They may not supply the body with all the essential aminocids. Again most of them may be predominantly acidic.

A large number of patients taking to Nature Cure adopt fasting, or reduce their food intake (in the words of experts, take to "low-calorie" foods) and recover their health. All of them disprove the calorie theory. Even after getting radically cured, such people continue to eat little and maintain their health, again, disproving the theory.

On the other hand, those who eat according to the calorie theory continue to be ill and become worse progressively, instead of becoming more and more energetic. This again disproves the calorie theory.

There is a condition known as hypoglycaemia (low blood sugar) wherein due to the lower sugar content in the blood, the individual feels weak and listless. Quoting this as an instance, food scientists may argue that as starches and sugar provide the blood sugar, their calorie theory is correct. Yes, it is agreed that the blood requires the presence of sugar to the desired extent for energy to manifest itself. Even so, the body requires the requisite amount of bodily activity or exercise, for energy to manifest itself. When the basic needs, e.g., food, air water, sunshine, sleep, etc. are supplied properly to the body, the structural integrity of the different organs is maintained and then alone can energy manifest itself through them rightly. This does not mean that sugar, or for that matter any other substance, *supplies* energy to the body.

46

Once it is realised that energy does not come from food but that, in a limited sense, food acts as its medium of expression, in the human body, the calorie tables and all the present attempts to put dietetics on a calorie basis will be found useless.

The utter stupidity of the calorie theory was demonstrated by Dr Dewey. He pointed out the significant fact that *'Food is a tax on vitality'*. He also showed that the assumption underlying the calorie theory was absurd, because if it was correct there would be no cause for fatigue. A tired man must go to his bedroom and not to the dining-room, to recover his lost strength. We put it more strongly still by posing the question: Why death, if the theory be true?

There is also the testimony of Dr Barbara Moore, who carried out long-distance walks in Britain and the U.S.A. She was a frugal eater; she lived on fruit juices, vegetable juices and honey, sometimes taking nuts. She maintained her health and normal weight (126 lbs). She passed away at the ripe old age of 75.

There is again, the crucial test of the cure of dyspeptics. These are easily and radically cured by fasting or an approach to fasting and other hygienic measures. They cannot digest the heavy rations of high-calorie foods prescribed by the medicos. If treated on orthodox lines they *die* in three to six years, suffering terribly all the time. The author himself was a sufferer from dyspepsia and neurasthenia, and was reduced to a state of utter helplessness because of medical ignorance of the basic truth of the natural relation of food to life; but he got restored to very good health in two years, by hygienic measures.

Prof. Chittenden of the U.S. demolished the calorie theory by experiments on himself and some volunteers. He proved that one third of the number of calories medically prescribed produced better health and strength than was possible by taking the full amount. Horace Fletcher, advocate of thorough mastication, also proved the same truth by his own example. Dr. Lindlahr has said: *"One-third of what we eat nourishes us; the remaining two-thirds go to nourish the doctors."*

The facts of long fasts by patients for the recovery of health, as observed and recorded by the great pioneers, totally disprove the calorie theory. The medical view that a faster lives upon his own flesh until emaciation sets in, and then dies, is negatived by these facts. Medicos do not know the distinction between fasting and starvation. That distinction is real, though rather too subtle for the understanding of obtuse brains of these self-styled 'scientists'.

During a fast for a month or more, the body temperature as a rule remains constant; but the amount of body-substance lost during the fast is not the same all the time. It is more than half a kg. a day at first, but in the end it is a few mgms, too little to account for the heat. It is the electric currents flowing in the nerves that maintain the body heat, not the tissue substance that is consumed.

Also there is the curious fact that a man with an abnormally high temperature who fasts, gets into the normal, 98.4°F. It also happens that if a man with subnormal temperature fasts long enough, say, 40 days, his temperature *rises* to the normal. How do the medicos propose to explain this?

Prof. Arnold Ehret states that a faster can be stronger after 20 days of fasting than he was before he began fasting. How can this be explained on the basis of the calorie theory? If this theory were true then not one of those long fasts would have been possible. Dr Dubos, in his book *Basal Metabolism,* admits that long fasts are not fatal, because, as he puts it, some *mysterious power intervenes to establish the basal metabolism (rate of process of vital changes of food-substance) at a lower level so as to avoid disaster.* This means that life can survive without damage even when no food is taken for many weeks. Actually abstinence from food has positively beneficial effects, as will be shown later.

The food-load which advocates of the calorie theory prescribe for health and fitness is far too heavy; a great many people whose digestive power is limited are seriously injured by eating the recommended amounts. Those who are of robust health and are able to digest all they eat, being free from mental labour, may escape more or less unscathed, but only for a time. The notion that vitality is proportionate to the amount eaten is a gross error of gross minds.

All the scriptures of the world ordain that to maintain and improve health, one should be frugal in matters of diet. It is the overeater who suffers, not the frugal eater. The former may mock at the latter outwardly, perhaps without realising that his own stomach is deploring his ignorance. Immoderation in matters of diet — either eating too much at every meal, or eating too often— presents a very heavy "Energy Bill" and hence it should be avoided.

# TEN

# Vital Economy

An abundance of the power called Life is the indispensable condition for health because, as we have seen, it is through the instrumentality of life that all vital processes, whether of health or of disease, are possible and *this power resides, not in the gross body built up from food, but in the subtle body,* of which scientists know nothing. We have also taken note of the fact that the amount of life-power that is present at any time in the body is limited by the encumbrances in it. Since the reduction of encumbrances needs time and effort the life-power in the body cannot be *increased* all at once. Hence, to maintain a sufficiency of vital power always, the only way is Vital Economy.

That food cannot be the source of vital power has been dealt with in the preceding chapter.

That which maintains health and restores it when lost, is *life*. The fivefold food-medicine furnishes only the needed repair material. The power that accomplishes these ends is life and life alone. This is evident from the fact that, *without the vital response to the measures of health or cure, there is no cure.* Those who ignore the life-power in their care of the sick do no good to them; on the other hand they do harm. Life it is that does all the work, prompted and guided by Mother Nature, the handmaid of God. When health is below par, it is life that restores it by eliminating foreign matter and reducing the encumbrances obstructing its proper functioning. A high level of health and ease in the cure of disease are possible only when the life-power is abundant, more than needful.

Those having an abundance of vital power enjoy a high degree of the Natural Happiness mentioned before, and are therefore always content and cheerful and free from the grossly weakening slavery to the desire for mere pleasures. On the other hand, those with low vitality are miserable, whether engaged in work or not, as remarked by Milton, who composed *Paradise Lost.*

If the vital power is insufficient, due to improper and excessive expenditure of energy, it can be made to suffice through sensible economy, by reducing the waste of vitality through channels that can be profitably closed. For this purpose, measures like continence (Brahmacharya), fasting or abstemious eating are useful and necessary. By these measures the foreign matter is eliminated and the body lightened. Then more vital power flows into the body from its mysterious Source, whatever it may be.

## How Vitality is Wasted

When there is abundant vitality, the body *feels* light, the tissues are clean, and the figure is normal and comely. Quite otherwise are the effects if the life-power is reduced to a low level by filthy foreign matter and drug-poisons. Herein we must remember the categorical statement of Dr Alonzo Clark that "every dose (of 'medicine') diminishes the patient's vitality".

The greatest waste of power occurs in the work of food disposal. By this waste life is greatly weakened, encumbrances increase and diseases occur again and again, become worse and worse.

It is true that weakness of life occurs after sexual indulgence also. But men become victims of lust, chiefly because they overeat, thereby poisoning their brains and thus producing discontent and cravings. Hence the practice of Dietetic Righteousness is fundamental to the health of mind and body. And of Dietetic Righteousness, Vital Economy is the chief part.

The practice of moderation and self-control in sex life is usually understood to be the meaning of the term 'Brahmacharya'. But we may consider self-control in *all* kinds of indulgence as included in the meaning of that word. It is the non-observance of Brahmacharya in this wide sense that leads to loss of health. And if the same course of wrong conduct is persisted in, where is the chance of the person recovering good health? But if he submits himself to the discipline that will be detailed here, and thus increase his store of vitality — his Vital Reserve — then to him Nature will vouchsafe good health.

By excessive attachment to enjoyments one comes to disregard the rules of hygienic living; and this leads to loss of vitality. By communion with the four higher sources of health, namely Ether, Air, Light and Water, Vital Power is maintained. It is the encumbering toxic filth that hinders communion. Of the four higher sources of health, the Ether-power is the subtlest and most important. More of this power is received by observing Brahmacharya in the wider sense of the term. Perhaps Life is the same as this subtlest of all the five elements of creation. Hence access to this source of life must be kept up for the maintenance of a high level of vitality.

In sexual life the married man must economise his vitality. That is his Brahmacharya, not absolute continence. It is said that the waste of semen is a cause of weakening. But it is the waste of vital power that is the real cause of the weakening of life. It is through loss of vital power that the lustful man contracts horrible diseases, such as 'syphilis' that are treated by unlimited dosing with poisons like mercury, arsenic or antibiotics. But by Vital Economy and positive dieting the much-abused sufferers can be redeemed from the depths of incurable diseases to which they are reduced by medical violence.

## Dietetic Righteousness

Of all the disciplines prescribed for men, the most important is Dietetic Righteousness, for the reason stated before, namely that other forms of unrighteousness arise from the constitutional defects caused by unrighteous eating. He that eats rightly is able to observe *all* the laws of righteousness. Indeed, he is the all-round righteous man as stated in *Shri Bhagavatam:* "He that has conquered the sense of taste has conquered all his senses."

Food is eaten, and it eats; therefore its name is *Annam,* says the *Taittiriya Upanishad.* The significance of this text must be understood. What is eaten righteously is eaten and the end-products are eliminated and hence health is unaffected. But if there be wrong eating then it becomes toxic filth, which being retained is the cause of disease and death. Another text which says that food is both medicine and poison, means the same thing.

Even wholesome food, if eaten in excess and without hunger, becomes toxic filth. So wholesome food must be eaten righteously. What is wholesome food is explained in the next chapter. This rule is for both the healthy and the sick. The abstemious eater obtains all blessings, namely, health of body and mind, length of life and happiness. The unrighteous eater loses both bodily and mental health.

51

It happens that some unrighteous eaters are seemingly not seriously affected in health, so that doubts may arise as to the truth of the teachings of hygiene. These men boast of their "excellent health" in spite of wrong eating. But if studied ccording to the science of encumbrances, given later, they would found to be harbouring diseases in seed form. Often these men die suddenly and unexpectedly of diseases arising from these encumbrances. Also their progeny is far from healthy. We should rather look at instances of high level health and longevity of those that live righteously and at instances of renewed health by reform of habits according to hygiene.

## When to Eat

When to eat, how to eat and how much to eat are the questions to be dealt with in this chapter.

One should eat only after noticing the presence of sufficient power to digest the food to be eaten, and not before. And one should make sure that this power of digestion will be available until the process is completed, that is, that the power will not be withdrawn meanwhile at any time. On this qualification hangs a rule, which will be expounded in its proper place. If this power be withdrawn, so as not to be available for the digestive function, then digestion will be suspended and indigestion will result.

The sufficiency of the power to digest can be known by the feeling of *hunger*. Therefore, the follower must eat only after he is sure that *keen,* natural hunger is present. Those who eat without waiting for hunger lose what health they have. That being so, how can sufferers from long-standing, deep rooted diseases, who eat without waiting for hunger, become healthy again?

Also, when there is fatigue of the body, or perturbation of the mind, hunger will not be present, and eating at that time is wrong, and food eaten then will change into poison. True hunger arises only when the physical body is well rested and the mind is calm, free from tempestuous moods. Food eaten at that time is preventive of ill health.

Here is a translation of a verse from a standard textbook of Ayurveda, bearing on the question of when to eat:

When the stools and urine have been expelled, the mind is pure, the humours are functioning normally, when a clean wind has arisen from the stomach, when keen hunger is felt, and the vital airs are cooperative, when the digestive energy is at its height, the whole body is at its lightest, and the senses are clear and efficient, then one should eat the food ordained by hygiene. This is the rule as to the time of eating.

True hunger, say the hygienists, is not felt in the belly, nor anywhere below the neck. We believe that hunger is essentially a mental feeling, giving rise to the desire to eat. This may be accompanied by the flow of digestive saliva (spittle) at the thought of food, signifying that the whole system is ready to receive and act upon the food to be eaten.

The rising of a clean wind from the stomach is a sign that the organ has become empty of food and has begun to rest and recuperate.

The following order of events must therefore be observed by one that wants to eat for health: (1) the emptying of the stomach, (2) the rest and recuperation of all the digestive organs, (3) the elimination of all wastes which are toxic filth, (4) the feeling of bodily lightness, (5) the abundance of vital energy in the body, and therewith the ability to do work, which should be utilised at that time, (6) the birth of hunger and its maturing until full digestive power is developed. It is in this order that a true and effective demand for food, called 'hunger', becomes unmistakably manifest.

After the stomach becomes empty it begins to shrink in size by a series of contractions, expelling the air filling it. Hunger does not arise while these contractions are going on, but later, when the stomach has rested and recuperated, after attaining its minimum size. Those who eat soon after the rising of the first clean wind are eating without real hunger. They complain that the wind, named the stomach's veto, comes up too soon after beginning to eat. Eating at this stage is therefore a grave mistake.

It may be that some persons do not notice rising of the clean wind. However, lightness of the body and the abundance of vital power would be present in every case of genuine hunger.

It has been mentioned that after the stomach becomes empty the eliminations of wastes begins. While Life is engaged in disposing of the food eaten, it is unable to eliminate the waste. So, *while digestion proceeds elimination is at a standstill.* This fact is biologically of great importance.

Life cannot simultaneously carry out adequately more than one great activity. So it cannot digest a substantial meal and eliminate foreign matter at the same time. As a rule, therefore, Life begins the work of eliminations *after* the stomach is emptied and the digestion is over. But the work of eliminations is more important for health than that of digestion. If digestive work be heavy and takes too long a time, elimination is postponed, the foreign matter accumulates, and encumbrances are formed. This is a reason for limiting the stomach-load to the indispensable minimum. Let it be understood that the minimum of food is also the maximum.

It is by effective elimination that bodily lightness is maintained. This lightness is not a matter of weight, but a *feeling*, due to the abundance of vitality. Life, it must be remembered, has not only to carry the body, a load for four persons, but also to work within it. This it cannot do if the work of elimination falls into arrears. When, due to efficient elimination, the body is light and the vital power abundant, then there is the ability to do work. At that time one should get through the main part of one's day's work. A moderate amount of work has the effect of maturing hunger, so that, after work, hunger becomes keen and unmistakable. For the lazy, hunger does not come at all, or it is anything but keen. Hence, on noticing the presence of power to do work one should engage oneself in work, but one must cease from it as soon as keen hunger has developed. Continuing to work even after that would banish hunger and produce fatigue. If fatigue comes, one must rest until hunger revives and then eat. During the interval it would be proper to have a bath.

Two clear signs of keen hunger should be known: the presence of abundant vital power and the liking for some plain, non-appetising, natural food, the most wholesome of those one is accustomed to. Such food would be *Sattvic* food. A liking for non-*Sattvic* foods can arise without hunger. But *Sattvic,* 'unstimulating food' as Louis Kuhne calls it, needs the sauce of hunger to be relished.

So the eater must first see that the stomach and bowels are empty; he must wait for keen hunger to manifest and then sit down to his meal.

When the stools in the bowels are stagnant, true hunger is impossible. Hence one should see that the stools are passed out and the bowels emptied. The emptying of the bowel is the first of the conditions mentioned in the verse quoted from the Ayurveda textbook. This shows the connection between bowel health and natural hunger. Those who disregard this rule, and eat while the stools in the bowels are stagnant, are conservancy carts, carrying the foul refuse of three or four days' eating or perhaps a great deal more. Of course, these men are not models of health. Foul gases emitted by stagnant bowels pervade the bloodstream and enter even the brain and affect its efficiency and health. The belly and the brain become heated and more or less paralysed or made unfit for work.

Hence, all the work of elimination must be allowed to be completed before one can expect to be really hungry, for thus alone does one remain always healthy.

As a rule, intelligence declines in old age. But for those who live righteously, intelligence grows and becomes keen.

## No-Breakfast Plan

Now we shall consider the modern habit of eating heavily in the morning. For one who has slept at night after eating a substantial meal, hunger does not arise in the morning. Dr Dewey remarks that "Sleep is not a hunger-producing process". Hence if a person has taken a meal at night, for him food eaten in the morning is poison. The rule for him is that he should wait for hunger as explained above, and then eat, meanwhile doing work, enough to provoke natural hunger. Eating a heavy 'breakfast' of negative foods in the morning is one of the causes of the great decline in the health of civilised nations.

As Dr Dewey observes, work is best done on an empty stomach. It was Dr Dewey who proclaimed the *No-Breakfast Plan.* He had been in poor health for some time. One morning he suddenly noted that he had no real hunger. Then and there he stopped eating breakfast. This became a habit with him. The results proved to him that abstinence from eating in the morning is an ordinance of Natural Hygiene. Morning eating is also condemned in the Old Testament.

## Work and Digestion

Another very bad habit that has come into vogue among us is the eating of very substantial meal, the principal meal of the day, *before* going to one's work. Work is done on a loaded stomach. *Work and digestion cannot go on at the same time.* As work is done with the will, the vital power is monopolised by the work, and there is no vital power available for digestion of food, which then ferments and putrefies.

Scientists who believe in the calorie theory of food values say that very little vitality is spent in mental labour. But experience shows that such labour is far more exhausting than muscular work. The fact is that life is not within the scope of scientific study.

Work and digestion must be kept apart, so that there may be no competition between them. When digestive work is to be done, then Life must be left free to do that work; no other work must be imposed upon it till digestion is completed.

## When to Eat the Principal Meal

Thus, we have the following rule: that we should eat our principal meal, whether in the day or at night, only after finishing all our work, and not before. This means that if one is free to rest after the meal, enabling digestion to proceed unhindered, one may eat that meal at a suitable hour in the day. But if one is not free, and is obliged to work till the evening, one must postpone his principal meal to the night, eating just a little, once or twice during the day, or living on water alone, till his work is over.

This rule is especially binding on brain workers. It is they who become victims of chronic, difficult diseases in middle age due to neglect of this rule of health. Only those who have at least three hours of freedom from work after the meal should eat it at midday or at any time of the day. This period is to ensure a good start for digestion which, once started, will proceed smoothly, if only light work be done after the three hours.

Those who honour this rule enjoy positive health and exceptional longevity and retain their fitness for work even in old age.

## General Rules of Healthful Eating

Now, for the general rules of healthful eating. Only one *principal meal* a day must be eaten. Two substantial meals would soon destroy the sense of bodily lightness, which is the chief test of health. This loss of lightness, feeling that the body is a burden, is proof that eating is not right, and that health is being steadily lost.

A person who eats only a light meal when he eats at all may eat twice daily if he feels hungry twice. But a person who eats till his appetite is *fully sated* must eat only *one* meal a day.

Eating only one meal a day is the best habit. Eating twice is midway. Eating thrice is the worst habit.

For a person who wants to eat twice a day the rule is that only one of the meals – not both – must be the substantial principal meal of the day. The other must be a light one, not more than a third of the principal meal.

In summer, eating the light meal in the day and the heavier one at night enables one to escape the severe discomfort caused by seasonal heat. Eating heavily in the day makes one liable to suffer a "sunstroke," which may prove fatal.

In eating, one must consider the state of the mind also, because the quality of the mind depends very much upon the rightness or wrongness of the eating. The eater must understand the principles before he can apply them to suit his needs.

## Pleasure of Eating — A By -product

One should eat for the sake of health and efficiency, *not for the pleasure of eating.* The pleasure is just a by-product. If one observes health rules, the pleasure does come by eating, and with that pleasure one must be satisfied, without hankering for more. *One should not live to eat;* one must eat to live in health. He who eats for the pleasure of eating sooner or later loses his health and becomes a victim of deep-rooted diseases and· dies prematurely, meanwhile enriching the doctors.

## How Much to Eat

In eating one should provide for space in the stomach for the expansion and contraction of the lungs in breathing, and for water to satisfy genuine thirst. This rule applies chiefly to the principal meal. The ancients laid down this rule: "Two quarters of the belly space should be filled with food; one should be reserved for drinking water when needed; the fourth quarter should be left free for the movement of the breath." But this does not tell us when one should stop eating.

It should be noted that mealtime is not the proper time for drinking water freely. That comes later, as will be explained in its proper place.

Let those who labour with their gross bodies for their livelihood eat once a day as much as will satisfy them. But brain workers ought not to eat thus. They should always eat with self-restraint, and eat only unstimulating food, which we call *Sattvic* food. This will be explained later. Here we point out only that heavy eating degrades the person to the *Tamasic* level.

## The Minimum is the Maximum

For high-level health, only the *minimum* should be eaten. Eating more than that is overeating. *The minimum must be treated as the maximum.* Whether one is a worldly man, or one who aspires to achieve the State of Liberation one should practise abstemious eating.

So one should eat just so much as would not cause a feeling of heaviness after the lapse of the time specified above. Of course, bodily lightness will be affected even by a moderate meal. But the eater must take care not to eat so much as to completely lose that feeling of lightness. The sense of bodily lightness is also accompanied by a pleasant feeling in the mind, no clarity of the intellect. Eating within the natural limits is of very great importance, especially for brain workers.

If one habitually eats the minimum – which alone will be conducive to health – then the mind will be clear and efficient, and even without regular exercise there will be fitness of the body for work all the time. The need for special exercise arises chiefly from overeating. This will be explained in greater detail when dealing with exercise.

## Rules of Vital Economy

The following are the rules of Vital Economy:

One should chew each mouthful so well that the food is broken into small particles and becomes well mixed with the *saliva*. Food so eaten is easily digested by the organs lower down. In eating by this rule, less is eaten in more time.

One should not eat at meal time a number of *courses*, one after another, but eat only *one* course, into which may be mixed all the foods that need to be eaten. Eating many courses causes overeating by the revival of the appetite, due to the taste-stimulation in changing from one course to another.

Some say that if one eats only natural food, there can be no over-eating. This is absurd.

Another aid to the prevention of overeating is the signal that comes up from the stomach. This signal is a wind from the stomach which warns that eating should be stopped at once. Those who eat more than one course need to respect this rule religiously. It may appear to the novice that he has not eaten enough. But this is a mistake. If one gets accustomed to eating according to rules, this mistaken notion will fade away.

## Appetisers

Appetisers like salt, tamarind (or lime juice), chillies or pepper, asafoetida and the rest, which provoke overeating and irritate and inflame the stomach and other organs, must be greatly reduced, if they cannot be given up entirely. Incurable diseases like blood pressure become curable if salt and other appetisers are given up. Hunger is the best sauce.

But we do not say that food should not be tasty. The natural tastes of wholesome foods become obscured by the use of appetisers and, finally one loses the awareness of those tastes. By the practice of right eating this awareness is revived, and then food becomes enjoyable. In the transition period however the eater should curtail the use of appetisers. *Food that is relished in the eating is better digested.*

Sudden and wholesale renunciation of appetisers is not easy. The non-*Sattvic* who gives them up all at once is unable to persist in his resolution. So he resumes their use.

Extremely sweet food may also be a cause of overeating and imperfect digestion. Food eaten should be only mildly sweet. Artificial sweetening is best avoided.

## Vital Economy in Treatment too

The rules of Vital Economy in relation to food have been stated above. In the methods of treatment for the cure of disease also this principle applies. The treatment should be neither too little nor too much. It should be adjusted to the patient's vitality; this rule is specially to be observed in destructive cases.

## Benefits of Vital Economy

An immediate benefit from this reform is the *restoration of the lost balance between the food eaten and the oxygen breathed in; it was insufficient but now becomes sufficient, without better breathing.* Soon a process of rejuvenation begins, by which all the vital organs become more efficient. The improved lungs enable the eater to practise better breathing. The stomach, recovering its natural tone, refuses to submit tamely to ill-usage as before. This means that the eater has now a Monitor to keep him on the straight path.

# ELEVEN

# Food for Health

We have now to determine what, according to the Life Natural, is the food for Health. There are vegetarians who assert that their plain vegetarianism is the best regimen. But it is seen that vegetarians also are subject to disease through defects in their diet. They live principally on cereals, rice or wheat, which is their staple food, with a little quantity of vegetables for taste. This staple food does not appear to be good for health. Man can enjoy a very high-level of health without cereals or gram. The Maoris of the Polynesian Islands in their natural state lived on fruits and vegetables. They had no agriculture and therefore they had no cereals – no rice, no wheat, no maize, nor millets. It was only when they became converted to the Western way of life that they lost their health. The proper term to designate their dietary in their primitive state is not vegetarianism but *vegetablarianism*.

During the third decade of this century, when the author lived in Pondicherry, it occurred to him to try the effects of making vegetables the staple food in place of rice. At that time he did not know of the work of Prof. Arnold Ehret, who taught and practised what he called the "Mucusless Diet Healing System". Later the author came to read his book under that title. He found that his system of vegetablarianism was based on the same principles as those of Ehret. Vegatablarianism is conducive to a higher degree of the bodily tissues and thus vegetables are our food for Health, and not cereals. On such a dietary the body constitution is a healthy one, whereas, if vegetables be neglected, health is imperfect. The body gets loaded with mucus.

## Soil Health

At the very outset an important point to be borne in mind is the quality of soil, which depends chiefly on the kind of manure used on it. For more than 4,000 years, all over the world, farmyard manure, with green manure, has been used, with the best of results. Soil fertility, which tends to become exhausted by growing the same crops continually, is renewed and the fertility thus maintained confers very good health on the people who eat food grown on such a soil.

The fertility of soil depends on the presence in it of a substance called humus, which is produced as a result of the use of natural manures. The experiments conducted by Sir Albert Howard at Indore have clearly shown that by the use of chemical fertilisers the soil is robbed of its humus, that only very poor quality crops can be produced that way and that those who consume such products suffer in health. On the other hand, crops grown on compost manure are nutritionally of a high standard and hence good for health.

Chemical fertilisers destroy soil fertility in many ways. One of their evil effects is the destruction of the germ population of the soil which carries out important functions in ensuring a healthy growth of crops. A scientist, Hugh Nicol, in his book *Microbes and Us* writes that these organisms thrive on the soil and are able to do their good work for the cultivator, and that when the humus is absent they die off. Hence, it is a bad policy to use chemicals as manure.

Another effect of chemical fertilisers is the increase of insect-pests that invade the crops. To kill them, poisonous pesticides are sprayed on the plants and this poisons the food for those who eat it, sometimes resulting in their death. Plants growing on soil 'fertilised' with chemicals lose their stamina and attract the insect-pests, unlike those grown on soil not poisoned with chemicals. The remedy is to stop using fertilisers.

Vegetables and fruits raised on soils manured with chemicals are insipid – do not have the agreeable taste of those grown naturally. Hence they have little or no health value as diet for healing the sick.

Where the humus is not maintained in the soil by a sufficient use of compost manure, the soil deteriorates and goes out of cultivation and becomes a desert.

## Sir Robert McCarrison's Experiments

Howard's work and findings have corroborated those of Sir Robert McCarrison who studied the health of the Hunza people and later conducted experiments at the Nutrition Research Laboratory at Coonoor. His experiments showed that wholesome natural food, with plenty of vegetables and fruits, was ideal for health maintenance (and the consequent freedom from disease), while consumption of polished and refined foods, without practically any vegetables and fruits, made his rats sick with different types of diseases. As in his experiments with different groups of rats, the only difference was in the food given to them, it was indisputable that the difference in the food was the cause of the health or ill health produced and *the germ theory was disproved 'scientifically', that is, in a laboratory, on animals.* But this conclusive demonstration was ignored totally by the medicos.

## Classification of Foods

Vegetables and fruits have a higher value for health than cereals and other grains, such as grams. The foods that are healthful will be distinguished as *positive* foods and the rest as *negative.*

Positive foods are also distinguished as *primary* foods. Negative foods are *secondary* foods. These positive, primary foods have plenty of cellulose or roughage and a high water context. Hence, they are lighter and easier to digest, and act as laxatives, so that there is no need for laxative drugs if one lives on these bulky foods. On the other hand, negative, secondary foods are constipating, because they are highly concentrated, very rich in carbohydrates, protein or fat. Those who eat such foods in great excess, neglecting the positive foods, are sick most of the time. These food constituents are difficult to digest, unless taken in strictly limited quantities.

We must keep in mind this distinction between the postive food factors and the negative ones. The latter have been mentioned. The former, in scientific terms, are called vitamins and organic minerals or salts, which are alkaline, and help to maintain the alkalinity of the blood. The negative food factors are chemically the opposite to the alkalis, and are acid-forming and thus promote ill health.

While, positive foods ensure elimination of body-waste, which is filth, negative food factors produce waste-products which need to be eliminated with the help of the positive foods. Hence, negative foods, eaten in the slightest excess, are health destroying and disease promoting. It has been explained already that foods raised on soil poisoned with 'fertilisers' are poor in the positive food factors, and tend to cause obesity and other forms of ill health.

Refined, manufactured, tinned, bottled, preserved foods do not have any health value whatever. These are devitalising; they can only weaken the individual, leading to the developing of chronic and destructive diseases.

## Freshness Factor

Foods, to be healthful, should be fresh and alive when taken. When freshness is lost, the vitality of the food is also lost. It must be noted that foods have the quality of life, which means that aliveness of the food must not be lost. Food that has lost its aliveness has ceased to be food, and should not be eaten, however tasty it may be made by the addition of salt and spices or by frying.

## Composition of Food

The first rule of eating is, therefore, to make positive foods the staple food. Negative foods should be partaken sparingly, as otherwise there will be loss of health. About 80 per cent of the food eaten must be positive, the remainder constituting negative foods in good condition.

## Primary and Secondary Foods

Primary foods consist of tender leafy vegetables and fruits.

Secondary foods are milk, eggs and seeds or grains. These are intended by Nature to serve as sustenance of the young of the species. Cow's milk is for the calf, as mother's milk is for the infant, not for grown-ups. The eggs are for the chicks growing inside it. The seed is for the future plant to sprout and put forth leaves.

The seondary foods, which are rich in nourishing food factors, as sub-divided by scientists are heat-giving and muscle-building. The latter are called proteins. Starch, sugar and fat are heat-giving. This is not quite correct.

## Non-vegetarian Food

The reader may ask about the place of non-vegetarian food (flesh, fish and fowl) in human diet. If the question is looked at from the ethical angle, the answer is obvious. Even from the hygienic angle, non-vegetarian food cannot be recommended for the following reasons:

(i)    A comparison of the human anatomy with that of herbivorous, frugivorous and carnivorous animals shows that the human system resembles that of the frugivorous animals and not that of the carnivorous.

(ii)    Meat begins to putrefy the moment the animal is slaughtered and the longer the interval between the killing and the eating of the flesh the more filthy it becomes. The same applies to fish.

(iii)    Before animals are taken to the slaughter house, they are overfed and artificially fattened, so that more meat could be obtained therefrom. They are also drugged. Again, in most cases only old and sick animals are slaughtered. The meat of such animals cannot be health promoting.

(iv)    If the waters are chemically polluted, as is often the case, the fish taken out of them can be very harmful.

(v)    All types of non-vegetarian foods are very rich in saturated fatty acids, consumption of which can produce arteriosclerosis, fatty deposits in the liver, heart and kidneys.

## Facts to be Known

Among the 'heat-givers' there are those that contain fat, namely nuts and oil-seeds. The rest are free from fat. Fat is a disturbing food-factor and must be eaten sparingly, even less than the protein-bearing foods.

All foreign matter is of acid quality and to neutralise and eliminate it, the alkaline constituents of positive foods are available, not in negative ones. Acid-forming foods are therefore to be taken sparingly. Excess of these foods has a disease-producing effect.

Much of the foreign matter is in the form of *mucus*. In its natural state, it serves as a lubricant and is therefore harmless and useful. But in an abnormal state it becomes viscous and a cause of what are called catarrhal diseases, like cold and cough.

The alkalis needed for health must be obtained from positive foods. Inorganic alkalis are not used by the living body; they are but poisons, that can be eliminated only by fasting. Hence positive foods are medicine for health, not negative ones. The *Taittiriya Upanishad* says that Food is the Universal Medicine. In different words, Hippocrates said the same thing: *Let food be your medicine and let medicine be your food.* Here only positive foods are meant, not negative ones.

It is possible for one to live on positive food alone, without negative ones like rice or wheat, as demonstrated by the splendid health of the Maoris in their primitive state. Hence they are self-sufficient, not so the negatives.

Bodily organs, if built up with positive foods, are well formed and healthy. Negative foods disturb this healthy quality and so lower the quality of the constitution. Thus, it will be seen that positive and negative foods are opposites and, like plus and minus quantities in mathematics, cancel each other; the lesser, losing its vigour, has no effect as against the other. For this reason, the positive foods must be taken in much larger proportion than the negative ones, according to the needs of the constitution. For healthy persons a proportion of 2:1 or two-thirds, may suffice. For cure of ill health a large proportion, 4:1 or four fifths or even 5:1, may be needful. In many cases, in the initial stages, negative foods have to be excluded for some period.

What scientists have to say about the constituents of food, vitamins and minerals is not given here, as these have no practical value. If the rules of diet are observed, that is, if the food is fresh and complete, not tampered with by commercial agencies nothing is taken away and nothing added to it, and if variety is maintained, that will be enough.

Leafy vegetables contain an abundance of positive food factors with very little of the negative ones and hence are more highly positive than other vegetables and should be taken as part of a meal.

Among fats those that made of saturated fatty acid are derived from animal sources. Vegetable oils contain unsaturated fatty acids. So, while the latter may be used sparingly, the former must be strictly avoided. Hydrogenated oil, which goes by the name of Vanaspati in this country, is made by converting unsaturated fatty acids into saturated ones by a process called hydrogenation and should not be used. Its long use results in various diseases of a chronic nature.

Coconut is preferable to other nuts, because its protein is of a high class. Its fat content is low, and as it contains a lot of roughage it is safe. Nuts are easily digested. Each globule of nut-paste is made up of a spherical container built of protein, inside which there is the fat particle. This fat does not hinder the digestion of the food in the stomach. When protein is digested the oil that is set free at once goes into the small intestine where it is easily digested. This shows how Nature has adapted the food to suit the natural process of digestion. Fried foods are just the opposite. The fat is on the outside and the protein or starch on the inside. So fried food is unwholesome.

Eggs are not natural food. They are too heavy, consisting mostly of protein and some fat. They are not clean. They are indigestible and health destroying. They lead up to diseases of the heart and other diseases.

It should be noted that leaves (herbs and leafy vegetables), vegetables and fruits are the foods for health; they are also medicine.

Herbs of a Sattvic quality (which are non-poisonous, non-specifics) can be used as food supplements to aid the recovery of health in the treatment of chronic diseases and in sub-acute illnesses. If doubt arises whether a particular herb is Sattvic or not, the test to be applied is this: if it is eaten by a cow or goat, it is Sattvic; otherwise, it is not. Cows and goats avoid all non-Sattvic leaves.

Sattvic herbs may be dried in the shade for a week or more and then powdered. This powder can be taken by patients as a food supplement to hasten their recovery. It may also be used as a dentifrice for cleaning the teeth.

## Cereals

Cereals which have been subjected to manufacturing processes, in which positive food factors that are of great value for health, like the bran and the germ of the grains, have been removed and some artificial, manufactured substitutes added to make good the loss, are not foods in any sense, but poisons and should be strictly avoided. Unpolished rice, ground in a wooden handmill, so that the germ and bran are not lost, may be used but in smaller rations because they are richer in all the essential food factors. If eaten in excess, even these may upset the digestive process.

Polished rice, if eaten without a sufficiency of vegetables, is the most unwholesome of all foods.

The same rule applies to wheat and other grains. The germ and bran of the wheat must be preserved. That is, the grain must be ground in domestic stone mills, and the coarser particles must not be separated by sieving, as is done now.

## Fruits

Among fruits, the sweet ones, and those that are only slightly sour, should be eaten, not positively sour ones like lemon which are harmful to health. Sour fruits belongs to an inferior class of foods, according to the teachings of the *Gita*.

There are Nature Cureists who advise against the use of tamarind, but suggest lemon as a substitute. But how is lemon better than tamarind, which is also a fruit? The juice of the lemon is a stronger acid than that of the tamarind.

In the case of jaundice, lemon proves helpful. It is also useful in tickling a sluggish liver and in cases of fever when the patient has a bitter taste in the mouth. Such use of lemon is made on the dictates of Nature. The moment the trouble is over, the taste for lemon also goes.

Also, only naturally ripened fruits should be consumed. Artificially ripened fruits are harmful to health. Packed fruits transported from a long distance and kept in closed containers for quite some days or weeks, with chemicals sprayed over them to "preserve their freshness" are useless, and even harmful from the viewpoint of health.

## Sattvic, Rajasic and Tamasic Foods

In the *Sri Bhagavad Gita* foods are distinguished by three grades of goodness or otherwise as Sattvic, Rajasic and Tamasic, showing what foods are wholesome and what are not. The following verses from the 11th chapter of the *Gita* which describe these kinds of food:

> *Foods that are conducive to longevity, strength and purity of mind and body, freedom from disease, happiness, cheerfulness, which are juicy, containing lubricant fat, enduring and pleasant, are agreeable to the Sattvic man.*

> *Food that are very bitter, harsh or pungent are dear to the Rajasic kind of man, and are the causes of disease of body or depression of mind.*

*Foods which through lapse of time have lost their freshness and savour which have foul smell, as also those that are stale, are the remainder left over after eating, and which is unclean, are agreeable to the Tamasic man.*

Here it will be seen that the *eaters* of foods are designated as Sattvic, Rajasic or Tamasic. By implication, the foods also are of the same nature.

Men of Rajasa or passionate temperament are subject to desires, and are unsteady in their moods. They are inferior to those of the highest grade, the Sattvikas, restless in actions, covetous, arrogant and vain, undisciplined, and make no progress spiritually. They are selfish in their outlook and conduct.

The Tamasas are content to remain ignorant and indisciplined, are forgetful, lazy and mentally weak.

Because men prefer foods of their own level of character, these three qualities form a vicious circle, generally not permitting improvement. The effort to reform is always countered by the mind's opposition due to its love of pleasure. Will power is needed for successful reform.

The quality of a person depends on the grade of food he eats. So, if a person of lower grade takes to the eating of food of a higher grade, then in course of time his character is raised to that superior grade.

For the sake of health it is necessary to eat only Sattvic foods. Abstemiousness in eating should be practised at all times.

Since it is said that even the food of middling quality is disease promoting, if follows that food of the lowest grade is even worse in its ill effects on health.

## Tamasic Foods

Foods that are by nature, or passage of time, foul-smelling are Tamasic. Since Tamasic food generates forgetfulness, disinclination to work and delusions, the man who desires to improve himself must renounce the food of the lowest grade. All Tamasic food is laden with filth, and hence injurious to good health. Substances that are intoxicating are excessively Tamasic and debasing and are, therefore, destructive to health, namely, tobacco, alcoholic drinks,

69

etc. Such stuff poisons and weakens the brain. Of course, it affects other organs also. To emancipate oneself from addiction to such drugs, one will have to practise fasting and abstemious eating. This clears the brain of the poison and then it is easy to renounce these evil things.

## Rajasic Foods

Now we come to Rajasic foods. Foods which are by nature sour or having other Rajasic characters, as enumerated before, or have been made so by additives, are Rajasic. They provoke over eating. Also, they irritate and injure the digestive organs and thus tend to set up disease.

Pepper, salt and sour sauces, if very very sparingly used, may be treated as Sattvic. Even a slight excess is injurious to health. If sourness be lessened, very little salt will be needed. Salt in excess is injurious even to the healthy. For chronic patients it is desirable to omit salt altogether.

Sweet stuff, it is assumed, is Sattvic. Excessively sweet things are not Sattvic. They should be treated as Rajasic, and should be used sparingly, not in excess. Refined, crystallised white sugar is not a food but poison, because the positive food factors of cane juice have been removed in the process of refining. Jaggery or unrefined sugar is permissible in moderation. Fresh cane juice is superior to jaggery, and may be taken when available.

Dates, being exceedingly sweet, must be taken sparingly.

## Stimulants

We now come to the so-called stimulating drinks: tea, coffee, cocoa, etc. These are poisons and depressants. They do not contribute anything to our vitality. They just unlock our own Vital Reserve, which is thus lost. Thus they are *thieves* of vitality. These drinks, given to children, hinder their normal growth and development. They are bad for adults also, especially when made strong, by allowing a longer time for the ingestion to take place.

## Sattvic Foods

Now we come to Sattvic foods. Foods which are mild in taste, are not irritating, are neither Tamasic nor Rajasic, are Sattvic. But Sattvic persons alone can appreciate their excellence. Body tissues and cells built up with such foods live long and are hence described as *'enduring'*. This quality makes it easy for the eater to be satisfied with eating the bare minimum. This interpretation was given by Acharya Sankara Bhagavatpada in his commentary on the *Bhagavad Gita*.

If Sattvic food is eaten in excess it ceases to be Sattvic. Therefore, Sattvic food also must be eaten with self-restraint, sparingly, not more than the minimum needed. It should be understood that this *minimum is itself the maximum*. To eat even a single mouthful more than the minimum is over eating and will tend to upset the Vital Economy. This is the teaching of our ancients.

## Milk

We should now consider the milk problem. In the light of our principle of Vegetablarianism, milk is not a positive food, but a negative one. As such it must be taken, if at all, sparingly. Innumerable cases of loss of health are traceable to excessive consumption of this negative food. Some, feeling that the drinking of milk is morally wrong, put the question, "what is the substitute for milk?" The question does not arise at all.

Milk, according to Arnold Ehret, is a mucus-forming food, giving rise to what are called catarrhal diseases, such as cold and cough in the early stages, later bronchitis and pneumonia. If milk and milk-products are given up and a positive course of diet is adopted, these diseases are got over. Chronic catarrah takes a longer time to cure.

A test was made, on the suggestion of Mahatma Gandhi, on a person who had fasted for 28 days. On breaking the fast, instead of milk and milk products he was given only vegetable soup flavoured with a little coconut milk. Within a week he regained his strength and vitality, and was able to walk to and fro, five miles, both morning and evening.

Since milk is a product of grass or green leaves (herbs) those who chew a few tender green leaves will get greater benefit of health from them than from milk. Whatever good there is in milk is present in grass or other herbs. Proof of the goodness that is there in herbs is provided by the following example. A woman who had just been delivered of a baby had no milk in her breasts, and consulted the author's son L. Kamesvara Sarma, who prescribed drinking of a cup of grass juice a day on an empty stomach. After three days she reported that milk had been formed in the breasts and she was able to feed the child in the natural way.

Goat's milk is more positive than that of cow's, because goats eat a greater variety of green herbs. Also cows in the countryside give better milk than cows fed unnaturally in cities.

It may be noted that milk must not be boiled, not pasteurised, as this destroys its good qualities. Fresh, raw milk alone may be taken, by a healthy individual, if he wants to have it, but in strict moderation, in place of a meal and not in addition to it. But excess of milk can harm health. If the milk is free from bad smell or taste, it is all right. Actually, the germs present in milk are friendly ones, not dangerous to health. Pasteurisation takes away the freshness and many nutrients of milk, so that it is no longer milk, but a dead substance. Milk that has been pasteurised is stale.

## Food Combinations

For easy and quick digestion of food it is necessary to observe the rules of food combination. These rules have application only to the principal or substantial meal of the day, not to the light repasts at other times. One rule is that solid and liquid foods should not be eaten during a single meal, since digestion is delayed unnecessarily by this combination. It is for this reason that drinking water with meals is prohibited.

It is stated as a rule of food combination that protein and starch should not be eaten at the same meal. The proponents of this rule say that starch is digested in the mouth by the action of the saliva which is alkaline and has an enzyme, ptyalin, which acts upon and splits the molecules of starch while protein is digested in an acid medium — the gastric juice — whose active principal is pepsin. So when the starch, whose digestion begins in the mouth, when swallowed, gets mixed with the acid gastric juice, the digestion of starch cannot be completed. Hence, they say, starch and protein should not be eaten together at one meal.

They are however, mistaken in this, because Nature has made provision for the continuation of starch digestion in the stomach itself. The stomach is in practice not a single organ, but has two distinct parts. The left half of the stomach, which is spherical, serves as a reservoir or holder of the food for some time. The right half, smaller but more muscular, secretes gastric juice which digests the protein in the food, when it comes into it and then pushes it into the intestine, the digestive organ next to the stomach. Meanwhile, there is an interval varying from half an hour to two hours, during which the salivary digestion of the starch continues, because the gastric juice takes time to penetrate the food-mass in the left half of the stomach, called the 'fundus'. So the case is not so bad as made out by proponents of the protein or starch rule. The utmost disadvantage of taking protein and starch together, as when one is eating wheat *roti* is that it delays digestion. It does not cause indigestion. Still, it is a good rule not to complicate the process by adding more starch or more protein to the meal by eating some other food which will increase the protein or the starch already in the wheat *roti*. Cereals like wheat and rice, are concentrated foods, and hence at the principal meal, only one concentrated food should be eaten, not more.

Another rule is that, as starch is digested in an alkaline medium, no highly sour sauce or other stuff should be eaten along with a starch meal. Excess of protein is not good for health, as stated before. Also, foods having different degrees of ease in digestibility should be eaten at different times, not at the same meal. Thus fruits should be eaten at different meals. Fruit and milk — if the latter be taken sparingly — is a good combination.

Vegetables combine well with protein or with starch.

Oil, if limited in quantity, goes well with protein or with starch. Oil should, however, not be used for frying.

## Salads

Because in cooking positive foods lose some of their health promoting food factors — vitamins, organic minerals and perhaps, other yet unknown elements — one should as far as possible take them uncooked, prepared as salads. For this purpose they should be tender, not mature. It is generally agreed that about half the meal should consist of salads — raw foods. Salads are prepared by washing the vegetables and then cutting them into small pieces, and then flavouring them with a few drops of lime juice, coriander leaves and coconut scrapings. Some may prefer to add fresh sweet curds; if this is done the quantity used should be small, not more than an ounce. An excess of curds is not good.

## Alkaline Vegetable Juices

The juice of ash pumpkin has been found very effective in relieving discomforts in the digestive system due to excessive acidity. For acute stomach pains due to indigestion about 4 oz. of diluted juice can be taken in the morning on an empty stomach.

Juice extracted from banana stem is a well known remedy for digestive and urinary disorders. It improves the functional efficiency of the kidneys and the liver thereby alleviating the discomforts and diseased conditions in them. It also improves the functioning of the prostate, gall bladder and urinary tract. In short, it clears the excretary organs in the abdominal cavity of toxins. It helps to eliminate the toxins in the form of urine. It has been found of great help in the treatment of prostate troubles as also for the removal of stones in the kidneys and gall bladder. Banana stem juice also reduces blood cholesterol and clears the arteries. Even blood clots are dissolved. The juice has been found to be a good remedy also for reducing obesity.

Whenever possible it should be mixed with juice of ash pumpkin.

Tender coconut water is a subsistence food containing electrolytes like sodium chloride and potassium, with potassium in its highest concentration. It has been found equal to blood plasma in its qualities and action on the human body. It has a soothing effect on the digestive system. During illness, this drink acts as an effective agent for reducing inflammation, both internal and external. In cases of acute diseases like diarrhoea, cholera, dysentery, etc., it has been found to replace the lost body fluids due to dehydration very effectively.

The water of tender coconuts provides a good approach to fasting. If drunk for a month or more, it produces beneficial results. It suits patients of chronic or destructive diseases, such as consumption or TB of lungs.

## Sattvic Herbs

Due to unnatural methods of cultivation foodstuffs available in the market are gradually losing their food values, which are being replaced by chemical poisons as a result of the use of fertilisers, pesticides, fungicides, etc. Mankind is also threatened by pollution of all sorts. The general health level of the people is rather low.

In such circumstances use of Sattvic herbs, both in health and in illness, becomes very necessary. Sattvic herbs have a high potency of food values and partaking of even small quantities of these herbs will ensure health to the human body. They also cleanse the system more effectively than cultivated vegetables and fruits.

Some of the common Sattvic herbs are: (i) aegle marmelous corea, (ii) basilicum citratum, (iii), centella asiatica; (iv) eclipta alba hassk; (v) eravatamia coronaria stape; (vi), euphorbia hirta linn; (vii) evolvulus alsinoides linn; (viii) holy basil; (ix) boerhavia diffusa; and (x) Solanum nigrum.

We have described only a very few Sattvic herbs. The reader is encouraged to use any edible herb which will satisfy the stipulations of universality and non-specific quality. Sattvic herbs are by nature universal; They will do only good to the healthy and the diseased when taken and can be recommended for the treatment of any form of disease, be it fever or asthma. Though all Sattvic herbs satisfy these stipulations it must be borne in mind that each herb possesses certain individual qualities.

Some Sattvic herbs are available at every place in our country. To take a few leaves of them every day will keep people healthy.

## Indian Gooseberry

Premature grey hair, heaviness of head or dullness of brain (including lunacy), irritable temper, loss of patience, etc., have been relieved by use of the Indian gooseberry (phyllanthus emblica, which is the richest source of vitamin C or ascorbic acid. The raw fruit is crushed and applied over the head, and allowed to dry while basking in the sun followed by a full bath.

## Cyndon Dactylon Bermuda Grass)

Known in this country as Dhurwa Grass, this herb is very effective in the cure of all stages of a disease. As it contains a lot of calcium, it is highly recommended for regular use, particularly by young children and expectant mothers. It promotes lactation in the case of mothers to breast-feed their infants with abundance of milk. It removes the causes of calcification of bones.

## Cooking

The amount of loss of positive food factors differs with different methods of cooking. The following are the chief cooking methods, in order of merit: 1) Baking in a closed oven, with a cover over the vessel; 2) Steaming in a closed receptacle; and 3) Boiling with minimum of water, the escape of vapour being controlled by a close-fitting lid. These are called conservative methods of cooking.

Roasting and frying in oil or ghee are wasteful and should not be resorted to. But slight roasting of nuts for a very short time, so as not to discolour them — so that their natural white colour is not lost — is permissible. In tne context it must be remembered that since nuts are negative foods, they should be eaten sparingly. In excess nuts are health disturbers.

Foods are rendered poisonous and bad for health by being cooked in metallic vessels. Among these are aluminium vessels. Brass or copper vessels, if tinned with *pure* tin, not with tin mixed with lead or zinc, are safe to use. Stainless steel vessels are suitable for keeping food after cooking, but not good enough for use in cooking. Earthen vessels are the best of all. Enamelled vessels of superior quality may be used.

In preparing dishes, care should be taken to see that there is minimum loss of nutrients.

## Water

Water used for cooking or drinking should be free of all inorganic substance, as these affect health. Water which has been treated with alum or chlorine is not safe. The former is used for clarifying water containing clay. Seeds of *kataka* should be used for precipitating clay, if necessary; but water red with suspended clay is harmless and may be drunk unclarified; the clay is not absorbed into the blood, but passes out in the stools.

Chlorine is a poisonous susbtance, and hence chlorinated water should not be consumed. To be on the safe side, one should consume plenty of vegetables and fruits, as these supply water of the best quality. Also, reduction of the salt added to food for taste will reduce the need for drinking water.

The best water for drinking is rain water. Also water of rivers and tanks that are well conserved and free from pollution. Well water may also be used. Water exposed to sunlight is good for health, not water which has not been so exposed.

Water which has been heated and kept for some time and thereafter drunk is not good; for heated water if kept for some time, loses some of its subtle essence which is necessary for health.

Excessive drinking of water is bad for health. As a rule, water should be drunk only when there is a feeling of thirst. Those who practise vegetablarianism do not need water at all.

Water should not be drunk at the commencement of a meal. A little water may be drunk at the end of the meal, not freely. About half hour before meals, and for two or three hours after meals, no water should be drunk; water may be drunk freely more than half an hour before eating and two or three hours after meals, where there is difficulty of digestion.

Excessive water drinking causes flatulence (gas formation).

Sipping cold water in small doses — called *achamana* — is good for reducing internal heat.

## Adopting Diet Reform Cheerfully

The health-seeker should reform his diet on the above lines cheerfully, with full mental cooperation, so that he can derive the maximum benefit therefrom. What is done superficially or mechanically, and hence without cheer, brings about restlessness of the mind resulting in loss of health.

# TWELVE

# Fasting

In fasting there is abundant rest--for recuperation and radical cure of diseases--and hence we shall discuss how and when to fast, so as to get the best results and avoid the dangers that beset this measure of our hygienic practice. In fasting, the vital power released from its usual heavy labour of digestion becomes available for lightening the encumbrances of toxic filth deposited in various parts of the living body.

## Necessity for Fasting

The necessity for fasting is this. A man who treats his stomach unfairly, by eating without hunger, by overeating, etc., becomes sick. He can get rid of his illness only be fasting and by eating abstemiously so as to maintain the highest possible level of Vital Economy. In some cases, by eating sparingly one can get better health without fasting. In other cases, this will not be sufficient; it will become necessary to give a more complete rest, and this can be done by fasting. This fasting must be looked upon as an expiatory activity called *prayaschitta,* for eating contrary to the Divine Laws of Health.

## When to Fast

Unmistakably, in acute conditions of ill health, Nature says, "Don't eat". Those who disregard Nature's Voice are inferior even to animals.

Keen hunger does not come to patients of chronic disease. For such persons, short fasts at intervals are necessary for recovery of hunger.

## What Sustains Life?

It has been shown in the *Chhandogya Upanishad* that Life has its source in water, and hence a faster who takes sufficient water will not die. In this holy book is narrated the story of a fast undertaken by one Svetaketu for 15 days. The fast was prescribed for him by his father to convince him that Life is made up of water, and so one can fast on water alone, but for not too long a time.

Not water alone, but also the three higher primaries of creation--sunlight, air and ether--sustain life during a fast.

## Objections Answered

Now we shall consider the main objections to fasting set forth by medicos. The statement that a faster lives upon his own flesh during fasting is not true. What happens is that during the fast, Life itself gets rid of the flesh tainted with toxic filth, because it is a hindrance. When by such vital effort the tainted flesh is eliminated, no more flesh is lost, even if the fast be continued for some time longer. We ask, Where is the harm if sickly flesh is 'lost'? When the body is purified by fasting, then healthy flesh is formed, which will be serviceable to Life.

In the case of a person who takes no food for three months, the vital organs do not lose much of their substance. About one-third — 30 per cent of the muscles are lost. There is no loss of brain tissue. So wrote Dr Dewey, citing Yeo, author of a textbook on Physiology. Our fasts do not exceed three days at a time.

The next objection is that fasting weakens the faster. This feeling of weakness is due to the fact that in fasting the Life Force is engaged in eliminating the encumbering foreign matter. So the weakness is unreal; it is also only temporary. After a time, the weakness abates and strength returns. Also, not all fasters experience a feeling of weakness. The return of strength occurs even during the pendency of the fast.

It is said that men who are obese, with much fat deposited in many parts of their bodies, can fast, but not lean men. This is not true. The obese may feel a lot of discomfort while fasting, but fast they must for recovering their health. The lean ones can fast comfortably.

## Fasting in Acute Disease

In acute cases one must fast until the disease abates and there is a sense of lightness. Thereafter one must break the fast in the proper way so as not to prevent the re-establishment of health.

## Long Fasts not Recommended

As a rule, in chronic cases long fasts are not to be undertaken. Short fasts are proper and should be gone through many times at intervals. When the patient is not fasting, positive foods (which will not form deposits of foreign matter in the body) should be taken frugally to provide a sufficiency of positive food factors, organic alkaline salts and vitamins.

In chronic patients, there is considerable morbid matter inside the body to be eliminated. The Life Force is weakened due to years of unhygienic living. There is insufficiency of the cleansing alkalines in the body. If, in such circumstances, a long fast is undertaken, then any disease, lurking latent, may manifest itself and prove fatal. Latent diseases should not be allowed prematurely to change into patent forms and *they would so change* if non-violent, safe, methods of fasting are not followed. It must be noted that diseases do subsist in a latent form in most cases. They should not be stirred up prematurely, when the conditions are not favourable to their cure. A premature crisis of health may have a fatal tendency; in all cases there is difficulty in curing them. But if the safe methods advocated here are followed, the latent disease will become alleviated by right dieting and occasional fasting and then favourable conditions will be established, so that there will be no danger if the disease becomes manifest.

Again, the patient may not be mentally prepared to undertake a long fast. If he is compelled to do so, his mind will get upset and this may make the condition worse. If we let him alone, relying on a restricted diet of positive foods, with short spells of fasts off and on, the latent disease will become less severe and come out in a patent form only when Nature is ready to start a curative crisis, not a destructive one.

If, as is usually the case, a patient of chronic or destructive disease does not have natural hunger, then to correct that defect , it would be right for him to fast for not more than three days, or at the most for five days. If even then hunger does not return, the patient may take to a course of positive dieting which needs no digestive labour; for a few days, and fast again, and this may go on until hunger is regained.

The wise patient, therefore, must achieve depuration of the body and an increase of vitality, during the first stage of the treatment. Just as a bird needs two wings, one on each side, to fly, so the patient needs both fasting and dieting, alternately, not simultaneously.

The ability to fast can be increased by resort to progressive fasting, increasing the period slowly, stage by stage, repeating the fast many times in each stage.

## Hints on Fasting

A question arises, "when does fasting begin?" Fasting begins, not from the time the last meal is taken, but when a meal that is to be taken is omitted, that is, after the previous meal has been digested and the resulting wastes expelled, and hunger for the next meal is felt. This hunger is satisfied by drinking some water, not by eating. In the beginning for a day or two, hunger may arise now and then at the usual meal-times but each time is must be turned off by drinking water alone.

Every day, beginning from sunrise, the faster should go without food for six hours or more, until natural hunger is felt and then eat a light meal of positive food. If hunger comes the same day again, a much lighter meal of positive food may be taken, or the fast may be kept on till some time in the afternoon or in the evening. If the patient takes two principal meals daily, he is unlikely to make any appreciable progress to a cure, or the cure may be slowed down, and postponed to a far-off date.

Generally, if it be possible, the chronic patient must not engage in strenuous labour of any kind. If he is able to work, he must not work for too long a time. Also, he must refrain from work after taking a meal, according to the rule stated in the chapter on Vital Economy. For weak patients more rest and relaxation are necessary, if they are not to suffer injury to health. After months or years of such treatment, a high level of bodily lightness will be noticed, and from that time onwards there may be *curative crises,* which will take the form of 'acute' diseases, as in the first stage of disease progression. The curative crises are a sign that the vital power has increased, and the load of foreign matter has been greatly lessened. So these crises are not to be feared but welcomed and gone through with fasting, as prescribed for acute conditions. By this process health is recovered and the disease comes to an end. In some cases recovery of health comes without noticeable curative crises.

Another mode of fasting is possible and may be resorted to by patients of chronic ill health. In this method some highly positive drink is taken not more than four times a day. This mode is suitable for weak patients who feel that absolute fasting is beyond their capacity to go through.

It has been stated by L. Kamesvara Sarma that patients must

fast for some hours daily, and for a few days monthly. In many cases the former alone may suffice. In others, both should be put into practice. These instructions are for the cure of chronic diseases and those of *degeneracy,* explained before.

In fasting the patient should drink water as often as necessary, when thirst is felt. Also, it is proper for the fasting patient to take non-violent enemas to keep the bowels clean and empty. The same methods are necessary for *local* diseases, causes by accident or injury, or a local eliminatory effort of life. A local disease may be utilised by Nature for effecting elimination of matter, and this must be aided by several health building measures.

## Fasting in Destructive Disease

In diseases of degeneracy — of the third and last stage of disease-progression — fasting of some kind must be gone through, as explained for chronic cases.

Every day, fasting until noon or longer, waiting for hunger, partake sparingly of some light, positive food — fruits or vegetables, raw — uncooked. He should only so eat, a little each time, that the sense of bodily lightness is not lost, as in chronic cases.

In allopathic practice these rules are disregarded and the patient is fed on flesh, milk and other heavy foods, which he cannot digest, or eliminate, and this too many times a day. Patients who are thus overfed, ultimately die due to exhaustion of their vitality. There are, even among professors of our own system, many who feed their patients on the same lines as the allopaths, thereby killing them, not knowing the basic principles of our hygienic system.

The truth is that in chronic and destructive diseases there is dyspepsia and consequently an inability to digest heavy foods. Hence patients suffering from such diseases need to be treated like dyspeptics.

## Fasting in Mental Disorders

Mental disorders are also curable by resort to fasting, because these are due to the presence of toxic foreign matter deposited in their brains. When the brain is freed from this encumbrance, it becomes normal. There is no need to employ a psychopathic physician. It is however needful to state in this context that if some virulent poison, such as vaccine, has entered the brain, the cure of the disease may prove difficult, or even impossible.

## Fasting in Addiction

Addiction to the use of tobacco or other poisonous stuff can be got rid of by resort to fasting. For such patients both fasting and dieting are necessary as also other hygienic measures.

## Mental Poise Necessary

One should take to fasting only after studying and understanding the theory and practice of the system, and firmly believing in it, not at the command of a 'doctor' of Nature Cure; one must rely upon oneself and God and use his own discretion.

While fasting, the patient must not engage in talks with anyone who might frighten or discourage him. But if the patient is equipped with knowledge and strength of mind, and if not influenced by others, he may do so.

In latent and chronic disease conditions, one should fast only with a pure and strong mind, not otherwise. Purity and strength of mind are to be achieved by having faith in this true science, surrendering oneself to God and being fearless. This means and implies that one should be a devotee of God.

If, during fasting, the mind gets upset or is weakened, the fast should be given up at once, and dieting carried out as described for breaking the fast.

## Breaking the Fast

Most persons are able to go through a fast. The difference between a man of superior mind and one with an inferior mind will show itself in the breaking of a fast. A fast should be broken according to the rules so as to ensure its good results. If the rules are not followed, no good results will be achieved even unfavourable results may follow.

After a fast one should not eat a heavy meal at once so as to ensure best results  The patient should, in the beginning, take a small quantity of some very light food, which can be digested with ease. The reason is that, during the fast, the digestive organs have very little power of digestion. They are unable to do this work then. They need to be trained by easy stages, so that they can recover their digestive capacity.

In the *Chhandogya Upanishad* there is an analogy which helps in the understanding of the right procedure. "Just as the bits of live charcoal left over in the ashes, after a big fire has consumed all the fuel, are not equal to the burning of heavy fuel, so the digestive power at the end of a fast is unequal to the work of digesting heavy meals. But the bits of burning charcoal can be made into a fire by first putting on very light material, such as dried grass or twigs, so the digestive organs can be fed with very light food in very small rations, the food being increased gradually, so as to become fit for digesting heavier food."

How can the digestive organs have more power of work than that there is in the body as a whole? So in this procedure, one should have regard for the vital power manifest in the body as a whole, and increase the digestive load accordingly. As the bodily vigour increases, so should the food-load be increased. If one, without having regard to the increase of vitality, eats food too heavy for the organs, he will become weaker and not stronger. If, by doing what is not proper, one gets worse, he should fast again and then proceed with the method of breaking the fast on the right lines.

We have heard reports of people starving during a famine; when available, they eat heavy food and die of indigestion. So those engaged in helping these people should give them only so much food as would ensure their survival.

While breaking a fast there often arises a voracious appetite which, if indulged, will prove fatal. So the faster should be on his guard. If he does not resist this onslaught of appetite and experience an upset of health he should fast again.

In breaking a fast, the faster should take diluted fruit juice, tender coconut water, soup of vegetables, or thin buttermilk*, which is curd mixed with water and churned. So long as there is no increase in the digestive power, the same food should be taken. If the power increases, there should be a changeover to heavier food. At this time, either fruit or conservatively cooked vegetables should be eaten sparingly. By this non-violent and safe procedure the fast should be ended. The food should be well chewed and insalivated, so as to avoid overeating.

---

* The curd should, for obvious reasons, be made from fresh milk and not from pasteurised milk or from powdered milk. The curd should not be sour. It should not be sweetened with sugar or salted.

## Stay Cured

The wise follower of Nature Cure who has recovered health by resort to fasting should thereafter model his mode of living on the lines taught here. He should not go back to his old, unhygienic ways. Whoever lives in the way taught here will enjoy the natural happiness of his own Real Self, as well as health and longevity.

Here is a warning. If ample vitality and good health have been won by following the Right Path, one should not be worried about the bodily weight being less than what the medicos say should be. The weight should be left to Nature. What the weight of a healthy man should be is known to Her alone.

# THIRTEEN

# Continence

Self-control in sex relations, it has already been noted, is a measure of Vital Economy, equal in importance to eating righteously. Vitality, if not wasted in the pursuit of vulgar pleasures, becomes the means of building up a high level of character and achievement. On the other hand, the self-indulgent remain at a low level of the finer faculties and are of little use to themselves or to the world.

If a foundation of good health is laid during the years of growth until maturity is achieved, then it will be easy to live a life of qualified continence, such as is needed for life in marriage. For most people, celibacy and absolute continence are not at all suitable, because of the Rajasa element in their character. Self-restraint in this kind of enjoyment for the sake of bodily and mental health is necessary for those who wish to avoid the ruinous effects of unrestrained indulgence. In this way the *Vital Reserve* is maintained at a high level and a useful and reasonably happy life extending into old age becomes possible.

## Developing Self-restraint

The problem of continence is difficult, since it will not do to fight the lustful urge of the mind directly. A mind that is slave to lust appropriates to itself more than half of the available mental energy; the will to reform is weakened and impotent, and the habit of lustfulness remains unconquered. So it would be useless to try self-denial just when the urge has come on. Efforts must be made to undermine the power of the foe in the intervals between the urges, when the mind is more amenable to discipline, that is, when a Sattvic mood prevails. Along with the hygienic habits of right eating and regular fasting, one should seek to purify the nervous system and habits of thought by means of Pranayama (breath control), meditation and other yogic and religious practices, *Satsang* (company of the Holy Ones), reading of sacred books in a religious frame of mind, reciting hymns of praise and prayer, and the like. This implies that the follower must also be a devotee of God in his own way and be an ardent lover of *Mukti* (deliverance of the Supreme State). Meanwhile, temptation must be avoided for 'Discretion is the better part of valour'

## Sex: Sane and Safe

The following rules should be observed by followers of Nature Cure.

1. There must be no kind of sexual indulgence before growth has been completed and maturity reached; the mind must be kept engaged in a pursuit proper for studenthood.

*The sexual organs are the last to be developed. Puberty is not the end, but the beginning of this growth as was well understood by the ancients. Side by side with sex, the mind also grows and becomes mature, and what is spent in vulgar pursuits is so much taken away from the possibilities of mental excellance. Physical maturity is reached about the 24th year of age for males and a little earlier for females.*

2. In married life and after full maturity is reached, it is proper to have regulated sexual relations, the right of initiative being allowed to the wife, especially the choice as to when she should become pregnant. Sexual intercourse should be had not oftener twice a month, until conception takes place.

3. After conception there should be continence for at least three years; this period is for ensuring the healthy growth of the new life in the womb and its proper feeding afterwards.

4. There should be perfect gentleness and non-violence in sexual intercourse. The couple must have a Sattvic mentality before and during the sexual congress.

These rules express the *ideal* that the follower must aim at, and try to live up to, to the best of his power; in spite of failures he must persevere to the end.

Men of Sattvic mind are instinctively aware of the need for gentleness in sexual intercourse. Rudeness and crudeness, together with selfishness and impatience cause great mischief, the wife suffers mental and physical injury. The wife, if she be of a refined nature, is disgusted and offended. This can lead to domestic unhappiness. It is the mark of a high level of culture of a man to treat his wife with extreme courtesy and unselfish love, with a desire that she should joyously participate in the process. For this purpose the husband should be a good master of the art of love.

Gentleness and courtesy are of the greatest importance at the first conjugal meeting and for some period thereafter, until there is established mutual understanding and cooperation. The wife has a personality of her own, which must be treated as sacred. She must not be regarded as a mere chattel slave, having no rights of her own. She should be honoured as the mistress of the house and as a comrade and copartner in life.

It is also proper that there should be only one single act of sexual intercourse at a time. The act must be gone through in a leisurely way, without impatience, so that there will be complete satisfaction. We have already noted that sexual meetings must be spaced out so as to allow of an ample interval for recuperation.

## Birth Control

The problem of birth control, or avoiding too frequent pregnancies, is a difficult one, and there are two extreme views. Being extreme views, they are probably both wrong or at least inappropriate and impracticable. One extreme view is that advocated by moralists who fail to the take account of the mental and bodily states of those for whom they legislate. The other is the way of artificial birth control through devices purchased in western countries, which are grossly unnatural and not free from risks to health. We believe there is a middle path, one which was followed by the author, thereby securing a minimum of a three-year interval between every two pregnancies.

Birth control is desired as a rule for economic reasons by people who are not going to deny themselves any pleasure which is within their reach. For them the middle path is recommended. The act of sexual intercourse really consists or ought to consist, of two parts. In the first part there are various acts constituting what is called love play — acts in which the organs connected with impregnation are not concerned. These are described as external procedures of sexuality. The male must be willing to forego the gross pleasure associated with the final act, which leads to impregnation and conception and be satisfied with the preceding part alone. It has been objected that this partial abstention could be injurious to health. But the author can affirm emphatically that it is not.

From the context it will be clear that this practice is not for those who choose the path of complete abstention. It may be noted that we do not impose anything by authority. Everyone is free to choose for himself as he thinks fit. In carrying out this process the parties must have a common understanding and purpose. Both must be vigilant and cease from the indulgence soon enough to avoid disaster, whereby the purpose in mind is defeated.

There are other methods of birth control expounded in books. One of them is based on the theory that there is a 'safe' period in the middle of every menstrual period of the female. It is said this safe period consists of nine days, preceding the last nine days of the menstural period, at the end of which the menstrual flow appears. To follow this method, the approximate length of the menstrual cycle of a woman needs to be determined, by observation for a number of months. Complaints have been publicised that this 'safe' period is not really safe in all cases.

## Health in Old Age

As soon as possible, before old age sets in, one should renounce indulgence in sexual intercourse. This, according to Sri Ramakrishna Paramahamsa, is a means of enduring formation of the spiritual centre in the brain. He said that the semen that is thus saved serves to build up a Medha Nadi

# FOURTEEN

# Pranayama and Air Baths

Since life depends on the supply of oxygen from the air by the breathing process, it is necessary to make sure that enough of this important food is obtained. Most people in the modern world — addicted as they are to the 'civilised' ways of eating and living and to the repeated use of stimulants, sedatives, drugs and the like — breathe subnormally. Their organs of breathing, the lungs, are almost always in a *depraved, rigid, inelastic state* due to severe encumbrances, and the *breathing cannot be improved without first restoring the lost elasticity of the lung tissue.* If breathing exercises be tried without setting right this serious abnormality, there may be injury to health. So *the first thing to be done is to reduce the encumbrances sufficiently to permit the practice of better breathing.*

So, taking into account his own physical limitations, every individual should seek to improve his lung tone by doing Pranayama (deep breathing) in the non-violent manner explained below.

## Where to do Pranayama

The air that is to be breathed in must be the purest available. And such air is to be had only in the open or in a room with good cross-ventilation. Walking out in the open air, practising better breathing in rhythm with the footsteps is also helpful.

Cold air is most wholesome for breathing. But care must be taken not to expose oneself to air that is too cold to bear. If the air happens to be very cold at any time, let it be breathed in through the nostrils alone. The nostrils in a healthy condition act as 'air conditioners'. Even very cold air as it passes through the nostrils is warmed up by the time it reaches the lungs and the individual need not be afraid of being 'affected' by it (Conversely, very warm the air as it passes through the nostrils, is cooled before it reaches the lungs). *Clean air is the finest medicine for the lungs, the throat and all the air-passages, and also for the body as a whole.*

## Posture

While doing Pranayama, the individual should sit or stand erect. Bedridden patients, can do it on the bed, but to ensure correct posture, they should be on a hard bed and not on a soft one.

## Dress

The dress worn at the waist should be kept slightly loose, so that no pressure is felt on the abdomen. The dress around the trunk, if any, should also be slightly loose to allow the lungs to expand and contract easily.

## When to do Pranayama

Pranayama should be done either early in the morning, or at dusk in the evening, when the stomach is empty. It should never be done when the stomach is loaded. A few rounds of Pranayama, say 10, 15 or 20 could be done each time.

## How to do Pranayama

The act of breathing consists of four parts: (i) expulsion of foul air from the lungs; (ii) a brief pause for resting the lungs; (iii) drawing in of fresh, pure air from outside, and (iv) retention of it in the lungs, to allow the exchange of gases that takes place between the blood and the air breathed in, so that the blood could get rid of carbonic acid gas and take the life-giving oxygen in its place.

The four parts are named *rechaka, outer kumbhaka, puraka* and *inner kumbhaka. Of these, the rechaka* is biologically more important, because it is an act of *elimination* whereby the air spaces in the lungs are emptied of the foul air containing the carbonic acid gas thrown out from the blood. To the extent that the retained air is thrown out by *rechaka* — and only to that extent — can fresh air enter the lungs by the next *puraka,* the breathing in. If the emptying is defective, some of the foul air is retained and to that extent less fresh air comes in. Hence the great importance of *rechaka* in practising better breathing. If the emptying be made as thorough as possible, then more fresh air is drawn in and more oxygen is obtained by the next *puraka,* even though no effort is made to improve that part of the breathing. So it is recommended that, to begin with, the follower should confine his attention to the improvement of the *rechaka* and the *outer kumbhaka,* leaving the *puraka* and the *inner kumbhaka* to proceed automatically as before. This is in accordance with our basic policy of non-violence. By this alone a considerable improvement in health will come about in course of time. Efforts to improve all four at once should *not* be made unless the constitution is in a fit state for the practice. This must, as a rule, be thought of only after some years of natural living.

In the *puraka,* the air must be slowly and steadily drawn in, so that, first, the diaphragm, the bottom or the floor of the upper part of the trunk, is pressed down; the breathing should not now be stopped, but must be continued, so that the chest expands sideways, the ribs rising up, and allowing the top of the lungs to be filled with its proper share of the fresh air. In this latter process, the belly, which has been pushed outwards at first, is drawn in again. This is deep breathig. When this is mastered, then it will be time to take up improvement of the *kumbhaka.*

In the above method of *puraka,* two processes —usually considered to be alternative methods — are combined for the sake of perfection of breathing. In modern conditions many people have rigid chests, which do not allow chest breathing to be done; they do only abdominal breathing. To normalise their breathing they must recover elasticity of the lungs and then make special efforts to practise chest breathing, in which the ribs rising upwards cause the chest to expand sideways, thus increasing the spaces for air in the lungs; this can be tested by a tape, showing an expansion of the circumference of the chest. After gaining full control of chest breathing, they may try to combine the two, the abdominal and the chest breathing as described before. The rigidity of the chest ought not to be allowed to continue.

For patients and those of subnormal health, the practice of the *rechaka* alone will be sufficient. This they may practise on an empty stomach, while taking the spinal bath, or while walking. The pause after the *rechaka,* herein called the *outer kumbhaka,* must be attended to after the *rechaka,* as this is necessary for resting the lungs.

The mode of holding the fingers of the right hand for doing Pranayama should be as shown in Figure 1. With the right thumb, the right nostril is gently closed and the individual should do the *rechaka* through the left nostril slowly and gently, without feeling any kind of strain, but to the fullest extent possible. When the

92

*rechaka* is completed thus, the *outer kumbhaka* is done with the nostrils closed gently by the fingers as shown in Figure 2. The *puraka* is then done through the left nostril, pressing the right nostril gently and closing it. Then comes the *inner kumbhaka,* with both the nostrils gently closed. Again the *rechaka* is done gently but to the fullest extent possible. After one Pranayama is over, one can have a few normal breaths and then start the next Pranayama. For doing the *rechaka* and the *puraka,* breathing through the nostrils can be alternated by his own level of health and vital capacity. No exertion or force whatever is to be used for doing any one or more of its stages for a time longer than what can conveniently be endured by the individual.

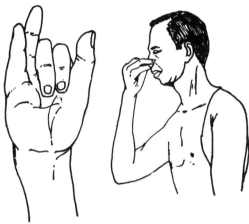

Fig. 1 – Fold in the index the middle finger; this becomes the mudra for Pranayama. The purpose of folding these two fingers is that there should not be undue pressure on the nostrils. The thumb will be used to close the right nostril and the little and second finger to close the left nostril.

Fig. 2 – Outer Kumbhaka. Rest to one of the vital organs, the lung, can be provided by introducing a pause between Rechaka and Puraka, when the lungs would remain empty.

With the regular practice of this kind of Pranayama and with the observance of the principles of Natural Hygiene in daily life, the health level of the follower would go up progressively and he would stand to benefit in every way.

## Caution on Hatha Yogic Pranayam

Having explained the technique of non-violent Pranayama, which can be ideally practised by everyone — ill or well — it becomes our painful duty to warn people against practising different types of Pranayama advocated by the Hatha Yogic school, e.g., Sitali,

Sitakari, Bhastrika, etc. While the select few who qualify themselves for the practice of Hatha Yoga, and later Raja Yoga, by observing the strict disciplines needed therefor at the physical, mental and spiritual levels, can doubtless practise such Pranayama, the common man, who cannot be deemed to be qualified for Hatha Yoga, should not attempt any of them. It is a pity that these types of Pranayama, as also complicated Yogic Kriyas and even Kundalini Yoga are demonstrated by 'Yogis' and 'Sannyasins' in public parks and through the mass media. The common man should not be tempted to do them.

These Yogic kriyas are far beyond the capacity of the modern man. Most of them are, strictly speaking, even uncecessary. Doing them might even harm the individuals concerned.

## Air Baths

Now, the manner of taking air baths — another useful means of utilising air for improving one's health level — is described. To take an air bath, the air should be comfortably cool, enjoyable. In summer, such a bath can be taken early in the morning and/or late in the evening, or even at night, when the breeze is pleasantly cool. In winter, air bath should be taken a little later in the day, when it is not very cold. It should always be had in the shade and not in sunshine.

An air bath is better taken when a breeze is on, so that one could feel it. If at any time, the air is still, it would be better for the bather either to walk about vigorously or to apply some slight friction to the skin by rubbing his body with his own hands (without the application of any oil, etc.).

During an air bath one should have the least possible clothing on the body so that the air could play upon the skin. Whatever clothes are worn should be of cotton, of the loosely woven variety, preferably white-coloured ones, so that even the covered portions of the body are not deprived of air and natural light.

An air bath may be taken for as long time as may be convenient. Half to one hour a day may be enough. It could be followed by a spinal bath or a regular bath in water.

Air baths tone up the skin, the nervous system and the circulatory system.

## Mode of Dressing

To have the beneficial effects of air baths throughout the day, it is necessary to so dress oneself that the skin is not deprived of light and air, even with the dress on. Clothes of white colour are worn best. If anyone wants to sport coloured clothes, they should not be of deep or bright colours. The dress should be as light as possible, with due regard to climatic conditions. Overdressing weakens the skin. It should not be worn so tight over the skin as to put undue pressure upon the skin and impede the functioning of the organs within. Trousers may be suspended by braces (*Figure 3, Page 120*).

The dress should be as loose as possible, so that there will be a column of air between it and the body. If the dress is made of a loosely woven material, there will be a constant interchange of air, leading to improvement of skin health. The column of air between the dress and the skin will keep the individual warm in winter and cool in summer.

The clothing should be such as to absorb what is eliminated by the skin throughout the day, be it summer or winter. Synthetic fibres, etc. lead to sluggishness of the skin. The best material to wear is cotton, loosely woven, not too closely knit. Where woollen clothes are necessary, these should be worn over the cotton ones and not straight on to the skin.

Care must be taken to see that the soap applied to the clothes for washing is removed completely and that no soap-film is allowed to remain on them. If detergent powders or soaps are used for washing, more care must be taken to wash off the clothes clean. If any soap-film is left over the clothes and they are worn straight over the skin health will be seriously affected.

If the above points are kept in mind, one can enjoy the benefits of air bathing, to some extent, even with the clothes on. The capacity to bear heat and cold improves progressively; neither summer nor winter will be intolerable and one can enjoy living, in the real sense of the term. Let everyone clothe himself or herself for comfort and keep away from "fashion" products.

# FIFTEEN

# Sleep and Relaxation

Sleep is Nature's device for restoring lost vitality, thereby refreshing and renovating both mind and body for the labours of the succeeding day. Nature confers this boon on those who maintain a reasonable level of health, physical and mental. During sleep mind and body merge into the Supreme Consicousness, though not completely. The subtle body acquires a greater access to the cosmic power known as ether or *Akasa* which replenishes the vital power. Access to the source of life and mind is greatest when there is the longest possible rest for life and mind, and in sound sleep there is such rest. There is a rhythm of work and rest, which has to be maintained for the continuance of life and health. Hence is the need for sleep.

## Ensure Sound Sleep

A unique quality of sleep is that it comes of itself and cannot be had unless the necessary condition is present, namely cessation of thought. When the mind is restless, the more one tries to sleep the more wakeful one becomes. *Sleeping is not an act: it is an event.*

When the brain and the rest of the nervous system is encumbered with toxic filth, due to disregard of the twin laws of health, namely. Vital Economy and Positive Feeding, the mind becomes abnormal, subject to restlessness and worry; so sleep fails to come, or if it comes, it is not restful and refreshing. Those who cannot sleep usually resort to the use of nervine poisons, such as barbiturates, which worsen the nervous condition; the semblance of sleep that comes by the aid of these poisons is not good for health; and even this semblance of sleep becomes unattainable later on.

Only those whose nerves are healthy, who have normal nutrition, whose bloodstream is clean, can sleep well. To ensure such a healthy condition, the individual, who may be having some degree of sleepless ness, must make use of all hygienic devices, namely, fasting, vegetablarianism and attention to Vital Economy. Improved breathing (in the manner explained in the preceding chapter) will also help. He must also restrict himself to one meal a day.

A hot foot bath for about 20 minutes, finished with a cold one for a few minutes, may be a good preparation for sleep.

Enema, used non-violently, will also help, to some extent, in clearing the colon of some of the clogging faecal matter.

The bedding should be firm, if not hard. Spring and sponge mattresses are highly undesirable as they make the body sink out of alignment. High pillows cause tension in the muscles of the neck and impede proper circulation of the blood to the head; hence,they are to be avoided. Bed clothing should be light, commensurate with the needs of the climate. If too many coverings are used, acute discomfort may be felt. Even in the choice of bed clothing, it is preferable to avoid closely woven materials. Bed clothes have to be aired and sunned as often as possible and there should be free ventilation in the sleeping room.

Mental poise is important for ensuring sound sleep. Mental tension undermines mental energy to a considerable extent and, hence, the health seeker should learn the art of keeping his mind calm at all times. Observance of the Law of Vital Economy in daily life, along with the practice of some spiritual discipline will greatly help in this direction.

It would not be advisable to go to bed immediately after taking a meal. Let an hour, or preferably two, elapse before going to sleep.

It is not good to sleep on one's back; nor is it proper to sleep always on the same side, whether right or left. As one lies down on the bed first on one's back and slips into sleep, he will be changing from one side to the other according to one's natural inclination.

Some people assume a rather zigzag posture when they sleep. Some have even the habit of placing their arms, turn by turn, over the pillow and resting their head over them. All such wrong postures are to be avoided.

It is advisable to lie in a relaxed position, with the legs stretched comfortably and with the upper arms kept on the two sides.

## Sleep Cannot be Conferred

Those having disturbed sleep should not be misguided by advertisements published in the newspapers, etc., about certain drinks said to be capable of 'conferring' sound sleep on the users. Let them master the art of relaxation. Let it be remembered that relaxation and stimulation are opposed to each other. Let them, therefore, give up addiction to tea, coffee, drinks, cigarettes, etc.

## If One has to Keep Awake

If one has to keep awake for long hours at night, it would be wiser on such occasions to avoid the usual meals. Either one could fast completely, or take some vegetable juices, raw salads or fruits, in small quantities. One can keep awake more comfortably on an empty, or lightly loaded stomach. For the same reason, night-shift workers should take their main meal not at night, before starting their work — or during their work — but during the day, for work and digestion do not go together.

## How to Feel Refreshed after Sleep

A person who sleeps soundly should feel refreshed on getting up. But many people do not experience this feeling; they feel weak in the mornings. As the day advances, they seem to experience increasing vigour. It would be necessary to know why people feel this way and how they should rectify their defects, so that they could experience freshness in the mornings, on getting up from bed.

How the body is recharged with energy during sleep may continue to be a mystery. Observations made by sane men through the ages have however given us a yardstick to go by. We now know fairly clearly the conditions in which alone the body can be fully, or satisfactorily, recharged with energy during sleep and, conversely, the conditions in which the body cannot be recharged. The body can be recharged to the fullest possible extent during sleep only when:

i)  the individual concerned is relaxed in mind and body at the time of going to bed, or is, at any rate, free from any kind of oppressive tension;

ii)  he does not overeat at night;

iii) he has spent his time and energy during the preceding 12-15 hours in a most constructive way and has derived therefrom a sense of fulfilment and happiness at the time of going to sleep;

iv)  he is free from feelings of mental and physical discomfort when going to sleep; and

v)   he is not mentally excited or depressed at the time of going to sleep.

So, anyone feeling weak early in the mornings has to find out for himself as to what, in his case, are the factors impeding the recharging of energy during sleep. If these are found out and removed fundamentally, the individual will start sleeping better and then he will realise the difference; he will wake up vigorous and very much refreshed.

It is not the quantity of sleep that matters, it is the quality. The quality of sleep can be improved only by building up the health level by adopting Nature Cure methods.

## Relaxation

Sleep implies relaxation and an individual who sleeps well at night can manage to be relaxed throughout the following day. But, there may be occasions when a person might feel the need to relax for a little while during the daytime, without going to sleep. One should know how to relax on such occasions.

Relaxation can be had by the individual by

i)    doing *savasasana* or having a spinal bath; or

ii)   having the cooling (or the stimulating) abdominal wet pack with a wet pack over the forehead; or

iii)  taking a cooling head bath and a few sips of achamana of cold water; or

iv)   going out into the open (provided it is cool outside) and doing the non-violent pranayama;

v     either one self singing, or intently listening to classical (ennobling) music; or

vi)   repeating the name of God, or some hymns or studying a holy book; or

vii)  spending time in some all-absorbing hobby, such as painting and sculpture; or

viii)    losing oneself totally 'in the company of' an infant or of a young child; or

ix)    spending time in the company of a holy personage, enriching oneself spiritually.

What has been suggested above is only illustrative. Any similar method, constructive in nature, could be thought of and adopted, to obtain relaxation. On no account should the individual indulge, on such occasions, in stimulants, sedatives or tranquillisers of any type.

What has been suggested here is the only sensible method of overcoming tension. Let this be noted by every health-seeker.

# SIXTEEN

# Exercise and Other Aids

There would be no need for any special exercise for those practising Vital Economy and eating positive foods. The ordinary movements necessitated in the course of an active life in which one does nearly everything for oneself, would suffice to maintain muscular efficiency. The need for regular exercise arises as a result of eating more food than is needed for replacing waste. The notion that muscles that are not exercised will atrophy and be lost in a short time is not based on facts. But because very few people are abstemious in their eating, exercise is necessary for most of us. We have now to discuss the principles which should be borne in mind while exercising.

Like food, exercise is also a tax on vitality, and hence there is a limit beyond which exercise will fail to do good. Mr Purinton, author of *Philosophy of Fasting,* says, "A man can eat a lot if he exercises a lot; but to eat less and also exercise less comes to the same end, with a saving of time, money, thought and vitality."

Another snag in exercising is that it often stimulates and sharpens the appetite for food, leading to formation of the habit of eating heavier meals. So long as the exercises are kept up, there is no noticeable harm done; but when the exercise habit is dropped, the eater does not take to eating less, as he should, and this may lead to chronic diseases, such as rheumatism.

It is a fact that exercise taken up in a wave of enthusiasm is in most cases difficult to carry out steadily; a time comes when the exercise is neglected. Hence the best policy is to rely more upon Vital Economy in eating than upon exercise. Also, it is better to take the minimum of exercise, not the maximum. This would enable the person to keep it up for a very long time. For students especially, the minimum of exercise is more beneficial than an excess of it. The excess leads to eating heavier meals upsetting the Vital Economy and leaving little vitality for studies, which ought to be the main concern of a student. The author's son Kameshvara discovered this truth, when he was a student at a university in the South.

One reason for many people giving up the habit of exercise is its monotony. This monotony can be avoided by mastering a variety of systems and changing them now and then.

We must distinguish between exercise that is natural and exercise that is not. Natural exercise is useful work, such as drawing water from a well, washing one's own clothes, or cultivating vegetables in one's own garden for the kitchen. Also there is the difference between exercising for health and exercising for increasing muscular strength. The former is a necessity; the latter, as a rule, a luxury or an act of vanity.

## Yogasanas

There are some simple poses known as Yogasanas. These form part of Hatha Yoga. They should be practised in the proper manner, steadiness rather than movement being the basic principle of Hatha Yoga. There must be no hurried, rapid or jerky movements though sometimes it may be found easy to assume the required pose.

Nowadays, Yogasana classes are conducted with the learners following the 'commands' given by the instructor, in the style of a mass drill. It may be necessary to educate people on a mass scale. But once the Yogasanas have been learnt, it is not proper to follow the regimental manner. One should do them by oneself moving the body in the manner required for any pose at a time when one feels he should or he could do without much strain. Regimentalisation ignores Vital Economy and non-violence and can never be termed Sattvic.

Do it yourself as best as you can. You will be benefited most.

Some of the simple Yogasanas that could be recommended for the health seeker are Sarvangasana, Matsyasana, Bhujangasana, Salabhasana and Savasana, but let it be clearly understood that these are not a very necessary part of Natural Hygiene. The more difficult asanas recommended in Hatha Yoga are not at all advocated by us, as attempting to do them might well involve violation of Vital Economy.

The Yogasana enthusiasts assert that to practise these poses is to practise Yoga and claim that it is a cure for all diseases. This is taking the part for the whole. It only leads the students to disappointment with just an initial degree of success. It earns discredit for real Yoga, which is far, far beyond Hatha Yoga. It should be remembered that practice of Yoga is not merely practice of Yogasans. Living the Life Natural is the first and foremost necessity in the real practice of Yoga.

Again, under the name of Yoga, a number of practices which are contrary to the Creator's aims are being taught. These only lead the follower far away from the Life Natural. To be more precise, practices like *neti, dhauti, kunjal kriya, sankaprakshalana,* etc., do help to remove quite a lot of foul matter in quite a short time. But it cannot be denied that they have a tendency to make the follower believe that he can afford to go wrong and yet to free from the punishment for his physiological sins. They cannot go scot-free for long. And when they are punished, they do suffer much.

## Corrective Exercises

There is a group of exercises termed "Corrective Exercises" which are to be done by people who are developing, or have developed, spinal or other deformities. The main object behind these exercises is to correct the deformity, to try to restore normalcy within.

## Massage

Massage may be useful adjunct for those who are too weak to take sufficient exercise and for those having fatty encumbrances. Massage may be described as a passive exercise. But it would be a serious mistake for anyone to become a slave to massage, because on the whole it is not as natural and useful as exercise combined with the baths. One who craves for massage is a sickly person; hence one must aim at becoming independent of it by acquiring a degree of positive health.

It must be noted that the safest massage is self-massage. Massage must be done non-violently. Very few professionals, it would seem, are aware of this basic principle. Massage done on safe lines improves skin health, making it softer and more elastic and efficient. It affects blood circulation, provides the relief from fatigue, weakness and pain.

The instructions given here are for self-massage. But if on any occasion it becomes necessary to have it done by another person, it is necessary to ensure the following conditions:

1. The masseur should possess better health than the massaged. Otherwise, the massage will be ineffective, and may result in a lowering of vitality.

2. Even if he be a mercenary, the masseur should have an obliging temperament.

3. The masseur should have good endurance to be able to carry on with the massage till the patient experiences some relief.

4. The nails on the hand of the masseur should be cleanly cut so that they do not injure the patient, even unknowingly.

5. The masseur should always be attentive in watching the reactions of the patient as to the extent of force or pressure applied and be alert enough to alter it suitably.

A massage well done often lulls the patient to sleep.

While doing self-massage, parts of the body which cannot be reached by one's own hands can be treated in a slightly modified manner with the aid of a string of beads of about ½" or more in diameter. Alternatively, simple friction with a wet towel held by the ends in both hands would suffice.

In massaging, the hands and the parts to be treated must be oiled lightly so that the hands may move smoothly over the skin. Only mild vegetable oils should be used, not vaseline or other mineral grease. Some 'experts' prefer 'dry' massage, using talcum powder. This power contains boric acid, some colouring matter and a synthetic scent, which are poisons; also, the tiny particles of the powder get into the skin pores and close them, so that sweat cannot come out freely. Hence the use of talcum powder is unsafe. Oiling is needed not for procedures called *static* but only for those called *dynamic*.

The following are the procedures of massage. Straight and simple English names are given to indicate the processes:

| Dynamic | Static |
|---------|--------|
| Tickling | Pressing |
| Stroking | Squeezing |
| Rubbing | Pinching |
| Kneading | Beating |
| Vibrating | Tapping |
| Drawing | Poking |
| Stretching | Clapping |

The order given here need not be strictly followed, except for tickling, which should also be the very last procedure.

An important caution to observe is that massage of the abdomen, self or passive, should be commenced only after clearing the bladder and the bowels. At least there should have been an attempt for a bowel evacuation. This type of abdominal massage, at first anticlockwise and, after a little pause, clockwise, after taking a small enema, will be helpful in inducing a good motion and in bringing about a feeling of lightness. This will be specially helpful when there is a headache or any pain as a result of clogged bowels.

For massage in general, the dynamic movements that are chosen should be gone through first, and then the static ones.

As the capillaries are to be relieved first, there must be superficial massage first, in which the outer skin is treated by tickling without any pressure, and thereafter massage of the deeper parts. As told earlier, tickling should be repeated at the end also.

Tickling is passing the outstretched fingers over the skin surface with no pressure, but with a very light touch, as if with a feather. If in doubt, one may do the tickling by gently passing the soft edge of a bunch of feathers over the skin surface. This rouses the stagnant blood in the superficial venules. The mode of operation of other procedures is explicit enough from their names.

If a particular part or region of the body is to be massaged to give relief from pain due to swelling or a sprain, the parts around it, especially those nearer to the heart, must first be massaged in a centripetal direction so that it is ready to receive the accumulation for onward transmission in the circulation. Then only should the affected part be massaged.

Foreign matter in the body is stirred up by massage: it is displaced and distributed in the surrounding areas and so there is a feeling of lightness in the affected area. It is left to a larger area to dispose of the foreign matter. That is made possible only by dietetic righteousness. Massage alone will not be able to produce any lasting benefit. The reader should dispel from his mind any illusion.

Massage stirs up heat in the system. It is not proper to leave it like that, because that will induce a tired feeling afterwards. It is good to finish the massage with a cool bath, chiefly the Spinal Bath. It is good to repeat that Vital Economy and Positive Feeding are of prime importance. Else, dependence on massage will become permanent.

## Proper Attitude towards One's Work

We, the Natural Hygienists, hold that like food, water, air, sunshine, etc., work is a basic need of living and that it is impossible for any individual to be healthy without an adequate amount of work and without a proper attitude towards it. The day-to-day work should not be looked upon as a drudgery. To dislike it intensely and yet continue doing it would put the individual to the greatest possible amount of mental and physical strain, affecting his health adversely.

There are many people who do their work in a routine, uninteresting, way. They are often reduced to mere machines, sans initiative, sans commonsense. Their work becomes 'boring' and they lose all interest in life. Their health is thus affected.

Repetitive work done mechanically day after day cannot confer any health on the individual. It is like consuming devitalised stale foods. It could only result in progressively the physical and mental health of the individual.

*Let it be remembered that the sense of fulfilment arising out of a job well done is like a multivitamin tablet.* This will enrich the personality in every way. Let each piece of work which an individual has to do--either at home, in office or elsewhere--be done with the full attention it deserves. One can then observe how it helps in improving one's physical and mental health. This is Yoga. In the words of the *Bhagavad Gita,* "Yoga is efficiency in action."

No work should be looked upon as dull. What is ordinarily deemed to be a dull job can be made interesting by the individual if he makes up his mind to do it better than anyone else. Even an uncongenial job can be used as a means of strenghthening one's character since, as William James put it, doing every day something for no other reason than its difficulty tends to add to one's stores of courage and will power.

Whether or not health is regained, retained or improved will in many cases depend on whether or not the individual has emotionally adjusted himself to his environment. Neglect of this all-important factor would mean slow but sure disaster. Many cases of nervous breakdown, heart disease, digestive disorders, etc., can be attributed to emotional maladjustment. The individual who cannot adjust himself emotionally to his environment or his daily job will develop depression, irritability, etc.

*Let shirkers know that their illness is most likely the result of their wrong attitude towards their environment and work.* Let them change their attitude and start liking their jobs. Let them take real interest in their work and do it with all the attention they can bestow on it. Let them do a little more work each day than they think they possibly can. Let them not be deterred by obstacles, real or imaginary. Let them reflect over the statement of Dorothy Carnegie· "The mature individual is so intent or overcoming a handicap that he never thinks of using it as an excuse for failure." Let them remember that the greater the obstacle the more glory there is in overcoming it. Let them know that a healthy attitude towards their daily work has a very constructive contribution to make towards their own physical and mental health.

There is another important aspect of work. It is its Social value If each citizen has the right attitude to work and if each one works towards the common good — Sarvodaya — the nation will prosper. Workers are an asset to the nation; shirkers are the greatest liability to it.

At this stage, a note of caution has to be sounded. Quite a few people — generally from among politicians, executives, social workers and businessmen — become "addicted" to work. To them work means only their professional work and nothing else. They want to outrival each other in the rat race and work under terrific tension. All the work is done mechanically — there is no time to

107

think! Subjected to constant pulls and pressures, they are like ship wrecked sailors, feeling insecure at every moment!

They would like to work off their fatigue through stimulants. They would try to soothe their frayed nerves by tranquillisers and sleeping pills. They cannot enjoy normal sleep. Their 'addiction' to work really isolates them from their families and even society. The little 'social life' they have is all mechanical.

People who indulge in high-pressure living may be leading a 'successful' life in the accepted sense of the term but they will progressively worsen their health.

Let every health seeker, therefore, avoid either of the two extremes, shirking work and "workaholism" and adopt a balanced view of life, taking care not to deny any basic needs of living to his body and mind. Let everyone adopt an integrated, total, approach to life as advocated by the Science of Natural Hygiene.

## Happiness

Happiness is a basic need of living. It is a health-maintaining, health-promoting factor. Pleasure resulting from sensual indulgence of one or the other kind should not be mistaken for happiness. All great thinkers have proclaimed the great truth that happiness lies in self control, that sorrow and misery are the lot of the pleasure seekers. All indulgence is at the cost of health and happiness. Happiness can never be achieved at the expense of health. This is a truth, the significance of which should be recognised by every health seeker.

Physical health provides the basis for happiness, but even with physical health an individual can still be unhappy for psychological or social reasons. If anyone loses happiness he would lose physical health too, in due course of time. Hence, it is necessary to know in some depth how to be really happy all the time.

*Happiness consists in being perfectly satisfied with what one has got and equally with what one has not got.* It is not how much one has, but how much one enjoys that makes for happiness — the term 'enjoyment' here is not used in the vulgar sense. Happiness is the reward for successful living — living unselfishly, productively, amicably. Those having a behaviour pattern primarily charaterised by intense ambition, competitive drive, constant preoccupation with occupational deadlines and a sense of urgency are very likely to be in a state of constant tension. Happiness will elude them for ever. Such people sacrifice their health and happiness in acquiring 'the more material and tangible gains', with the result that life becomes a failure. For, without real-life enjoyment, what is the point in living?

True happiness makes a man sensible; such happiness is always shared with others. Share your happiness with others, in all humility, without creating the impression in them that you are more fortunate than them. Happiness is a sunbeam which may pass through a thousand bosoms without a particle of its original ray; nay, when it strikes a kindred heart, like the converged light on a mirror, it reflects itself with redoubled brightness. It is not perfected till it is shared. Hence, share it with others.

## Character Development

Those who do their daily work with devotion and dedication and cultivate real happiness develop all the good qualities of character what is described in the *Bhagavad Gita* as *Daivi Sampat* — like serenity, sincerity, simplicity, veracity, equanimity, nobility, non-irritability, fixity, generosity, purity, integrity, magnanimity, each one of which has an immense health value, far more important to human health than vitamins and mineral salts. Inattention to the development of such qualities in daily life has made the modern man the world over miserable and sickly. So, let health seekers pay full attention to this aspect of development of the human personality.

## Bowel Health

A stagnant bowel is a source of disease. It leads to malformation of the lower part of the belly, affects the digestive organs, the stomach and the intestines by its backward kick, and may lead to dyspepsia with neurasthenia or other diseases which would seem to be located elsewhere. The cause of stagnation is neglect of Vital Economy and Non-violence. Abnormal bowels should be made natural again by right application of these two principles, with the aid of fasting as described before and non-violent enemas, whenever necessary.

At this stage, it becomes necessary to state what the constipated individual should not do. He should not use any kind of laxative or purgative. These may irritate the mucus membranes of the colon and, in course of time, the individual may develop appendicitis, colitis, etc. He should not also strain himself while going to stool. By such strain the muscles of the sigmoid colon and anus are considerably weakened, leading to the prolapse of the rectum and even to the development of piles.

If the straining habit is continued over a period of time, the colon might be deformed. The individual may develop diverticulosis (a condition in which small outpockets are formed on the colonic wall, like blebs or sacs). The part of the colon so affected may get inflamed and even develop perforation (diverticulitis). The symptoms of diverticulitis are a low, cramping, abdominal pain and tenderness in the area of involvement. If the condition worsens, the inflammatory mass may mechanically obstruct the passage of faecal matter or, worse still, perforations may occur.

The constipated individual should not do *yogic kriyas* like Sankaprakshalan. Such *kriyas* are very violent and can adversely affect the peristaltic movements of the alimentary canal. The enema recommended by the medicos, as also the one used by most naturopaths, with plenty of water (sometimes mixed with soap or glycerine) and a long tube, is equally objectionable from the hygienic point of view. To the extent needed, the non-violent enema (described in the chapter on Water Cure) may be used. This type of enema is not habit forming.

## Skin Health

The health of the skin does not exist as somethig apart from the health of the whole body and mind. Skin health is an integral part of health. But here we should take note of a few expedients primarily related to the outer skin, which is the boundary of the physical body, serving as a rampart against harmful influences or outside factors and as a receptacle for supplies of light, air and water.

Sensible diet reform, air and sun baths are vital for improving skin health.

Ordinary bathing should be done in soft water — free from dissolved earthy substances that would irritate the body. The dirt on the skin should first be removed by rubbing it well with a wet towel wrung out almost dry, or with wet earth — a mixture of pure clay and fine sand. This is needful especially before taking a cooling bath. The water should not be unbearably cold. Patients with delicate health would do well not to take cold baths in the beginning but may do so after their general health level is raised. It is desirable not to use soap on the body, as its particles are liable to stick to the skin, due to carelessness or the hardness of the water. The habitual use of soap spoils the skin. Instead flour of grams may be used.

## Helping the Digestion

Digestion is often delayed or made impossible by the contents of the stomach becoming overheated or by the irritating quality of the meal taken. If the condition is not serious, slow sipping of small quantities of cold water will allay the heat and irritation. In more serious conditions the only way is to vomit at least a part of the stomach contents by profuse drinking of lukewarm water and then provoking a vomit* by tickling the throat with two or three fingers. When enough of the irritating liquid has been thus got out, there will be relief and the digestion will proceed easily. A spinal bath or a hip bath may suffice in some cases. But prevention is better than cure.

## Care of the Teeth

Good teeth are formed only if the feeding is right. An excess of sweets made from commercial white sugar is chiefly to blame for the bad teeth of children. This defect continues throughout life. It has been found that the teeth of people living in places where the water contains fluoride, even so little as one part to a million parts, grow abnormally. Positive food supplies all the right materials for forming good teeth.

Tooth-paste advertisements proclaim a lie: 'A clean tooth never decays'. Caries of the teeth, in which cavities form, are formed by eating defective food and tooth-pastes cannot prevent them.

It is not proper to apply any inorganic substance on the teeth for cleansing them. Plain water, or water with a trace of lime-juice in it, and a brush are enough for doing this. No tooth-paste need be used. The green herbal powder, described in the Chapter Food For

* This type of forced vomiting (called *gaja-kriya, hasti-kriva* or **kunjara-kriya** or *kunjal* by the yogas is recommended indiscriminately and many people indulge in it a little too often. The author recommends it here to be taken resort to very very occasionally. If it is repeated too often, the tone of the alimentary canal is adversely affected and the individual may develop conditions like hiatus hernia. This caution may be noted by readers).

Health!, mixed with an equal part of powder of charred rice-chaff or of almond shells, may be used, if preferred.

## Old Age

Old age can be postponed. It can also be made more like youth by Vital Economy and positive feeding. The age of a man depends much more on his mind than on his body. Ignorance and self-centeredness are the chief causes of an unhappy and burdensome old age. Cheerfulness and acceptance of whatever comes, with complete reliance on God, are the means of growing old without being infirm or depressed. The temper of renunciation, with the aid of discrimination between the real and the unreal--which means, between the unchanging eternal and what is transitory and perishable--is also necessary. This comes by the study and practice of philosophy. The problem of death must be faced and settled according to the teaching of one's own religion. Death is only a bugbear. Lucretius, who started the pseudo-philosophy called Epicurianism, made a sensible observation: *"Where we are, death is not; where death is, we are not."* But there is more to this saying than he knew. We are not the body, nor the mind. We are the Life behind life, the Mind behind mind. We are only witnesses of the world, to which our bodies and minds belong. Our Nature is Pure Happiness, and nothing can put an end to us. God is our Eternal Friend and Companion, and He will see to our future welfare. Death is but a sleep, from which we awake, not in this body, but in another or perhaps in God himself. This mentality, or whatever else is the highest in one's own religion, should be cultivated. Then death will be seen for what it is, a figment of our worldly imagination.

A warning needs to be given. As age advances, vitality becomes less, and with it the digestive power. This means that the food load must be reduced so that the Vital Economy is maintained. Activity also must be curtailed. Thus there will be a greater access to the uncaused Happiness of the Self, which is the real food for the soul.

# SEVENTEEN

# Sun Cure

Almost equal to air in value for health is sunlight. This can be seen in young plants that grow in a dark place; they are white and sickly. It must be realised that it is hygienically a sin to live in a house devoid of sufficient sunlight.

A sun bath may be taken by merely basking in the sun, as animals do in the morning* when there is a pleasant feeling of warmth. Such basking could be had for such time as would suffice for getting warm. In the beginning, this may be done in mild sunlight, and later, as one gets habituated to it, in warmer sunshine. A sun bath can be had while walking, sitting or lying down on the ground. The head and face should in the beginning be shaded from the sun, until the whole bodily condition becomes attuned to its light and heat, so that there is no injury. Here the policy of Non-violence needs to be observed for a considerable time, because the body may at first be unable to assimilate this unaccustomed food, but would be able to do so after gradual practice. The head and face should at first be in the shade, or should be protected by a green banana or other leaf, or a white or green wet cloth.

At first, basking in the sun should be practised until a pleasant warmth is obtained. Later it may be continued till the onset of sweating. Still later it may be continued for some time after sweating has begun. Then the sweat should be wiped off with a wet towel that has been wrung out almost dry. After this, if the bather likes, he may take a spinal bath, which will be described in the next chapter. Only fairly robust persons should take the ordinary full cold

---

* The actual time for a sun bath will be different at different places, depending upon the local weather.

bath; those of a delicate health should observe the hints and cautions given in the section on Skin Health in the previous chapter.

In severe cases, where there is great weakness and little response to the methods employed, a *prolonged* exposure to the sun is recommended, but the fierceness of sunshine should be softened by covering the body with a piece of cloth kept wet by drenching it just sufficiently in cold water.

In the use of sunlight the patient's feeling must be chief guide. What is unpleasant must be avoided. There ought to be no hurry to get well. It may be assumed that what makes the patient feel good is doing good.

The good effects of Sun Cure depend to a considerable extent on the use of methods of Water Cure also, described in the next chapter.

One of the good effects of sunlight is improvement of the blood circulation and the consequent equalisation of heat throughout the body, due to an increase in vitality and its penetration in all parts of the body, including the extremities. If the patient suffers from cold hands and feet he experiences relief from the symptoms which finally disappear in most cases.

The following methods of taking the sun bath are given as general guidance. Everyone should choose for himself the method or methods most suitable to his own constitution.

## The Mild Sun Bath

This may be taken when the sun has risen somewhat high in the sky and the heat is mild, that is, within three hours after sunrise. The patient should lie down on a bed-sheet spread on the ground, and for some time remain almost naked, wearing minimum clothes but covered with a thin dry cloth or shawl, till he gets well warmed. Then he must have a wet cloth, wetted and wrung out nearly dry, or a green banana leaf or other leaves, spread over him from the neck down to the knees, the face being kept in the shade, and the parts below the knees being covered with a dry cloth. If the face also is in the sun, it must be covered with a green leaf or with two pieces of folded wet cloth, one covering the upper part of the face and the head, and the other the lower part, so as to leave the nostrils open for breathing. The patient may begin with 15 minutes of sunbathing and gradually increase it up to 40 minutes, having regard to the principle of Non-violence. After this the skin surface should be wiped clean with a nearly dry cloth. A trunk bath or a spinal bath should then follow.

## The Walking Sun Bath

Walking in warm sunshine at any time when the sun is rather hot, with the head and upper parts of the body protected from the heat by a wet cloth, is an easy way of sun bathing in the open. This may be done when going to and returning from a plunge bath in a tank or river.

## Hamsa Water

Sunlight can be used indirectly also, by charging drinking water with it. The proper way is to expose the water to sunlight in a shallow and wide-mouthed vessel, covered over with a plantain leaf or other green leaf. Over this may be placed a thin porous cloth, secured on the sides so that the covering leaf is not blown away by the wind. The exposure is maintained for the whole day. The vessel is left in the open all night, so that the cold air and the night dew may add their own qualities to the water. Water so treated is called *Hamsodakam,* Hamsa being one of the names of the sun. The water may be drunk in small doses at intervals the next day. It may also be smeared on the body, or used for bandages or packs, if possible, or for the abdominal wet massage and the piecemeal cold friction bath mentioned in the next chapter.

## Steam Bath

The following methods of bathing do not strictly belong to this chapter; but since they serve nearly the same purpose as sun baths, they are given here. They serve to raise the vital power of reaction to the cooling baths that are given in the next chapter.

In many Nature Cure institutions in this country and outside it, full steam baths are given to most patients, ostensibly "to improve their powers of reaction and to enable their skin to eliminate the toxic matter quickly." Such baths are given even in summer months and to very weak patients. A note of caution is to be made in this regard.

Full steam baths are very violent and in Sarma's Nature Cure

Sanatorium we have found them unnecessary. It is a well known fact that only serious cases — medical failures — take to Nature Cure treatment and the patients, in practically all cases, have very little vitality left in them. Steam baths given to such patients may even harm them

Local steam baths, where found necessary, may be taken in a convenient posture, sitting in a chair or on the floor, so that particular parts of the body are exposed to the hot vapour, the face being kept open, and the rest of the body being covered so as to confine the vapour. If the face needs to be steamed, as when there is a cold, or a severe headache, the exposure must be very short. Immediately after such a local steam bath, it would be advisable for the patient to take either a spinal bath or a cooling abdominal wet pack, with a wet pack over the forehead, and rest.

## The Hot Foot Bath

A hot foot bath can be taken for a duration of 10 to 30 minutes, with the body well covered so as to promote sweating. *It is a safe, convenient and sufficient substitute for the steam bath.* It warms up the body, producing a reasonable amount of perspiration. Thus it is a good preparation for a spinal bath or a hip bath (described later). The foot bath can be taken simultaneously with any of the cooling baths with great advantage. Such a combination is essential for patients with chilly extremities. They will find no difference in temperature between that part of the body which is placed in cold water and the rest of the body. This helps in artificially creating that difference without which cooling baths are of no benefit (may also be seemingly harmful). This bath is absolutely non-violent and can also be taken by weak patients by suitably adjusting the temperature of the hot water. It is remarkably helpful in relieving cold or heaviness of the head.

The feet must be dipped in as hot a water as the patient can comfortably bear. It will not be proper to prescribe any temperature, as it might possibly prove violent to some and insufficient to others. The decision must be left to the patient. Any suitable vessel in which both the feet can be comfortably placed will be good enough. Also, it will be advantageous to have as deep a vessel as possible. In the beginning the temperature should be low. More hot water may have to be added as time passes and as the patient gets his lower extremity warmed up. Sipping cold water very slowly at intervals during the bath makes it more non-violent, and more advantageous.

It would not be advisable to give hot foot baths to patients suffering from high blood pressure, heart trouble and kidney or liver disorders. In such cases, if the feet of the patient happen to be cold, two hot water bottles (with a towel wrapped over them) may be placed on the bed, on either side of the legs, and a bed-sheet (or woollen sheet, if need be) may be used to cover the patient's body (keeping the face exposed) to keep the bed warm.

## Hot and Cold Fomentation

Normally, for the relief of pain, cooling of the affected part of the body by the application of a local wet pack (as explained in the next chapter) should do. Where the pain is severe and unbearable, other methods, suggested in the next chapter, may be followed.

In cases of unbearable pain in any particular parts of the body, hot and cold fomentation may prove of great use. *This could be a very good substitute for, and even better than, the local steam bath.* The manner in which hot and cold fomentation should be done is explained below.

Prepare hot water (as hot as may be conveniently bearable by the patient) in a wide-mouthed vessel and have cold water (bearably cold but not ice-cold) in another wide-mouthed vessel. Have two towels to a size suitable for fomentation over the affected area. Dip one that would produce a little friction over the skin. Fold each of the towels to a size suitable fomentation over the affected area. Dip one towel in the hot water, rinse it fairly well and apply it over the affected area (preferably three or four inches above or below it), keep it there for a minute applying a little gentle pressure over it by the hand. Immediately thereafter take the other towel (suitably folded, dipped in the cold water and rinsed fairly well) and apply it over the same area. As a rule, hot fomentation is applied for a minute and cold one for twenty seconds or so. Start with hot fomentation, go on repeating hot and cold ones alternately ending with the latter. Afterwards, apply a wet pack over the area.

117

# EIGHTEEN

# Water Cure

The good effects of water cure methods are equalisation of the bodily heat, relief of pain by the dispersal of congestions and temporary increase of vitality. These emerge from the vital reaction they produce. If there is no vital reaction, there is no benefit to health. Hence, it must be understood that these methods must be so used as to obtain the vital reaction. Though cold water is chiefly used in them, the purpose is not to take away or reduce the bodily heat, but to rouse the vital power to generate more heat than which is lost. For, heat is Life, that is, it is by generating heat that life possesses and controls the body. In an abnormal body there is unequal heat distribution, whereby some parts are congested, with stagnant blood, and therefore hot, while others are poorly supplied with blood, and so are cold. This has to be corrected. The baths described here are well suited for achieving this purpose. They are non-violent, if rightly used.

In acute conditions, these baths are very useful; in chronic ones, they are less useful. In the latter cases, packs are more useful because they are milder in their application.

For water cure baths and packs, soft water is to be preferred. Water that is not too hard can be used if it is treated with herbal juices, and some lime juice. It may be better to expose the water, before thus treating it, to the sun for a whole day and then let it cool in the open during the night.

## The Tub

A special tub has been devised for the principal water cure bath, the spinal bath. This tub can be used for all the other baths such as the hip bath etc. Made to accommodate an adult, it can also be used for a child by placing a thick plank of wood across its width at the leg side, so that the child bather can keep his legs over the plank to keep his lower extremities dry.

For the benefit of those who would like to have this tub manufactured at their own places, full instructions are given in the appendix to this chapter.

## Cloth

The cloth to be used for bandages or packs should be reasonably clean, free from grease and dirt, but preferably not new, as new cloth is not so absorbent as old cloth. The cloth need not be sterilised, as done in hospitals. It should be soft, so as to absorb and retain the water.

## Earth for Packs or Bandages

The earth to be used for bandages must be a mixture of clay and fine sand in nearly equal parts. This must be obtained from ant-hills or from high ground rendered clean by rain. The earth must be pounded well and sieved through a wire- sieve to remove the stones or coarse particles of sand in it. Fine sand must be mixed with the earth after washing and drying it.

The following are the general cooling baths: (1) The spinal bath, (2) the head bath, (3) the full hip bath, (4) the shallow hip bath, (5) the trunk bath, (6) the piecemeal cold friction bath, (7) the sitz bath. With some of these baths the hot foot bath may be combined; that is, the baths may be taken simultaneously, with great benefit.

## The Spinal Bath

Of all the baths, this is the most useful as a tonic for the nervous system and through it for the whole body. It gives the good effects of all the other baths. The best place to take it is in a tub of the pattern referred to earlier. The figure shows the posture of the bather in the tub. The bather lies down in the tub with his head on the side that is most slanted, his buttocks at the opposite end and his feet outside it. If the weather is cold or chilly, a blanket is used to cover the body from the neck down to the feet, the sides of the blanket hanging outside the tub. If a slit is provided in the blanket just over the face, then it may cover the face also, so as to leave the nose free for breathing. For beginners a thick wet cushion of folded towel, about an inch in thickness, is placed of the bottom of the tub on which the bather lies down. To begin with, an inch of cold water is poured for the bath; this may be moderately cold at first. Later it may be made colder, but not unbearably so. Gradually the bather will come to prefer water which has been cooled by evaporation in earthen pots for not less than six hours. The bather may gradually increase the level of the water up to four inches if he likes. A folded wet cloth should be placed on the front of the trunk, covering the chest and the belly. The bath may be taken for 15 to 45 minutes, or, if the bather falls asleep till he awakes, which could be after an hour. This sleep is most refreshing and is the most perfect sleep possible, because in it the time sense is completely lost, which is very rarely experienced in bed sleep.

Fig. 3 — Spinal Bath

During the bath, about once in five or ten minutes the bather may sit up and rub his back thoroughly with a dry towel. After allowing some time for the back to become warm he should lie down again and continue the bath. This, it seems, is not absolutely necessary, except at the end of the bath.

The spinal bath can be taken at any time as one likes, even immediately before or immediately after a meal. If taken after a meal, no wet cloth should be placed over the abdomen. The spinal bath must be finished with a head-bath, as described below.

The spinal bath is perhaps the best — and the easiest — method to relieve tension. The bather feels perfectly relaxed when he gets up from the tub. Patients as well as healthy persons by benefit taking the spinal baths daily as it is essentially a health-promoting measure. It is a 'must' for the so-called busybodies, executives, etc., who are subjected to tension during their daily work.

## The Head Bath

This is a very simple bath. It is just cooling the head and the face by pouring cold water over them with a kettle or other vessel 10 to 20 times. Beginners taking the spinal bath may feel hot in the head. The head bath useful for quickly bringing down the heat. It may also be taken at other times, if found needful. But it is most useful after a spinal bath or any other bath in which the central part of the body, the belly, is cooled.

## The Full Hip Bath

This bath is taken sitting in the tub, as shown in the *Figure 4,* with the two ends of the tub at the two sides of the bather. The latter may have the tub placed adjacent to a wall, and lean on a plank placed against the wall, so that he can lean on it comfortably while bathing. The water should be moderately cold, not as cold as required for the spinal bath, and should, if possible, come up to the bather's navel. Bathing is done by friction with a small square towel under the water, from side to side and from top to bottom of the whole body so as to agitate the internal organs and blood circulation. This has a tonic effect on the digestive organs. In the case of beginners, internal inflammations may be brought to the surface, which becomes sore; this must not be taken as an injury caused by the friction. It is a curative crisis. The bath should not, therefore, be discontinued on this account; but till the soreness passes away, there need be no application of friction at all, that is, immersion alone will be sufficient. The bath is suitable for patients who are not so weak as to be bed-ridden. For the latter, packs are more suitable.

The full hip bath should not be taken within two hours of eating meals, nor should meals be had within two hours of taking bath. There can be only one exception to this rule, that is, when there is any abdominal distress within two hours of taking a meal.

## The Shallow Hip Bath

While the full hip bath is recommended by Louis Kuhne, the author has found that the shallow hip bath is far better, especially for patients with a weak reaction. In it no more water than required for the spinal bath, i.e., about 1½ to 2 inches depth in the tub, should be used. The water should just touch the buttocks, the abdomen remaining above the water. The water may be as cold as that used for the spinal bath, because only a small quantity of water is used.

Fig. 4 — Hip Bath

The posture of sitting in the tub is the same as for the full hip bath. Instead of a small square napkin, thick cotton socks can be slipped over the right hand for rubbing the abdomen. The hand is dipped in the water and the abdomen rubbed in a clockwise direction around the navel. After a few rounds, of rubbing a sense of warmth will be felt. The hand is again dipped in the water and the process repeated. Thus, there is alternate heating and cooling. Even the heat produced is the result of vital reaction, as at each moment only a very small part of the hip is treated. The expected relief is attained in just half the time taken in mere cooling. Also, there is no violence to the system.

As in the spinal bath, the bather feels a little warmth in the head at the end of this bath also. The same precaution of a full bath or at least a head wash as prescribed for finishing the spinal bath should be followed after the shallow hip bath.

Here, there is no feeling of chillness as is felt after the full hip bath and, therefore, there is no need for any exercise or warming up in bed. Because of the quick result that the shallow hip bath yields, it is not necessary to take it for as long a time as the full hip bath.

The author would even recommend taking this shallow hip bath for about 5 to 10 minutes, follow it by a spinal bath for about 20 minutes and finish it with a normal bath. The little tiresomeness caused by the rubbing of the abdomen (during the course of the shallow hip bath) will be relieved by the spinal bath. There is thus a saving of time and energy and, at the same time, a greater gain.

As the shallow hip bath is far more effective, the full hip bath need not be taken at any time. The former should not also be taken within two hours after meals, nor should meals be taken within two hours after the bath.

## The Trunk Bath

In this bath the water should be just bearably cool. The bather lies down as in the spinal bath. The quantity of the water should be enough for him to immerse his whole trunk. The bather should now and then rub the parts immersed in water with his hands, or with a rough piece of cloth. He may remain in the bath for 15 minutes or as long as he likes. He should then get up and wipe himself dry and get warm as may find convenient. The bath is suitable for persons who are weak, but not so weak as to be bed-ridden.

## The Piecemeal Cold Friction Bath

There is a substitute for the common full cold bath. It is suitable for those whose vital reaction is not good enough because in it the whole body surface is chilled at the same time. In the piecemeal bath only a part of the skin surface is bathed at one time, different parts being bathed one by one. Each part is rubbed with a wet cloth, and bathed and wiped dry before the next part is bathed. Hence, even weak persons obtain a good reaction, improving their skin health in a reasonably short time. This bath can also be taken after a spinal bath so as to increase its good effects. There is no rule as to the order in which the various parts are to be bathed. The feet may be left out and bathed separately some time later, if the patient prefers to do so. Warming up after the bath is necessary. The bath relieves the pain of mosquito-stings; it relieves itching also.

## The Abdominal Wet Massage

In this process the bather wets his hands in cold water and gently, but with some pressure, massages the belly from the side and below upwards, wetting the hands now and then, to cool the body. By doing so, the internal organs are agitated and roused into greater activity. This may be taken as a substitute for the hip bath or the trunk bath, when the bather is disnclined to take them.

## The Sitz Bath

This was invented by Louis Kuhne as a stimulant for the nervous system. As both hands have to be kept in cold water, very weak persons find it unpleasant. This is the reason why the author invented the spinal bath which is far more pleasant to take, and at the same time is more efficient in toning up the nervous system. For the patient taking the spinal bath, the sitz bath is unnecessary. But the latter is useful for women suffering from menstrual disorders, pain or diseases of the womb. The bath is taken sitting on a small seat shaped like a stool and placed in very cold water in a tub, the water being at level with the seat or a few inches higher. The bather rubs, with a rough cloth, the outer surface of the genitals taking care not to rub the opening between the two sides of the organ. The bath should last 15 to 45 minutes, or until the bather feels a definite sense of relief.

## The Tonic Abdominal Wet Bandage

A broad bandage or pack of wet earth or cloth around the whole of the belly, so as to cover the back part also, provides a tonic of great efficacy, both in acute and chronic afflictions, whether or not localised in the digestive organs. The bandage should be more than half an inch thick. In acute cases it may be left exposed to the air, while the patient lies down on a wooden plank or cot. In chronic conditions the bandage should be covered with a coarse woollen wrapper, so as to allow the water to evaporate. The internal organs are thus relieved of their abnormal heat; the bandage becomes warm. This may happen after two hours or more, and then an itching sensation may be felt, which is a sign that the bandage should be removed. Then a short spinal bath, a trunk bath or a hip bath will be very useful, and should be had, unless the patient feels disinclined to do so. Where the lungs are diseased the bandage should be alternated with stimulating wet bandages for the chest. Bed-ridden patients may have a wet pack of earth or folded cloth laid on the belly, covering only its front. The patient should be covered with woollen blanket so that the reaction is generalised and increased.

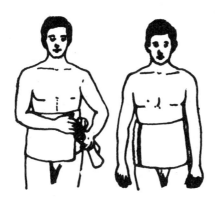

Fig. 5 — The Tonic Abdominal Wet Bandage

The wet abdominal bandage — as well as other bandages — can be worn inside the usual dress, if there be a dry protecting woollen wrapper as prescribed above, while the person attends to his daily work, if he is able to do so.

## The Local Cooling Wet Bandages

In addition to some suitable general treatment, cooling or stimulating wet bandages can be applied and great relief obtained in cases of local troubles, such as sprains, boils, fractures, wounds, stings, burns, carbuncle, sores and ulcers. Where there is no pain a stimulating wet bandage may be more suitable. Even in cases of serious injuries, the patient is able to almost forget the pain as a result of the cooling bandage.

125

If there be bleeding, the bandage should be made rather tight in the beginning, specially so a little above the place of the injury, so as to stop draining of the blood. A continuous flow of very cold water should be maintained over the place of injury and about it. When the bleeding has stopped and a pain owing to tightness of the bandage is felt, the bandage should be remade a little loosely.

Bandages not only need the cooling effect of the water, but also access to external air. It is the movement of air over and through the bandages that ensures better cooling.

## The Stimulating Wet Bandage

This is also applied in the same manner as the cooling wet bandage, but it is not drenched so much nor is it left exposed. It should be covered up with a dry coarse woollen cloth. Wet cloth alone should be used. It may be kept on for three to six hours at a time. This bandage is useful for cases in which there is no pain and for those in which pain is mild and bearable.

## Poultice for the Eyes

For sore eyes and other types of eye inflammation, not excluding formation of granules. a poultice of mashed ripe banana or other neutral vegetable like cucumber, carrot (which has been reduced to a very fine and soft condition by grating or mashing) or a paste of the leaves of Ervatamia Coronaria stapi, is placed over thin piece of clean wet cloth over the eyes and bandaged to retain it in position. The vegetable or the Sattvic herbs should be washed well with clean cold water, before grating or mashing it. The poultice can be had at night, while going to sleep. If the condition is severe, it can be had during daytime too. But there should be a gap of about two hours between two bandages.

Where there is irritation in the eyes, due to dryness a few minutes of mild hot fomentation before application of the poultice will provide more relief. For this purpose, freshly cooked whole (wholesome) rice is put in a small square cloth and fresh butter added to it, as an emolient. It will directly soothe the eyes.

## For Cooling the Brain

The temples are gateways of the brain. Apply masses of wet cloth on the temples to cool the brain, and keep them in position by tying a bandage around the head.

## The Achamana

This is a means of internal cooling of very great efficacy and an aid to other cooling methods. In high fever it may prove a sufficient remedy along with intake of pure air and fasting, without baths or packs, except where the sun-cure is also needed. But there is a risk that the patient may not be given the achamana often enough. Fever may easily prove dangerous if sufficient water is not given. The process of the achamana is to give the patient cold water in very small doses so that it is fully assimilated. Often enough it is the simplest of all cooling methods. Very cold water, such as is obtained by storing it in earthen pots, is either sipped by the patient or given to him with a teaspoon, allowing an interval of two or three seconds after every sip or spoonful. Every single sip or spoonful should be of less than ten drops, that is, one-sixth of a teaspoonful. Not less than ten such doses should be given or taken in succession *at a time* — with the intervals between the doses as prescribed. All the doses so given at a time are together called an achamana. In fevers at least twenty doses should be given in a single achamana. But if the patient likes he may have *more* at each time. The treatment should be repeated every five minutes until the fever gets milder and safer. In other cases achamanas are of great value before a meal for refreshing the nerves, or for curing or preventing fatigue, and also after a meal for protecting the digestion.

## Relief of Pain

Pain is caused by heat due to the pressure of fermenting foreign matter upon the nerves. The pressure is relieved in a natural way by cooling off the excess of heat and by improving the blood circulation. Where the pain is not of a persistent kind, it is easily relieved by gushing with cold water or by the application of a cooling wet bandage. The bandage should be made so thick and extensive as to keep down the heat that causes the pain. In severe cases like scorpion stings, an extensive bandage, covering a considerable part of the affected limb, is needed to give relief. Non-violent enemas may also help. If the pain re-appears, the bandage may be gushed again or wetted with cold water. Until the pain is fully cured, the bandage must be kept on or renewed from time to time. If the pain is serious or persistent, some general treatment, such as a local steam bath, alternate hot and cold fomentations, a sun bath, a hot water foot bath, an immersion bath in sufficiently warm or hot water as desired, followed by a *series* of spinal baths or trunk baths will be necessary. *Fasting* should be strictly observed till the pain ceases, or at least till it becomes bearable. Strict diet should be observed until the cure is complete. In many cases cooling baths may suffice, without steam baths or the like. *Warmth* should be applied to the adjacent parts also, or to the body as a whole, and not to the sick part alone. The latter can be better helped indirectly through the healthier parts. Enemas may also be taken as often as needful to cleanse the bowel thoroughly, for a bowel encumbered with stagnating stools is likely to be one of the chief causes of the pain.

When there is an injury caused by a severe blow, as with a hammer, pressure must at once be applied to the affected part and maintained for some time, either by hand or by immediately tying a bandage wet or dry. The pressure should be enough to prevent the rush of blood to the injured part. If this is not done at once, not only will the pain become more severe and last longer, but a swelling will gather at the site of injury, which will prove intractable. After 15 to 30 minutes, when the pain has subsided, the bandage must be untied and a wet bandage tied, with minimum pressure, covering a sufficient extent of the surface. This will serve to prevent the pain from returning.

In some rare cases it happens that relief is not attained by these methods. In such cases, relief may be attained by a local steam bath or a hot bath of sufficient duration, and then lying in bed well wrapped up till the pain disappears. This is recommended only in cases where other methods have tried in vain. After the pain has become bearable a cooling bath should be taken.

## The Enema, Its Use and Abuse

An objection raised against the use of enema is that it tends to become a habit. This is absurd. It does not apply to the *non-violent* enema that we advocate. We consider the bowel to be an *eliminating* organ on the same level of importance as the skin, the kidneys or the lungs. If its functioning is allowed to fall in arrears, the general health of a person and even his nervous system may be affected. We do not teach that it is sufficient to use the enema to restore bowel health. We say that the sufferer must take to the practice of the *whole* of Hygiene as taught here, especially the eating of an

128

129

abundance of positive foods in strict accordance with the Law of Vital Economy, together with occasional fasting whenever proper. If a person finds that he can get on without the enema, he is not asked to use it; the choice whether to use it or not is left to *him*. The following instructions are given for followers of Nature Cure.

## The Tonic Enema

The object of this method is not to clear out the whole bowel, which ought not to be done often, but only the end part of it. As a rule, moderately cold water* should be used. Its quantity should not be more than half a pint (10 ounces) and it should be retained for five to ten minutes, or until the water becomes warm. In course of time the amount of water should be reduced little by little until only 6 ounces are found sufficient. We assure the reader that this enema, far from becoming a habit, has the effect, if taken daily, of toning up the bowels, enabling him to dispense with all artificial aid in course of time. It helps to cure that heat and dryness of the internal surface of the bowel, which is the cause of chronic constipation. The patient should lie down on his right side and bring the buttocks close to a wall, bending the legs to the right. Or he may lie down on his back, with his legs bent at the knees, and move close to the wall, or he may raise his legs so as to rest them against it. The can of the enema must be placed at such a height on the wall that the nozzle or end of the tube is a little lower than the anus in the position taken. The enema tube need not be more than three feet in length. The patient can help the passing in of the water by breathing out and keeping the lungs empty. Reciting aloud of verses or the like would be a great help. If there is pain from any obstruction of the stools inside, the water may be shut off for a few seconds and then opened again. The obstruction may be due to the blocking of the nozzle by faecal matter entering into it. In that case the nozzle must be taken out, cleaned and inserted again. Retention of the water is helped by massaging the abdomen with wet hands. The patient may practise retaining the water and gradually increasing it. The enema can be taken after the regular daily movement of the bowel, so as to bring out the remnants of stools that may be in it. It may be repeated 2 or 3 times at intervals until the bowel is fully cleared.

* Only plain water should be used. No soap, glycerine or castor oil should be used for any kind of enema. If preferred, filtered lime-juice may be added to the water.

## The Retained Enema

Most chronic patients carry in their colon matter that is very many years old — perhaps claiming tenancy rights! Fasting helps in the removal of such matter. The retained enema would also help such individuals considerably in regaining their bowel health. A retained enema of about two ounces of cold water taken through a syringe at night before retiring to bed is not difficult to hold for the whole night. The water may be wholly absorbed by the dry, hard matter sticking in layers over the inside walls of the colon. It will get swollen and, in due course will be detached and eliminated. Small balls, like the goat's excreta, black and stinking, will come out. The fact that these are *old stools can be verified by the fact that they sink in water. As explained earlier, a tonic enema can also be taken after a natural bowel evacuation.

## Vaginal Douche

Gushing water — cold or alternately hot and cold introduced into the vagina greatly helps in the treatment of leucorrhoea (sticky whitish discharge from the vagina). This process is known as vaginal douche.

The rectal nozzle of the enema is removed and the vaginal douche fitting is attached to the stopcock of the enema. The can is held at a moderate height. It is filled with water — hot or cold and the stopcock is opened to see that the air remaining in the tube is expelled and the water starts flowing. The vaginal nozzle is inserted into the vagina in such a manner that its bent end part points towards the top side. The stopcock is then opened. The water flows into the vagina and runs out. When the can is almost empty, it is filled again. In the case of alternate hot and cold douche, the beginning should be made with the hot douche, followed by the cold douche, then alternately repeating hot and cold douches for some time, say about 15 to 20 minutes. The process is terminated after a few repeated douches with cold water.

Disintegration of the membranes of the uterus weakens the vagina and this is manifested in the form of leucorrhoea. Pregnancy, in such a condition, often results in an abortion. The vaginal douche, along with dietetic reform, is helpful in ensuring safe delivery.

* Fresh stools float on water and old stools sink in it.

## A Rule to Follow

An even distribution of the bodily heat to all parts of the body from head to foot is an important condition of health and vitality. The rule is *to keep the head cool and feet warm.* If the feet are felt to be cold in any degree, the warmth must be increased to normal by the use of every possible method: foot baths, woollen socks, warm clothing for the legs, use of woollen shawls or blankets for the lower half of the body, as and when necessary. This will be conducive to a better functioning of all the organs of the body and to a more rapid recovery of health and cessation of disease. Some people might have a feeling of 'too much heat' in their lower extremities. In such cases, walking barefoot on a lawn every day, early in the morning, or taking alternate hot and cold foot baths will be helpful, in addition to the adoption of dietetic reform and other hygienic measures.

Various water cure applications—baths, packs, bandages, enema, etc. — have been described earlier. The following test may be used to determine the suitability or unsuitability of a water cure application. If the patient finds it pleasant — or at least not unpleas-and—the method is good for him; if unpleasant, it is not suitable for him. No treatment must be imposed on the patient if he does not like it. Care should be taken to avoid overtreatment, i.e., a number of applications or methods should not be used. The principle of Non-violence, stressed in this chapter and earlier, should be borne in mind fully.

# NINETEEN

# Motherhood and Child Care

There are problems of womanhood, namely, pregnancy, giving birth to children and caring for them in the right way, which, when solved, would improve their health progressively, until they become able to take care of themselves. The basic principles and methods heretofore expounded can be applied to these problems. By dealing with them in this way the family as a whole would enjoy freedom from medicos and hospitals. In particular, dangers said to be related to childbirth—common in modern days—could be overcome. This Hygienic Science will thus prove to be means of raising the health level of the human race.

The mother-to-be must take good care of her health for the sake of her own self and that of the future child. This implies that she must eat an abundance of positive foods—vegetables, fruits and herbal supplements and observe the Laws of Vital Economy in eating them. Women who live thus need have no fear of pregnancy and of the process of giving birth to the child. Those who disregard these laws of health will face the risks attendant on motherhood.

Those who follow this way, are very likely to have children who will be more healthy than themselves and will hereby escape the diseases they may tend to inherit by birth. For it is a fact that the seeds of disease--in the shape of encumbering foreign matter, together with weaknesses of particular organs are passed on to the children while they remain integral parts of the maternal bodies.

A woman should look after her health much before she conceives. She should bear in mind the following:

i) She should avoid the habit of tying undergarments tight about the waist.

ii) She should ensure that the monthly menstrual flow is as normal as possible. Any disturbance in it should be set right not through any kind of symptomatic treatment but by Natural Hygiene

iii) She should give up the habit of chewing betel leaves and avoid eating its arecanut and inorganic lime.

iv) She should not use cosmetics as these would harm not only her skin health but general health too. (The best of cosmetics is wet clay or the juice of baked lime. This is to be applied and kept on for some time and then washed off.)

v) She should not wear high-heeled footwear.

Pregnancy is not to be looked upon as a period during which constant, or even occasional, medical attention is to be sought. If the pregnant woman happens to be healthy, all that she need do is to have proper prenatal care, as explained in this chapter, so that she can maintain her health and have a healthy baby after a safe and easy delivery. She does not need any kind of medical interference whatever.

## Diagnostic X-rays — Exposure Hazardous

If the pregnant woman is unhealthy, let her not be exposed to the so-called diagnostic X-rays, as exposure to them may be dangerous. According to Alice Stewart, M.D., of England, the link between childhood malignancies and X-ray examination during the early part of pregnancy has been fully established. He says that a radiation-induced mishap in the D.N.A. of the rapidly dividing prenatal cells can be translated into cancer after birth. Dr Irwin D.J. Bross, Director of Biostatistics of the Rosell Park Memorial Insititute of Bufallo, New York, has found that the offspring of persons exposed to X-rays, before and after conception, showed a five-fold increase in diseases like asthma, urticaria, eczema, pneumonia, dysentery and rheumatic fever.

Even an unintended exposure to X-rays — as might occur to a woman in an early stage of pregnancy stopping by an improperly installed X-ray unit in a roadside shop — may lead to her giving birth to a congenitally deformed child or to one who would develop blood cancer early in life.

## No Drug Treatments Either

Let not the pregnant woman be subiected to drug treatments of different kinds. Even if she happens to fall ill, let the sane and safe way of Basic Nature-Cure be adopted. Let the proper prenatal care, as set out in this chapter, be given to her.

## Smoking

It is necessary to refer to one more important point. The pregnant woman must understand the enormous complications that she exposes herself to by her taking to cigarette (or *beedi)* smoking or by allowing herself to be affected by passive smoking, i.e., by being by the side of, or very near to, smoking individuals. It might affect her health, as also that of the growing foetus, in ever so many ways. It may even lead to stillbirth or perinatal death.

## Why Aversion to Food?

In the beginning of pregnancy, due to ill-health, errors in eating or other causes, there often arises a period of acute dyspepsia, manifested by aversion to food, and in a few cases, even to water. This is Nature's hint that the digestive organs need rest, and if this hint be heeded the dyspepsia will pass away.

## Diet During Pregnancy

A grave error propagated by ignorant medicos is that a pregnant woman must eat a meal for two. What is eaten according to the rules of Vital Economy is quite sufficient for all purposes. The meals must be predominantly positive, especially where these been negative before. Along with salads of non-starchy tender vegetables, it would be desirable to partake of ripe, sweet fruits. Subacid fruits may be taken very moderately.

The ancients laid great stress on the maintenance of a happy, healthy mentality by the mother during pregnancy. Among the means for achieving this end is the eating of the right food at the right time in the right ratio. Indulgence in eating improper food is as bad for the pregnant woman as for anybody else; indeed worse.

## Other Helpful Hints

Along with druglessness and sensible diet reform on the lines suggested earlier, the pregnant woman should, for improvement of her general health and that of growing foetus, take take regular spinal baths, or at least have the cooling (or the stimulating) abdominal wet packs daily. She should not strain her bowels at stools; as often as needed, she may use the non-violent enema. She may practise the non-violent Pranayama regularly. Normal physical activity must be continued and physical strain avoided.

## Labour Pains

It takes approximately 9 months and 7 days from the first day of the last menstrual period for the delivery to take place. As the expected date of delivery draws nearer, the pregnant woman may get apprehensive, but there need be no such anxiety. If she has taken proper prenatal care, the delivery can be a natural, normal one, needing very little help from others. Caesarian delivery becomes necessary when the baby is very large (and hence of a great body weight) or when it is not possible to deliver it by natural means through the birth canal. Proper diet (strictly no overeating), moderate physical activity every day (with spinal baths or cooling packs, Pranayama, occasional non-violent enema, etc.) should avoid the need for a caesarian delivery. It should be stressed here that wearing high-heeled footwear is one of the factors necessitating a caesarian delivery, as the abdominal muscles are hardened and placed abnormally to thwart the scope for the normal and easy delivery.

Labour is the process by which a mother expels her baby and, later, the placenta and membranes from the uterus. Before labour actually begins, more changes take place in her baby. One of them is called 'lightening'. This is the lowering of the uterus when the baby moves down and locks its head into the pelvis, thereby restricting its movement. Now the mother can breathe more easily as the pressure on the lungs has lessened and the digestion improved. Moving about or walking becomes difficult after this, as lightening is a pressure on the pelvic region, producing an urge to urinate more frequently. Lightening may occur about two weeks before actual labour, or just before it.

As the belly moves or pushes against the cervix, the cervix opens and a mucus plug comes loose causing some mucus mixed with blood to come out of the vagina. Another sign of labour is rupture of membranes and gushing of water, which is the amniotic fluid surrounding the baby during pregnancy. After breaking of the 'bag of waters', labour begins and contraction may start any time.

Contractions should be steady and regular in time. They should occur at definite intervals. Some contractions do not persist. This is what is called 'false labour' and will go away if the woman walks for some time. It is more pronounced in the second or third pregnancy.

Contractions of true labour are regular in time. They last 10 to 30 seconds, with an interval of 15 to 20 minutes, in the first stage of labour. In the mid-phase, the contractions last 30 to 45 seconds with a similar interval of three to four minutes. In the transition phase the contractions last 45 to 60 seconds with an interval of three to four minutes.

Breathing and relaxing during the three stages of labour help the mother to conserve her energy and direct — or concentrate — it at a definite point. However, breathing should not be started immediately at the beginning of contractions as she may waste energy that she will need badly in the other stages of labour. The mother should go about her normal household chores, listen to music, go for a short walk, have a bath, etc., in fact do everything slowly, not giving the contractions much thought. Let her not get panicky or excited during this stage. The midwife, or the elderly lady attending on the pregnant woman at the time of delivery, will be able to help her only after she completes the three phases of labour.

If the mother is physically and mentally relaxed, she will experience less pain. Contractions are involuntary and the uterus is not connected with many nerve endings like any other involuntary muscles in the body. Only the surrounding tissues that are connected experience the changes and pain. So, if these can be relaxed, or pain controlled with breathing, child birth will be less painful.

In the early or first phase of labour, for every contraction breathing should be slow, shallow and effortless, beginning and ending with a deep breath. The pregnant mother may slightly massage her abdomen during contractions with her palms starting from the lower end of the abdomen, circling outwardly both sides meeting at the centre of the abdomen and sliding down the other above the centres of the abdomen. This can be repeated several times during contractions but no pressure should be applied to the abdomen. Or, in place of the massage recommended, she can be helped by the application of a cooling wet pack on the whole of the belly, renewed every few seconds, or even oftener. In doing this her preference for cold or hot water must be ascertained and respected. When hot water is preferred, it means that hot and cold packs should be alternated. This aid is generally so reliable that forcible delivery, which is often resorted to by so-called trained midwives or surgeons, can be avoided.

During labour the mother may want to have a bowel movement; she should then be provided with a towel on which she can evacuate. She should not be encouraged to go to the toilet as the baby may be born any time now. Sometimes, the bowel movement and the childbirth occur simultaneously.

During the transitionary stage when the contractions are more frequent and well pronounced the mother should continue with deep breathing. She should start deep breathing, follow it up with mouth breathing and end with a deep breath. After this she may not have any contraction pain when the baby is about to be born. She may then be taken to the delivery room and placed in a position easy to deliver the baby. She may be on her side with one leg bent towards her.

When the head of the infant has presented itself, she may feel the urge to expel the baby. If she is asked to wait for a minute by the midwife attending on her, let her do so. This will give her time to adjust herself to receive the baby, that is, hold it at the armpits to let it slide through when she expels. During this last stage, let her take a deep breath, hold for some time and expel the baby with all the force she can, as she would a very hard bowel movement. The baby is then born easily.

## Immediately after Delivery

To restore the womb and other related organs to their normal form the allopathic practice is to tie a tight dry bandage for a number of days. This is a wrong thing to do. The proper remedy is to give the mother a pack spinal bath and an abdominal wet pack. These must be tied with a little pressure. The diet must be as light as possible consisting of positive foods, including tender coconut water, vegetable soup or diluted fruit juice, for a few weeks, until the organs recover their normal form and tone. No solid food should be given until the third day of the child birth.

## Breast-feeding

In the post-natal stage, woman should follow Natural Hygiene fully. Breast-feeding has several advantages. It benefits the baby and the mother too. During the first three days after the delivery, a fluid called colostrum is produced by the breasts, which is good for the health of the baby.

A working mother can also breastfeed, though not completely. It is better to have as much maternity leave as she can the baby is born. This would help to have a longer duration to feed her baby completely. During the last week of her leave period, let her feed the baby at a time when she will be able to do so when she goes to her place of work. On resuming duty she may find it difficult during the first few weeks to feed the baby till she gets adjusted to the routine. At her place of work she may have to expel some milk from her breasts at times when she cannot bear to hold it any more. The same procedure is to be repeated by her as soon as she reaches home--expel a little milk, wash the breasts and then feed her baby. During office hours, the baby can be given diluted goat's milk. Cow's milk comes next, and if it is given, its defects should be countered by giving the baby herbal or grass juice. Dr Teofilo de la Torre, of Edenia, Central America, suggests coconut milk diluted with coconut water. This mixture is definitely better than cow's milk. These instructions also hold good in feeding a baby which cannot, for any reason, be breastfed throughout the day.

There will be sufficient milk in the breasts for the new-born babe, if the mother's feeding has been right. If there is no milk, or if there is not enough of it, the remedy is to resort eating highly positive meals, and to supplement them with the juice of grass or other herbs, as was done in a case in *Bombay, if, due to ill-health, the mother's milk suspected to be defective, the remedy is not artificial

After a week, the patient telephoned Kamesvara that she had chosen the last alternative and had the best result-there was milk enought for the baby.

* In this case, the author's son Kamesvara Sarma suggested the adoption of way of the following three alternatives:

i)   milk of groundnuts, extracted by wet-crushing of groundnut soaked previously for 24 hours, and diluting it; or, better still,

ii)  milk of cotton seeds, prepared in a similar manner, or, best of all,

iii) diluted grass juice of Dhurvagrass, referred to earlier. Any one of these foods has to be taken as the first feed for the mother; nothing else has to be consumed by her for at least two hours thereafter — to allow for sufficient time for digesting and assimilating the food completely.

139

feeding. Breast-feeding should be continued, the defect in milk being countered by giving diluted herbal juice to the baby and the mother.

The next question is how long breast-feeding should be kept up. Many fantastic reasons are put forward for weaning the baby after nine months, or at the most one year. One of them is that the teeth *begin* to be formed then. But *complete* formation of all the teeth, called the *molars,* by which alone chewing is possible. appear *last of all.* Hence this argument about the teeth indicates the naturalness of breast-feeding for three years. There have been cases where, because the mother did not become pregnant, the child was given the breast for four years or more, and in all of them the child was the better for this prolonged breast-feeding; of course in such cases the child has other foods also, which means that for a considerable time it takes both mother's milk and other foods, which provide an easy transition. In the opinion of Dr. Lakshmi Narayan Chowdhury, retired Civil Surgeon of Jabalpur, expressed in his book *Ideal Children* the *minimum* period of breast-feeding should be two years.

## Why Does the Baby Cry?

It is wrong to feed the baby every time he cries. A baby cries because he needs attention. There may be many reasons for it. He may cry –

i) if he is ill or is feeling pain or discomfort in any part of his body;

ii) if his dress is very tight;

iii) if his bed is inconvenient, having too little room to lie comfortably, move his limbs freely;

iv) if the weather be very unpleasant, too hot or too cold;

v) if he is mentally upset or if he feels very tired, may be because of lying in the same position for a long time;

vi) if there is any loud noise;

vii) if he is left alone or if he feels insecure in any manner; or

viii) if there any outsiders present in the room.

There could also be other reasons for the child to cry. The mother could make an intelligent guess as to why the child is crying. She should not stuff him with more milk or other food. Giving the baby food every time he cries may apparently pacify him for the moment but it would affect his health adversely.

## No "Pacifiers"

When the baby cries a little too often, parents instead of attending to its basic cause and helping him, resort to the use of a "pacifier"--a rubber nipple or a similar object. This habit, if persisted in, will lower the health of the baby progressively.

## Number of Feedings Per Day

How many times the baby should be fed is the next question. Three feeds a day is the optimum. This is well in accordance with the principal of Vital Economy. But it would be more convenient to so fix the intervals between the feeds so that the number of feeds is not more than three. As interval of six hours between two feeds will be right. But, in between, the baby should be given something to supplement of mother's milk, so that its defects, if any, are neutralised. This must, therefore, be something highly *positive,* herbal juice diluted with water and some fruit juice or coconut water, if available.

Excessive feeding should be avoided at all costs. Failure of digestion and a great many satellite diseases arise from it.

When the baby is fed with some substitute for mother's milk, a mistake often committed is that it is forced to swallow the food rapidly. This must not be done. The food should be given to the infant slowly giving it enough time to suck or sip it.

## Baby's Bowel-Health

If the child is fed naturally and sufficient positive food supplements are also given, the bowels will move by themselves. Non-violent enemas may be given if required. A simple tonic measure for the child is the wet abdominal bandage. If he is constipated, resort should not be taken to the purgatives. Care should be taken to see that he does not strain himself while passing stools. If the child is cared for hygienically, his constipation can be radically cured before long.

Children of delicate health need all the sunlight they can get as well as occasional exposure to the cold air outside. They should also have plenty of pure air to breathe.

141

## No Stimulants

An important caution to take is against the formation of a craving for so-called stimulants. These unnatural drinks hinder proper growth of the child's vital organs. Even among allopaths there are some who hold the view that tea and coffee are bad for children while they are growing.

It is also desirable to bring up children on Sattvic food alone, if possible, and for as long as possible. They should not be allowed to acquire a taste for oversalted, pungent and otherwise appetising foods.

## Children's Diseases

Children's diseases in their very nature are acute, such as fevers, measles, eruptions on the skin and so on. These crises lessen the inherited encumbranes, whereby the latent seeds of disease are destroyed. Hence suppressive treatment of children's diseases is a crime. It has been remarked even by some allopaths that the chronic diseases of adulthood are the effects of suppressed diseases of childhood.

Where children fall ill, the non-violent methods of Basic Nature Cure will yield beneficial results. There is very little difference between adults and children in the modes of treatment. To give them baths, five to ten minutes are sufficient. These should however be repeated much oftener than for adults. In Nature Cure there is no need for specialism as there is in allopathy.

## Let the Children Grow Healthy

If parents want their children to grow into healthy adults, physically and mentally fit to deal with the problems of life and livelihood in the civilized world of today, it is necessary that the children should be afforded an opportunity to learn the practical details of the Life Natural and the Natural Cure of illness so that they may become their own doctors when they grow up. Theoretical instruction should be given as part of their education. Thus alone can a healhty society, free from chronic and destructive diseases, be brought into being.

# TWENTY

# Varieties of Encumbrances

We have seen that the names and forms of diseases--which alone are looked at by allopathic medicos--are misleading, serving only to conceal the substratum of the disease-form, namely, the health level of the patient. In hygiene it is the patient that is treated, not his disease. Different patients having apparently the same disease as medically diagnosed are not equally curable. Some may be curable with great ease, others with difficulty, and a few not at all. The difference is due to the difference in their encumbrances. Those who are lightly encumbered are easily curable, while those who are heavily encumbered are curable with difficulty, or are incurable. Hence it becomes necessary, or at least useful to diagnose the encumbrances. We are indebted to the great pioneer, Louis Kuhne, for a knowledge of these encumbrances and of the signs by which they can be diagnosed. Kuhne called it the Science of Facial Expression.

## Encumbrances

Knowledge of the encumbrances enables us to estimate the length of time needed for a patient to reach a radical cure, which is the recovery of health. It also helps us to recognise a disease in its latent stage, so that we need not wait for it to manifest itself in a patent from in order to deal with it. The patient can at once start on a process of health recovery by adopting the hygienic measures taught here.

Encumbrances are of four kinds: encumbrances of the front or back or either of the two sides, right or left. They are of three stages of seriousness; light, medium and advanced. Thus, we have at least twelve varieties of encumbrances.

The first stage of an encumbrance is manifested as by an increase of bulk. The medium stage is shown by tension. In the advanced stage there is thinness of the body, due to the destruction and replacement of live tissue cells by foreign matter, with a tendency to emaciation.

## Front Encumbrance

A front encumbrance is verified by the deformity of the curved line that begins below the ear and merges in the chin.

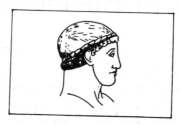

Fig. 10 — Back Encumbrance

Fig. 11 — Front Encumbrance

*Forehead:* Bald on top; no adipose cushion. *Eyes:* Dull. *Mouth:* Lower lip swollen, whole mouth too much forward. *Chin:* Enlarged and receding. *Face:* Line of demarcation far behind the ear, lower half of the face too full. *Neck:* Much Enlarged in front, line of demarcation of nape normal.

## Back Encumbrance

A back encumbrance causes disappearance of the line of demarcation between the back of the head and the nape of the neck. It is also to be inferred by a lessening of the convexity of the back of the head, or by a curvature of the back, with the shoulders bent forward.

## Side Encumbrance

Side encumbrances cause a deformity of the neck on the affected side and also a difficulty in turning the whole body.

144

Fig. 12 —·Front and Side Encumbrance.
*Head:* Too large. *Eyes:* Not quite normal. *Face:* Nearly square, no line of demarcation *Neck:* Too short and too thick.

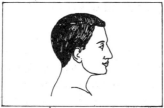

Fig. 13 — Normal Figure
*Forehead:* Smooth, no adipose cushion. *Eyes:* Large and tree. *Nose:* Well-formed. *Face:* Oval, clear of demarcation below the ear. *Neck:* Round, normal length.

## How Health is Affected

In the early stage of encumbrances of the front and right side, as a rule, only acute diseases arise. Advanced left and back encumbrances are at the root of chronic diseases. Back encumbrances affect the brain and the nervous system and are hence the worst. Pictures given in this book will help the reader to recognise the encumbrances by the signs described here.

It may be noted that foreign matter obeys the law of gravity and thus tends to occupy the side that is lowest in sleeping.

## Hints for Patients

The severity of the encumbrances determines the time needed for their cure. Chronic and destructive cases need a long course of treatment. (There is no sense in calling Nature Cure 'slow' on that account, because there is no other means of attaining a real cure.) The treatment can be shortened by judicious fasting. Without fasting the cure may take any time up to twelve years, or may not come at all. Treatment must be neither too much, nor too little. Excessive treatment would exhaust the patient's vital power and may kill rather than cure him.

145

Let it be noted, however, that even in a very slow case the patient will be having some improvement from time to time, so that he will be able to get on in life. He must be content with that and be patient.

Diseases become complicated and difficult and even incurable, due to the presence of two or more encumbrances, all in an advanced stage. But even the incurables may be benefitted, so that they get on through life with a degree of comfort, freedom from suffering and fitness for work.

There is also the problem of staying cured. This means that the patient must not go back to his old ways of life.

## Ayurveda

A word about the Ayurvedic theory of the three *doshas* or defects. We take no note of them in our practice. The *doshas*--which are called 'wind', 'bile' and 'phlegm', are possible only in an encumbered body when the vital power is low. With Vital Economy and positive foods we reach a cure of all diseases; nothing else is needed. Our methods are based on the Unity of Disease, and our success proves the unimportance of the *doshas*.

## Pot-Belly

Among the deformities due to encumbrances with foreign matter, the most common, and perhaps therefore the least regarded, is the pot-belly. An excess of fat deposits is one of the causes. Another cause is the retention of arrears of stools of a great many years, whereby the bowel is distended and weighted down, so that the middle part of it, the transverse colon, falls lower and comes to occupy a position at the navel level. The truth about constipation is given in full in the author's book *Cure of Constipation and Dyspepsia*. Apart from restoring bowel health, the Sarvangasana and exercises such as lying head downwards on a slanting board (the head being three to four inches lower than the feet) would be useful for reducing this deformity, along with the practice of Vital Economy and Vegetablarianism.

# TWENTY-ONE

# Diagnosis

Laymen and doctors (many 'naturopaths' included) agree that before a disease is treated, it should be 'properly' diagnosed. For diagnosis allopathic methods are as a rule employed. This is not the correct approach. Let us explain our stand fully.

The term 'diagnosis' is defined as the art of distinguishing one disease from another. This 'art' as practised by the allopaths, is based on the fallacy that there are thousands of diseases affecting one or more parts of the human anatomy, that each disease has some characteristic symptoms of its own and that each disease is to be 'treated' differently through specific drugs.

We shall proceed on the basis that this approach is 'scientific' and correct and examine matters on that presumption.

## What is to be Diagnosed?

The object of diagnosis is to know the type of disease the patient is suffering from. For this purpose, physicians study all the relevant symptoms the patient has at the time of examination. They subject him to an elaborate series of laboratory tests including X-ray. Can any, or all, of these tests and laboratory tests and examinations indicate the real cause of the fall in the health level of the patient? The answer is clearly in the negative. One may perhaps make a *guess* in regard to the causes leading to a pathological development, but the correctness or otherwise of such a guess will totally depend upon the intellectual approach of the physician. If he chooses to be a germ-virus hunter, as it happens to be in a vast majority of cases, he will surely mislead the patient.

# Can Diagnosis be fool-proof?

Once a 'diagnosis' is made, it is generally taken that it is correct, that it is fool-proof. But is it so? Could it be so in every case? That a diagnosis, made even after so-called diagnostic tests by modern methods, can never be fool-proof will be clear from the following.

In quite a number of cases, testing for cholesterol level in the blood is done. But many people may not know that this test is, in most cases, far from accurate. A very eminent medico, Dr E.R. Pinckney of U.S.A. recently observed: "It is probably one of the most inaccurate individual tests we have to do. If I say 'tsk!' tsk!' while taking a sample of blood for cholesterol analysis, I could raise your cholesterol 20 points."

Very often, the blood pressure of the patient is checked by the sphygmomanometer. Where the instrument is mechanically defective, as it happens to be in a large number of cases, both in public hospitals and private clinics, there could be significant errors in measurement of blood pressure and risk appraisal. Faults in the inflation/deflation system, caused mainly by dirt and wear and tear, with the resultant leakage, may result in giving misleading readings. According to the *British Medical Journal* (August 14, 1982), 94% of all the machines had cuff-widths shorter than the length recommended for usual use of adults.

The glucose-tolerance test (considered the best for the purpose of diagnosing *diabetes*) is of doubtful accuracy. It is extremely non-specific. It can be falsely influenced by age, inactivity, obesity, stress and drug consumption. There is also disagreement about what constitutes normal glucose level. Dr Marvin D. Siperstein, M.D., Professor of Medicine at the University of California, San Francisco School of Medicine, asserts that most Americans diagnosed as diabetic don't have diabetes and never will have!

As for diagnosing lung cancer by X-ray screening, it is admitted that 20 to 50% of detectable malignant tumors are completely missed, detected but not reported or reported but misinterpreted when they first appear on X-ray. Researchers have concluded (*Western Journal of Medicine,* June 1983) that "an error rate of about 30 per cent appears to be an unavoidable aspect of chest radiology, as it is currently practised."

As for the stress electrocardiogram (which is meant to show potential heart damage as well as previously undetected minimal heart damage), in more than half the number of cases the test fails to show abnormalities in patients who have them. What is more, where the stress test is given to those with no heart disease at all, more than half get false positive results, indicating that they do have some pathology.

Reference has been made only to a few of the common tests, each of which proves unreliable in most cases. Where then is the infallibility of diagnostic tests? Let us see what Dr Ivan Ilich says on this subject in his brilliant masterpiece *Medical Nemesis — The Expropriation of Health.*

> "Diagnostic bias in *favour* of sickness combines with frequent diagnostic error. Medicine not only imputes questionable categories with inquisitorial enthusiasm; it does so at a rate of miscarriage that no court system could tolerate. In one instance, autopsies showed that more than half the patients who died in a British University clinic with a diagnosis of specific heart failure had in fact died of something else. In another instance, the same series of chest X-rays shown to the same team of specialists on different occasions led them change their mind on 20 per cent of all cases. Up to three times as many patients will tell Dr Smith that they cough, produce sputum, or suffer from stomach cramps as will tell Dr Jones. Up to one-quarter of simple hospital tests show seriously divergent results when done from the same sample in two different laboratories. Nor do machines seem to be any more infallible. In a competition between diagnostic machines and human diagonisticians, in 83 cases recommended for pelvic surgery, pathology showed that both men and machines were correct in 22 instances; in 11 instances the computer correctly rejected the doctor's diagnosis; in 37 instances the doctors proved the computer wrong; and in 10 cases both were in error."

In cases where man or machine has (or where both have) erred, the wrong 'diagnosis' would inevitably lead to treatment that is 'wrong' even according to medical standards with the inevitable adverse consequence of further lowering the health level

Even where the 'diagnosis' is said to be correct, the naming of the disease does *not* indicate the cause for the fall in the health level of the patient. Where the 'correct' drugs are prescribed by the doctor for the patient, only the symptoms are dealt with, the cause is not at all attended to and there is no question of the health level of the patient being raised. The inevitable side-effects and after-effects of the drugs are there to add to the misery of the patient later.

## Is 'Diagnosis' Really Necessary?

So far as the patient is concerned, he is personally aware of the fact that his physical condition is not normal. Even if his pathological condition has been 'correctly' named, this would not help him, so long as he is not guided as to how he could restore his health. If, on the other hand, he is told that he is only imagining disease, or if different experts pronounce different opinions as to the 'nature' of the disease he is supposed to be suffering from, he gets more and more confused. 'Diagnosis', as done today, is hardly necessary. The patient should be helped to restore his health level the hygienic way.

## Does one Gain Anything by being 'Diagnosed'?

As would be clear from the above discussion, nothing could be gained by the patient by his being 'diagnosed'. He might get either terrified by the high-sounding names given to his disease or confused. The mental upset that might follow such a situation would inevitably worsen his health. And if, as is likely, he chooses to drug himself as per the prescriptions of the physician, his sufferings will know no end.

## Do not Diagnostic Tests Cause Health Hazards?

Again, we quote from Dr Ivan Illich:

> "In addition to diagnostic bias and error, there is wanton aggression. A cardiac catheterization, used to determine if patient is suffering from cardiomyopathy — admittedly this is not done routinely — costs 350 dollars and kills one patient in fifty. Yet there is no evidence that a *differential diagnosis* based on its results extends either the life expectancy or the comfort of the patient. Most tests are less murderous and much more commonly performed but many still involve known risks to the individual or his offspring which are high enough to obscure the value of whatever information they can provide. Many routine uses of X-ray and fluoroscope on the young, the injection or ingestion of reagents and tracers and the use of Ritalin to diagonse hyperactivity in children are

examples. Attendance in public schools where teachers are vested with delegated medical powers constitutes a major health risk for children. Even a simple and otherwise benign examination turns into risks when multiplied. When a test is associated with several others, it has considerably greater power to harm than when it is conducted by itself. Often tests provide guidance in the choice of therapy. Unfortunately, as the tests turn more complex and are multiplied, their results frequently provide guidance only in selecting the form of intervention on which the patient may survive and not necessarily that which will help him. Worst of all, when people have lived through complex positive laboratory diagnosis, unharmed or not, they have incurred a high risk of being submitted to therapy that is odious, painful, crippling and expensive....

"Diagnosis always intensifies stress, defines incapacity, imposes inactivity and focusses apprehension on non-recovery, on uncertainty, and on one's dependence upon future medical findings, all of which amounts to a loss of autonomy for self-definition. It also isolates a person in a special role, separates him from the normal and healthy, and regulates submission to the authority of specialised personnel. Once a society organizes for a preventive disease-hunt, it gives epidemic proportions to diagnosis. This ultimate triumph of therapeutic culture turns the independence of the average healthy person into an intolerant from of deviance."
average healthy person into an intolerant form of deviance."

That different kinds of tests could adversely affect the health of the patient, sometime very seriously, should be clear from the following:

i)   Exposure to radiation (through procedures like tomography) can produce complications inside;

ii)  In gastroscopy, as also in esophagoscopy and dudenoscopy, perforations could occur. Administration of local anaesthesia might lead to pulmonary aspiration and even cardiac arrhythmia.

iii) Sigmoidoscopy might not only involve stretching the sharp angulations in the rectum and sigmoid colon but might even result in perforation.

iv) In the elderly, the barium meal may stagnate in the colon and may even cause obstruction in a few cases. Barium may enter the peritoneum, if given inadvertently where perforation exists. It can also precipitate colon volvulus.

v) Where the barium enema is given, perforation, usually of the rectosigmoid, due to excess pressure, may occur. Where the ordinary saline enema (with a good quantity of hot water mixed with glycerine or soap) is given, perforation may be caused where there is pathological change such as diverticular disease.

vi) The hazards that may follow jejunal biopsy are haemorrhage and perforation.

vii) In rectal biopsy, there could be perforation.

viii) Oral cholecystography may lead to renal failure. Patients may develop rashes or sensitivity reactions after ingestion of iodine-containing oral cholecystographic media. Cases of iodine-induced hyperthyroidism have been seen following oral cholecystography.

ix) By submitting the patient to bronchoscopy, complications such as trauma to the teeth, neck, larynx and mediastium, bronchospasm, bronchial and tracheal perforation and sub-glottal oedema and sometimes even fatal haemorrhages due to trauma may occur.

x) Lung biopsy of every type whether it is the open biopsy, ordinary needle biopsy or needle biopsy with a high speed drill, does result in some morbidity and some mortality too

xi) Pleural biopsy is painful and might cause haemoptysis pneumothorax or neoplastic seeding of the wall.

There could be several other complications arising from the application of diagnostic methods.

## The Right Method to Diagnose

From what has been stated above, it follows that the ritual of 'naming' the disease--which is what is ordinarily meant by the term 'diagnosis'--is not only meaningless but also unnecessary. While having this ritual performed, the patient might actually be creating more complications within himself and might thus be worsening his condition. The 'naming' of the disease-condition is not going to help the patient in any manner, for that will never indicate the cause of the fall in his health level.

Rightly speaking, diagnosis should be of the level of health that a patient is presently having. It may be that the level of health is low. Let the patient know the extent of encumbrance he is having in his body. Let the patient find out for himself how his different organs (stomach, lungs, skin, bowel, etc.) are working and take the right type of work from each of them, without taxing them in any manner, so that he could build up his health level, slowly and steadily by the application of the principles of Non-violence and Vital Economy.

Let him free himself from fear and become self-reliant. Let him clearly know whether his disease is acute, chronic or destructive. A study of his health history, his habits of living and the extent to which he has drugged himself to suppress his earlier disease-conditions will enable him to decide correctly.

Let him know that all he has to do is to build up his health, by giving up his unhygienic habits of living and start living rightly, in tune with the Laws of Life. He need not bother about the so-called diagnosis, let him simply rectify his habits of living. Before long, he will find his health level improving progressively. All the symptoms which he used to suffer from will disappear, for, where health has been restored, how can there be symptoms of disease?

# TWENTY-TWO

# Acute Disease

We have already seen that diseases of the first stage in disease-progression, which are called acute diseases, are themselves the *cure* of disease in its latent state, which is only defective health. They are efforts of Life, guided by Nature, to reduce the existing encumbrances of toxic filth. Because they arise when the encumbrances are light and vitality abundant, Life makes *vigorous* efforts, through these diseases, to restore health and for this reason they are called acute diseases. Generally speaking, in such cases all that is needed is to let the disease take its own course, taking care not to do anything to obstruct the process of health recovery, which the disease is.

In the civilised life of today, however, this would not be a safe policy to follow, for civilisation and the medical profession have so corrupted the sources of life that most children are born with an inheritance of disease with weakness and defects of vital organs. This makes purely acute diseases exceedingly rare. That is, most acute diseases of today have a background of chronic ill health, which greatly complicates the problem of health recovery. In a few cases, there is a background of disease of the third stage, destructive disease, in seed form, so that sufficient attention to the principle of Non-violence will be necessary to regulate the process of cure. Simple fevers, which were far from uncommon during the boyhood of the author, have now given place to subacute fevers, such as typhoïd, pneumonia, influenza, malaria and so on, and new varieties are originating every few years. In regard to many of these it has been said by competent witnesses that they are not natural, but iatrogenic, in the sense that an ordinary fever of no real seriousness is aggravated by medical malpractice and thereby assumes one of these forms. Among fevers the more serious one are the intermittent ones, which go into latency and come out again in patent form, at intervals, so that they are called periodical fevers; these partake of the nature of chronic disease, and hence the natural cure needs to be aided by the hygienic measures described before, among which fasting is the most important. It may be said that even such complicated illnesses will be disarmed of their alarming features and will cure themselves much sooner than by allopathy, if the Natural Way be followed.

Acute diseases are by themselves short-lived; they would not last long if they are not maltreated. This means that there should be no effect to suppress them by drug-poisons and that eating should not be resorted to unless there is hunger. As a rule, in an acute disease the patient has no hunger; he is also, as a rule, averse to food; this is because nature withdraws the vital power from the digestive organs and utilises it for eliminating the encumbering foreign matter. In purely acute illnesses fasting should be the rule till the illness abates. In sub-acute cases there need be only a very close approach to fasting for one to three weeks, by which time the background of chronic ill health will be cleared away. It may be better to fast on water alone in some cases. After this, light but highly positive food medicine should be given in restricted amounts.

Air and sunlight should be freely and abundantly availed of. The patient must be kept where pure air and sunlight are available. If the patient is weak, he should have sun-baths so as to augment his vital force. In some serious cases, it would be proper and necessary to place the patient in open sunshine for nearly the whole day, morning, forenoon, afternoon and evening, excluding the midday hours when the sun is too hot. Exposure to hot sunshine, when necessary, may be done by covering the patient with slightly wet cloth or green banana leaf.

Among the water-cure methods the spinal bath is the most useful and necessary of all. Weak patients would be benefited by taking it simultaneously with a hot foot bath, in the cold season a blanket may be used for preserving bodily warmth as indicated earlier. For weak patients the shallow hip bath is most suitable. To promote bowel movement enemas are helpful and in some cases may be absolutely necessary.

During fasting, herbal juice--about a teaspoon or two diluted in water may be given to the patient, and diluted in water until relief is felt.

Methods to obtain relief from painful conditions should be employed as described before.

## Feverishness

At least two or three days before the onset of a fever, the patient feels feverish. Though his body temperature is normal, he may be experiencing some of the following symptoms: a bad throat, dizziness, clogged nose, muscular pain, coated tongue, lack of hunger, constipation and a general feeling of uneasiness.

The patient is advised to heed the warning of feeling 'feverishness' as soon as he experiences it and take timely preventive action if he has not earlier been wise enough to keep his body internally clean. These symptoms are an indication that the individual would, if such preventive action is not taken immediately, develop fever in about 48 hours or so.

The moment feverishness is experienced, let the individual go on a complete fast or take only tender coconut water (or some other herbal juice) in a small quantity, twice or thrice in th e day. Let him either take the spinal bath or the abdominal wet pack twice or thrice a day. In the morning, after such water-cure application, let him take a piecemeal cold friction bath. Let him also take one non-violent enema once in early in the morning and then late in the evening. Above all, let him keep a way from all kinds of physical and mental strain, take a complete rest and keep himself mentally calm, as there is no reason to get perturbed, now that he is giving the maximum opportunity to the body to clean itself. If this is done, the condition of feverishness will disappear.

Readers are aware that many disease conditions like diphtheria, poliomyelitis. chickenpox, measles, etc., develop only after a spell of fever. If the above programme is followed in "feverishness" even the fever conditions would not follow, the patient may rest assured that he can also prevent diphtheria, poliomyelitis, etc.

If, in a few cases, where the bodily impurity is a little too much, fever does appear even after observing the required precautions, it will be mild and quite controllable. The body, having cleansed itself to some extent during the two or three days of feverishness, might not have the level of toxaemia necessitating the appearance of diptheria, poliomyelitis, etc. The mild fever that the patient gets can be radically cured in a very short time by Nature Cure methods.

## Fever

Among acute illnesses fever stands foremost, because it is most conducive to a rise in the health level, if naturally treated. Fevers are either simple or complicated. Typhoid, pneumonia and the like are of the latter sort. Simple fever yields to fasting on water alone and care in breaking the fast will ensure better health. Spinal baths or hip baths will be helpful, and may be taken with benefit.

Fevers complicated with latent defects of health, such as typhoid, paratyphoid, malaria, pneumonia, influenza, etc., can be treated on the same lines. Most of such fevers are intermittent and periodic; that is, they are alternately patent and latent. The great mistake usually committed is to give the patient substantial food on the days when the fever goes into latency. This prolongs the fever and leads up to some serious chronic disease. Fasting must be observed continuously in these fevers, both when the fever is patent and when it becomes latent. If the patient wants food, only diluted fruit juice, vegetable soup or tender coconut water may be given to him sparingly that is, there must be an *approach* to fasting and the food given must be positive. After the fever subsides, the same diet must be continued but more of the food may be given. Later, limited rations of cooked vegetables or salads may be given. The Water Cure administered must be adapted to the patient's powers of reaction. Baths will be suitable in some cases, and packs in others.

In some cases the fever remains partly or wholly internal, so that the fever-heat is unequally manifested in different parts of the body. In such cases the fever needs to be brought out and enabled to pervade the whole body. For this purpose, the trunk pack or other packs will be useful. Once the fever is brought out, the cure is easy.

## Headaches

It should be realised that headache is only a symptom. It can be present in different conditions--indigestion, constipation, eye-strain, catarrh, menstrual disorders, nervous disorders, high blood pressure, anaemia, fever, common cold, tension, etc.

Anyone wanting to get rid of the unpleasant and annoying symptom that headache is should realise that the sensation of pain in the head indicates a warning to be taken note of. He should not resort to the so-called 'headache remedies' must understand the cause of the trouble and reform his habits.

Habits such as taking meals hurriedly, working on a loaded stomach, eating wrongly-combined foods or stale foods, eating too often, eating beyond one's assimilative capacity, taking meals when one is excited or tired, addiction to stimulants, etc., tend to cause headaches. If some or all of them become regular habits, headache would become, so to say, one's constant companion.

Other factors that can cause headaches are: (1) emotional maladjustment, (2) wrong posture, (3) visual strain, (4) fatigue due to overexertion and (5) unhygienic environment.

The cause(s) of the headache must be investigated by studying the history of the patient in depth and steps taken to correct his habits. Wrong modes of eating and wrong choice of foods must be corrected.

If the cause of headache is emotional maladjustment, it must be attended to. There are numerous persons who have developed disgust for their work. Whatever may be the reasons for one developing this negative attitude--none of them may be justifiable--it is not going to help them. Instead of taking to tranquillisers, sedatives or stimulants, let them change their attitude towards work and environment.

Without compromising on principles, everyone should try to have emotional adjustment to the environment. For without it, the home could well be turned into a hell, the place of work into a gaol.

The habit of taking stimulants (coffee, tea, cola drinks, cigarettes, etc.) 'to relieve' headache is to be condemned outright. Continued addiction to any stimulant depletes vitality and is a major cause of chronic and destructive diseases. No stimulant can strengthen the body. No stimulant can relax the nerves. Let this be clearly understood. If anyone happens to be an addict to any of the stimulants, let him follow the Nature Cure methods and build up his health; the stimulants would 'leave' him.

Besides rectifying his habits of living, the patient should also take the spinal bath (or the abdominal wet packs) daily. To the extent needed, the non-violent enema may be had. Air baths and non-violent Pranayama would also help him to rebuild his general health. Occasional fasting should be practised

# Common Cold

There is no allopathic cure for the common cold. Everything has been tried, even vaccines and what are called antihistamines, and all have failed. Even among the medicos, some have come to see that what is needed is only a commonsense care of oneself. The comon cold is neither a cold, nor the effect of cold air or water. It is not a contagious, or very contagious, virus infection as some believe. It is caused by inflammation of the mucous membrane of the upper respiratory tract, brought about by wrong choice of foods and wrong modes of eating, as also other wrong, unhygienic, habits of living. In this condition, elimination of a more or less thick and viscous exudation called mucus is on. The process needs to be helped by general rest, including the digestive organs, by means of fasting which may have to be kept up for from three to five days or at the most a week.

The cause of a cold is the same as that of all acute conditions. It is more a cure than a disease. Vigorous walking, sleeping in the open air, spinal baths with hot foot baths, sun baths, fasting or at least a very close approach to fasting, enemas to keep the bowels clean and a cool mind, all these or most of these might be required.

If the cold is accompanied by fever or a headache, the patient should not get worried. Let him fast completely and avoid all kinds of strain.

Those who profess to follow the 'yogic' method of treating diseases recommend the *kriya* such as *jala neti, sutra neti* or *grta neti* as a 'cure' for the common cold. Nowadays even many 'naturopaths' in India have started recommending the adoption of these *kriyas* by patients and by even healthy persons.

By flushing water into one nostril and expelling it through the other — that is what *jala neti* means — symptomatic relief may be felt by the patient inasmuch as some mucus might be forced out. The water that is flushed through the nostril *also* removes even the minimum mucus that ought to be left over the nasal mucus membranes. The membranes dry up, as it were, for some time, and this affects general health. If warm water is used for *jala neti* or, worse still, if salt is added thereto, as some people do, the nasal mucous membranes will be injured all the more.

Some years ago, in the name of *sutra neti*, 'Yogis' used to insert a cotton thread (of moderate thickness) into one nostril and draw it out through the other. Nowadays, either small plastic or rubber tubes (of moderate thickness) are used for the purpose. Holding the extended portion of the tube outside each nostril, the patient is asked to draw the tube in and out, apparently to cleanse the nostrils. Though there may be apparent relief immediately, the irritation caused by this 'tug-of-war' process, in addition to injuring the fine cilia in the nostrils, aggravates the inflammatory condition in the nasal mucous membranes the patient becomes susceptible to repeated attacks of cold and related catarrhal diseases.

*Grta neti* is done by applying ghee in the nostrils (in place of water used in *jala neti),* though in a much smaller quantity. Some of the ghee used in the *kriya* would naturally get deposited over the nasal mucous membrane and the mucosa in such a condition would tends to draw more and more dirt over it. This worsens the condition of the patient.

For the reasons mentioned above, adoption of any of the 'neti' *kriyas* by the patient suffering from the common cold (or any other disease condition) is not recommended. Let the patient adopt the Basic Nature Cure methods and cure himself.

## Whooping Cough

Whooping cough is a disease of the respiratory tract, usually experienced in childhood. It is accompanied by convulsive coughing which manifests itself in a cold and sore throat. The cough (which, if not naturally treated, would last four to six weeks) is characterised by a 'whoop' and is sometimes accompanied by vomiting.

Dr. David Morris of London admits (in a letter published in the *British Medical Journal* dated April 10, 1982) that "there is really no effective treatment once the disease is caught, although claims are made constantly for a variety of remedies."

Even if drug systems claim that they have "very effective" remedies, the health seeker must keep away from drugs. By resorting to drugs, a patient cannot cure himself.

When a child suffers from a disease like whooping cough, the parents, worried very much, would like to help him to get over it as early as possible. Let there be no doubt about it; children respond to Natural treatment much more quickly than older people do. Let, therefore, the parents restore the health of the child through the sane, safe, Natural way.

Whenever food is taken into the stomach, the cough increases, the patient will have very poor digestion. If a little care is taken in feeding him sensibly, he can be cured very quickly and radically too. In the mornings, the patient could be given a very small quantity of ashgourd juice or some other herbal juice, freshly prepared. About 11 a.m., vegetable soup (without salt) could be given. At about 4 p.m., he could have either some seasonal fruit, or ashgourd juice or herbal juice. At night, vegetable soup could be repeated. Every time something is taken in, an abdominal wet pack could be had. Non-violent enemas may be given daily to the patient.

## Mumps

This is a condition normally characterized by swelling of the parotid gland(s), located beneath and in front of the ears. Normally, only one of the parotid glands is affected. In certain cases, the submaxillary (or submandibular) glands, situated on either side below the angle of the lower jaw, are also inflamed.

Whichever glands are affected, it is only inflammation that has occurred. Hence, it is an acute disease indicating that the digestive system of the patient is upset. One need not get concerned about it. The disease, as with every acute condition, works itself off. All the complications that are ordinarily associated with mumps are *not* caused by mumps but are due either to neglect of the condition or to suppressive drug treatment.

It occurs most often in children of school going age; it is uncommon in infants. Adults too may get the disease.

A tender swelling first appears in the recess behind the angle of the jaw (on one side) and is accompanied by malaise and fever. The swelling may or may not spread to the other side. Occasionally, the submandibular glands may also get inflamed. Pain and tenderness are felt in the affected parts. The pain may also spread to the throat and there may be fever. There is discomfort when opening the mouth, chewing or swallowing. Acid foods and 'beverages' cause an increase in the pain. There is no hunger. Headache and backache are also felt.

With the digestive system upset — and that is what has led to the development of the mumps — *Nature declares a lockout, as it were,*

*and makes it impossible for the person even to open his mouth!* There
is an aversion for food in such a condition. The patient should take
to fasting the moment any of the above symptoms develops. Cooling (or stimulating) wet packs with packs over the neck applied
thrice or four times a day, would greatly help the patient. Non-violent enema may be had once or twice a day for a few days. By following this regiman, the patient would become normal very
quickly.

## Hints on Treatment

In all acute diseases, only the five-fold food medicine is employed.
Under the head of Space (sky), fasting or an approach to fasting has
been prescribed. Air, sunlight and water are also made full use of.
Medicinal doses of highly positive food substances have also been
availed of. These represent the Earth's contribution.

Now the reader must not complain that his particular acute disease does not find a place in this book. Enough has been said to con-
vey the basic truth that substantially the same methods will aid the
cure of all acute diseases.

In each case there are two things to be attended to immediate
relief from painful or unpleasant symptoms and radical cure of the
condition by the recovery of health. The two will, as a rule, overlap.
For example, enemas or foot baths will give immediate relief as well
as final cure. Local and general restoratives, that is bandages and
cooling and other baths and packs, are necessary. Speaking generally, the care for any acute disease is substantially the same as the
care for a fever. Whoever understands this will know how to get
through any acute disease. The methods should be adjusted
to the patient's needs as explained before. It should be noted that
in the Natural way sleep comes naturally. Sleep is the best of
medicines for the sick. So the sleeping patient must not be disturbed
for giving treatment. After the cure is reached, the health that has
been recovered must be confirmed and enhanced by adopting a
programme or natural living according to the principles set forth in
the earlier chapterss, with special attention to Vital Economy and
the choice of positive foods.

The reader ought to know also, that patients of acute diseases
ought to abstain from sexual indulgence till they recover normal
health. Disastrous consequences are likely to follow if this rule is
violated.

# TWENTY-THREE

# Chronic Disease

The reader will have known from the preceding chapters that chronic disease in present-day civilisation is always *iatrogenic,* that is, it caused by medical incompetence. The persistent supression of acute diseases, thereby preventing reduction of the encumbering toxic filth, incidentally poisoning the nervous and other bodily tissues with deadly drugs — which the Life Principle is never given an opportunity to eliminate — brings about two untoward results: a great increase of encumbrances and an equally great reduction of vitality. The bodily constitution becomes affected and disabled, reducing the power to eliminate foreign matter greatly. Life, however, does not cease to make efforts to reduce the encumbrances; but these are not as vigorous as before. The disease *appears* comparatively mild. But because the twofold cause has become chronic, the disease is also chronic, that is to say, it is deep-rooted and tends to last for an indefinitely long time, as if it were an integral part of the patient's constitution.

Among the organs affected are, first and foremost, the organs of digestion. These are chronically disabled. Whereas in an acute disease there is only a temporary indigestion, in chronic disease there is a degree of chronic indigestion, called dyspepsia. This dyspepsia is almost always masked by disease of some other organ or part of the body, so that the patient and his doctor mostly tend to ignore this basic *defect* of health and concentrate their attention wholly "on the other disease".

A few doctors have however always been aware of this fact, among whom we may mention Dr Rabagliati, who wrote in the book *'Intis'* that practically all diseases, such as asthma, consumption or rheumatism, are really masked dyspepsia and are therefore, curable by reduction of the stomach-load or by fasting.

All chronic diseases alike need to be cared for only as varieties of dyspepsia, and are curable only by this plan. *What fever is to the totality of acute diseases, dyspepsia is to all the chronic ones.* It is because of this knowledge that the hygienic care of chronic disease is possible.

In chronic diseases there is not only a fall in the level of vitality, but also a change for the worse in the quality of the blood, due to the excessive eating of negative foods and the utter neglect of the positive ones. The blood loses its normal alkalinity. The patient's ability to fast and fitness for fasting are decidedly less than when the disease was acute.

For this reason, we do not think it proper for such patients to take to a long fast straightaway. Occasional short fasts in the beginning for recovering the submerged sense of hunger, and later for helping the elimination of foreign matter are necessary. This is *Instalmental Fasting.* Later, when the health is sufficiently improved, it would be proper to resort to Progressive Fasting. That is to say, for chronics, fasting and dieting must laternate, the intervals between any two fasts being long enough to improve the blood alkalinity and the general health.

In chronic conditions the water cure is not so effective as in acute cases, and hence resort to must not be as frequent as in the latter ones. The following hints may be borne in mind in this regard:

i) Instead of cooling packs, stimulating wet packs will prove more beneficial.

ii) Retained enema may be taken daily to clear the colon.

iii) Spinal baths taken along with hot water foot baths will be more effective.

iv) Sun baths taken a little earlier in the morning but for a somewhat longer period will do good. If the sun is a little too warm, it will be safe and advantageous to have a banana leaf or at least a well wrung or wet (white) sheet covering the body. The spinal bath may follow the sun bath.

The following examples will serve to familiarise the reader with the practical methods of hygienic cure of chronic cases.

## Constipation

The reader may bear in mind the hints on bowel health given in the chapter 'Exercise and Other Aids' and improve his general health by observing Vital Economy and Non- violence. It should not be forgotten that the *enema should only be availed of to supplement the natural motion and not to substitute it.*

The patient should attend to dyspepsia which is the main disease, whereof all others are only satellites. The reader is referred to the author's book *Constipation and Dyspepsia*. Care of the dyspepsia that is there will ultimately restore bowel health and then enemas will become unnecessary.

In some cases the retention of arrears of stools of a great many days causes the middle part of the bowel, called the *transverse colon,* to get detached from its proper position. It falls downward, manifesting as obesity of the part of the belly that is below the navel. To help restore this part of the bowel to its proper position, recourse may be had along with the above treatment, to one of the Hatayogic *asanas* called the *Sarvangasana.* An alternative is to lie head downwards on an inclined plane, on a board or wooden plank of about six feet in length, placed so that the upper end of it is about three or four inches, at may rate not more than a foot, higher than the lower end. The patient should do some simple exercises with his legs, imitating cycling, guided by his own natural instinct. This may have to be done regularly for a long time, at the end of which the bowel will be brought back to its natural position above the navel.

It may be stated here that as the dyspepsia — which is also present — is the cause of all other chronic diseases, the mode of treating it is also the means of curing them.

## Dyspepsia

The reader must understand that practically all that has been set forth before in Chapters 1 to 20 is relevant to the cure of this disease. To begin with, the patient must prepare his mind, as explained in Chapter 8, so that it may cooperate with him in the enterprise of recovering lost health. He must understand the truths of superscientific Biology as taught in Chapter 3 and the technique of using Nature's Fivefold Medicine, as expounded in Chapter 6. He must also master all that is taught in the chapters on Vital Economy, Vegetablarianism, and fasting, and all else that follows. Above all, he

165

must have a clear understanding of the Unity of Disease and Health as explained in the chapter on Unity. By knowing all this he is qualified to become his own doctor. He must then put into practice the No-breakfast Plan or its equivalent; he must practise waiting for hunger and eating no more than the minimum, knowing that it is also the maximum for positive health. He must also choose his foods correctly according to their health value and not their 'food value' He must also be able to decide when to fast and when to make only an approach to fasting, and when not to fast. He should become familiar with the practical effects of methods of Sun Cure and Water Cure wherein the enema is included and he must carry in his mind all that is said in the later chapters, about self-denial in sex, about breathing, exercise and so on. He must prepare a prescription sheet for himself in accordance with the principles of this science and alter it suitably from time to time. He must also know what to do in curative crises and what to do to *stay cured* after he is cured.

Strictly speaking, every follower of Nature Cure must prescribe the remedy for himself with the aid of the foregoing hints. It will be wrong to furnish him with a standard prescription which he can follow blindly without an understanding of the hygienic truths on which it is based. Nevertheless, hoping that after some personal experience he will make efforts to prepare a programme of treatment for himself and for others, if need be — so as to become, gradually, more and more self-reliant, we suggest the following measures, which will suit not only all dyspeptics and neurasthenics, but also all chronics, whatever be the medical label for their particular disease, which in the first place is only a defect of health primarily of the digestive system, and in the second place of the other systems also.

About 7 a.m., on an empty stomach, take a drink of herbal juice prepared as recommended.

Whether before or after taking the juice as may be convenient, clear the bowels with or without an enema; if the bowel seems not to have been fully emptied, take a non-violent enema.

Depending on the weather, some time in the forenoon when the sunlight is pleasantly warm, say between 8 a.m. and 9 a m., bask in the sun in a non-violent way as long as it feels comfortable. Then cleanse the skin surface either by wiping with a slightly wet towel, or by a lukewarm, tepid or cool bath, as preferred, finishing with a spinal bath with such precautions as have been described. About 10.30 a.m. or when hungry or at least when the stomach is empty and there is an unmistakable sense of lightness, take the principal meal, consisting of either a raw salad, or conservatively cooked non-starchy vegetables, to which coconut scrapings and a trace of lime-juice for taste may have been added. Where coconuts are not to be had, other nuts may be used. It will be ideal to have the dishes without salt, or with very little salt. The attempt should always be to go on minimising the salt content so that it could be given up. After the meal, a few ounces of much diluted buttermilk (not sour) may be drunk if preferred. No salt or sugar should be added to the buttermilk.

Between 2 and 3 p.m., a little buttermilk, of the kind described above, or some tender coconut water or diluted fruit juice may be drunk.

At any convenient time in the afternoon, a spinal bath for 15 minutes or more, followed immediately by a hip bath for 10 or 15 minutes should be taken.

In the evening or at night a very light repast, consisting of fruit or vegetables of one kind, followed by a drink of buttermilk, not sour, may be taken. This regimen may be added to other items, such as an abdominal wet bandage, as required. The regimen will have to be modified if the patient is able to attend to his daily work and has to do so. If this be the case, the principal meal must be taken at night and the light repast in the day. Also, exercise, Hatayogic *asanas,* and Pranayama, which have not been provided for in the regimen must be considered and provided for. If he can, the patient must take a walk, of not too great a distance either in the morning or in the evening, or at both times if he can, practising improved breathing while walking.

Before implementing the regimen the patient will do well to go through a period of an approach to fasting for at least three weeks--if possible for four weeks--subsisting on very light food of a positive quality, such as tender coconut water, juice of raw vegetables, preferably tender ones to the latter, a trace of lime juice may be added for taste.

Also, the patient must take to instalmental fasting, one day at a time; he may do so once a weak. If he does so for two or three days each time, the interval may be increased to two weeks. Later, he may take to Progressive Fasting to complete the cure.

167

## Varicose Veins

Varicose veins is a circulatory disorder primarily caused by lack of tone of the blood vessels. The veins become varicose, that is, distended, dilated, distorted.

While varicosity may occur anywhere in the veins of the body, it is most common only in the veins of the adbomen and the limbs. If varicosity occurs in the veins of the rectum, it is called haemorrhoids or piles. If it occurs in the veins of the scrotum, it is called varicocele. If the condition is found in other places, it is simply called varicose veins. The condition is most commonly found in the lower extremities of the body. Whatever the location of varicosity, the causes are the same.

When, due to a number of factors, some of them of a primary and others of a secondary nature, the veins lose their tone and the passage of blood through them onwards to the heart is affected, some of the veins (specially in the lower limbs or the abdomen) develop varicosity. The affected vein(s) can be seen prominently on the surface of the body. Ugly to look at, these enlarged veins allow the blood to stagnate in them. As more and more of the surrounding veins become varicose, hard and knotty lumps are formed.

For quite some time, this condition manifests no painful symptoms and there is a tendency on the part of the sufferer to neglect it. As the condition worsens, skin disorders may occur locally (such as varicose eczema). The distended blood vessels may develop a rupture and this will lead to haemorrhage, which may well prove fatal. Other complications that may develop in an advanced stage of varicose veins are phlebitis (inflammation of the veins) and varicose ulcers.

The supportive and compressive treatments suggested by medicos pay no regard to the primary causative factors and, hence, provide no radical cure. These may offer some relief, which is the reason why they are resorted to. It is well worth remembering that *if a part of the bodily economy is replaced by mechanical aid, regeneration can scarcely be expected.*

The 'sclerosant therapy' (this 'therapy' consists of injecting drugs intravenously for the purpose of effecting a shrinkage and fibrosis of the 'offending veins') injures the circulatory system seriously

Even the sorrounding veins may start developing varicosity. All such symptomatic treatments do not aim at removing the cause of varicosity and can do no good at any time.

It would be well worthwhile for the sufferer to begin with a short fast of two or three days. During the fast, the patient may take tender coconut water or raw (fresh) juice of vegetables or (fresh) fruit juices, twice or thrice a day, in a moderate quantity.

After this initial fast, the patient may live, say, for a period ranging from two to four weeks on a highly positive diet. Fresh, unspoilt foods, almost entirely consisting of raw salads and/or conservatively cooked vegetables and fruits, could be taken not more than twice daily, in strict moderation.

After this period, the patient should live on a predominantly positive diet, vegetables and fruits forming about 75 to 80 per cent of it, the secondary foods forming the remaining part. Fruits should not be consumed along with the meals. These could be taken either at breakfast (about 8.30 or 9 a.m.) or late in the evening (by 4.30 p.m.) when the stomach will be empty.

Occasional fasts for a day could be undertaken once a fortnight.

Vigorous walking is highly beneficial. Walking barefoot on grassy lawns or a sandy beach is very much recommended. The patient should avoid, as far as possible, standing for long hours. He should sleep on a hard bed. (In fact, a hard bed is recommended for everyone as sleeping on a soft bed can create circulatory problems and later, even of the joint diseases.)

For a patient suffering from varicose veins, it would be better if the 'leg side' of the bed is slightly raised (by three or four inches) by placing bricks below it. His head will be at a slightly lower level than the head, though the posture of the body will be straight. In early mornings, he can while lying on the bed, do the exercises suggested under the head 'Constipation' in this chapter.

Regular spinal baths, or at least cooling abdominal wet packs, may be taken daily. The non-violent enema may be used, to the extent needed. The patient may also do the non-violent Pranayama regularly.

The sufferer from varicose veins should avoid weaning tight belts, bands, garters, etc. The body should be as unhampered by clothing as possible.

# Haemorrhoids (Piles)

When the veins in the mucous membranes inside or just outside the rectum get inflamed (varicose), the condition is known as, haemorrhoids (piles). The veins may also become filled with blood clots (thrombosed).

The 'tumor-like' piles which appear at the edge of or just within the anus, cause intense pain, itching and discomfort, especially at the time of passing stools. They also bleed in quite a few cases. There may be rectal prolapse also.

The discomfort is felt in the form of soreness and irritation after the passage of the faeces. In some cases, a feeling of fullness or heaviness in the region of the rectum (with an ever-present 'urge to pass stools but with nothing coming out) is also there. There may be mucous discharges. Bleeding may occur during, or following, stools. Excessive or severe bleeding may result in anaemia.

If the condition is allowed to persist, with or without drug treatment, the rectal sphincters develop tenesmus; they lose their tone to an extent where they become ineffective in doing their function.

The causes underlying varicosity of the veins and prolapse of the rectum have been explained earlier. A study of the relevant portions will enable the reader to know the causative factors leading to the progressive weakening of the rectum and the anus. Haemorrhoids (or piles) form a link in the chain.

It is said that haemorrhoids sometimes occur in pregnancy because of pressure on the veins from the enlarged womb. The words "because of" are misleading. In a healthy woman, the enlarged womb at the time of pregnancy cannot *cause* pressure on the veins, leading to the development of haemorrhoids. It is the general lowered level of health, with chronic constipation and sluggish blood circulation, that causes haemorrhoids.

It is a mistake to regard this condition as a purely local disturbance and to resort to symptomatic treatments therefor. Injections, and not unoften surgical treatments, are recommended by medicos, but the sufferers know it to their cost that these do not effect any radical cure. Any immediate relief that may be felt does not last long; the suffering increases progressively.

Natural treatment for this condition should be more or less on the lines recommended for varicose veins.

## Asthma

From the medical point of view, asthma, like every other chronic disease, is an incurable condition. The medical profession spends all its time, energy and talent in looking for the causes of man's diseases in external agents whereas an unbiased scientific investigation would readily reveal that every disease can be traced to wrong eating habits, lack of emotional poise, addiction to unhygienic practices or some such factor having a close bearing upon man's living habits. If asthma cannot be cured medically or by other so-called healing systems — which are, in fact, nothing by 'symptom-cure-opathies' — it is because they have not, even on their own admission, ascertained the actual cause of the disease.

Asthma is due to loss of tone of the respiratory system (the lungs and the bronchial tubes) which, in turn, is the result of (i) imperfect elimination, (ii) a general state of enervation, (iii) improper eating habits, (iv) suppression of acute diseases by drugs, etc. (v) wrong posture while sitting, standing or sleeping and (vi) emotional upsets.

If the causes are understood, the cure becomes easy; for *the cure lies in removing the causes*. The sufferer should take to diet reform and observe Vital Economy. Occasional fasts of a short duration (of two to three days' each time) may be observed with great advantage. A non-violent enema may be taken daily at least for four or five weeks in the initial stages of the treatment. Regular sun baths may be taken at a convenient time in the mornings or late in the evenings. The spinal bath may be taken once or twice a day; this will tone up the nervous system and help in restoring health quickly. Herbal juices can be taken separately (in very small quantities) once or twice a day or they may be taken mixed with wheat flour for preparing composite rotis.

If this programme is followed in the sub-acute phase of the disease, it will help in restoring normalcy quickly. The sufferer should, however, conduct himself cautiously during the acute attacks, that may occur in the meantime. While, in a great many cases, the attacks cease completely after the commencement of the programme, it may happen in very severe cases that they continue, of course with less severity and for short periods of time, even after the commencement of the Nature Cure treatment.

If and when an acute attack occurs, the following measures will be of great help in lessening its severity. (A word of caution, however, is necessary here. None of the water cure methods to be outlined below is to be applied if the sufferer has any of the severer types of asthma, such as renal asthma, cardiac asthma or emphysematous asthma. In these cases, all other hygienic measures, e.g., approach to fast or complete fasting, mild sun bathing, non-violent enema, spinal baths, etc., may be applied.)

Hot chest and shoulder packs will give quick and satisfactory relief. These may be given continuously for half an hour or more, twice or thrice a day. Relief can also be afforded by giving hot foot baths.

Bernarr MacFadden recommended hot hand baths on such occasions. The hands and forearms up to the elbows are immersed in hot water. This might be done three or four times a day, for ten minutes each time. According to MacFadden, the hand bath has a reflex influence upon the respiratory function.

Hot immersion baths along with a cold head pack have been found to be of great benefit in the majority of cases. A full bath in cold water, or at least a head bath after the hot immersion baths, is necessary. This may be done once daily if the attack happens to be very severe. But, if the attacks are not severe, or few and far between, let the hot immersion bath be dispensed with.

Hot and cold fomentation of the upper part of the back along with a hot foot bath and placing of a wet cloth over the head will give instant relief in an acute attack.

Any of the above methods, as found suitable, may be adopted. As soon as relief is obtained, cold trunk packs (stimulating, if need be) should be given. After an acute attack, the patient is likely to feel prostrated for some time (usually for one to three days). During this period, the patient should live on an approach to fasting, taking only diluted herbal or fruit juices, tender coconut water or vegetable soup, in moderate doses, thrice or four times a day. If any solid diet (or so-called nourishing food) is taken during this period, the weakness will be aggravated, not lessened, and there is a possibility of recurrence of acute attacks.

Asthma could be redically cured by following the hygienic plan, outlined above.

# Bronchitis

The term 'bronchitis' means inflammation of the bronchi and bronchial tubes. It indicates a catarrhal condition of the mucous membranes lining the bronchi and bronchial tubes. It may be acute, i.e., without any previous history of the disease, or chronic. In the so-called 'acute' phase, it may be accompanied by cold and fever. It is, in this stage, nothing but an extension of the acute catarrhal condition down to the trachea and bronchial tubes. There may be frequent coughing resulting in soreness of the throat and perhaps of the trachea as well. Accumulation of mucus in these regions causes a wheezing or humming sound during inspiration. The other symptoms that may be present during the acute stage are headache, nausea, dizziness, etc.

Atmospheric pollution is an environmental factor in the causation of bronchitis. The pollution is an environmental factor in the causation of bronchitis. The pollution may be caused by domestic coal fire or smoke emitted by factory chimneys. Some of the air pollutants are highly irritant. Sulphur dioxide is one of them. This appears in the air of most urban communities. It is present in appreciable quantities in the air of communities in which coal, especially of lower grades, and fuel oils are the principal sources of heat and power.

There may be other pollutants, e.g., beryllium and its compounds, manganese compounds, carbon monoxide, radioactive isotopes, carcinogens and insecticides.

In industrial areas (even in the so-called smokeless zones), drop lets of mild sulphuric acid may condense and fall when there is "inversion" in the atmosphere. In such areas, people are compelled to breathe this acid air. Using an electron microscope, it is possible to demonstrate these acid praticles in the finest parts of the lungs.

If the bronchitis patient lives in a polluted atmosphere, the chances of his complete recovery are much less. Even if by diet reform and certain other methods he improves his health level to some extent, the chances of his suffering repeated bronchial attacks will be there as long as the atmospheric pollution persists.

If the patient happens to be a smoker or lives with smokers around him, it is very likely that this sole factor has caused the con dition. If he is a smoker, he should give up smoking. If he lives with smokers, he should move away to another place free from tobacco smoke.

Acute bronchitis would clear away by itself in a few days' time. The treatment may begin with a short fast of two or three days. Non-violent enemas may be taken once daily during this stage. A spinal bath could be had twice or thrice daily. A hot foot bath, preferably before going to bed, would be very much useful. The place where the patient rests should be well ventilated and clean. It would be wrong to shut out fresh air.

The short initial fast, with the programme outlined above, would bring about sufficient relief. Thereafter, the patient should either live on an approach to fast, on tender coconut water, diluted fruit juices and or herbal juices, vegetable soups, etc., or on a raw and conservatively cooked vegetable and fresh fruit diet, as the condition may demand. The spinal bath, the non-violent enema, the hot foot bath, sun bath, etc., may be continued as before.

By following the programme outlined above, the patient of acute bronchitis, should be all right well within two weeks' time. Thereafter, he would do well to follow the principles of Natural Hygiene, so that he could stay cured. Taking some herbal juice in the morning and later ashpumpkin and banana pith juice will help in staying cured.

The condition known as chronic bronchitis requires more or less the same treatment but spread over a slightly longer period. Alternate hot and cold compresses over the chest region would be very useful in helping clearance of the congestion in chronic bronchitis.

## Diabetes

We, the Natural Hygienists, are against any and every type of symptomatic treatment. We consider all of them as opposed to the Laws of Nature. In our view, the "complications" suffered by diabetics, e.g., diabetic cataract, diabetic retinopathy, diabetic neuropathy, various types of renal disease, cardiac neuropathy, etc., and "diabetic emergencies", e.g. hypoglycaemic coma, severe hyperglycaemic ketoacidosis, etc., are solely due to continued medical treatment which has nothing solid to offer to build up the health of the individual the rational way. Hence, we cannot advocate the use of any conventional drugs or remedies.

How, then, could diabetes be treated? Before we deal with this question, we would like to categorically say that diabetes could, and should be, prevented. Diabetes is an advanced chronic disease. A person can develop a chronic disease (including diabetes) *only* if he has failed to cure an acute disease naturally and sought to suppress it through the so-called drug therapies.

*So, let our readers clearly note that diabetes can be prevented.* If, however, anyone has already developed it, let him, before it is too late, give up all types of symptomatic treatment and take to Natural Hygiene.

As the patient's glycogenic function of the liver has been almost upset and as the ability of the pancreatic cells to secrete insulin is at a very low ebb, the diet recommended for diabetics is one which should be very light from the viewpoint of digestion, though rich in its positive, health-giving value. In a diabetic condition without any other serious complications, a diet of raw and conservatively cooked vegetables taken moderately twice a day would greatly help to relax and tone up the digestive organs. Naturally ripened (seasonal) fruits, including sweet ones, may be taken, again in moderate quantities. It would be advisable to take a herbal drink early in the mornings. As, in many cases, vegetables and fruits are grown with chemical manures, the author would suggest that at least the herbal drink should be of Sattvic herbs grown naturally with natural manure. The raw juice of the herb aegle marmelos correa (bel or bilva leaf) is found to act more effectively in diabetic cases.

For very weak patients with diabetic complaints for quite a length of time, with or without "complications", it would be wise to begin the treatment with an approach to fast for a week or ten days. During this period, herbal drinks, vegetable soups, diluted fruit juice, tender coconut water or juice of ashgourd may be taken. Only one of them should be taken at a time, in very moderate doses. Such a liquid diet may be taken three or four times a day. After this period, the diet suggested in the previous paragraph may be taken. Occasionally, however, it would be desirable to revert to the approach to fasting for a few days.

In the earlier stages of Nature Cure treatment, all proteins and fatty foods will have to be thoroughly eschewed till there is a definite improvement in the general bodily condition. It would not do if only starchy foods are avoided. In many cases, various complications follow the diabetic condition only because of indulgence in protein and fatty foods under the mistaken notion that the calories (which the body is deprived of due to lack of starchy foods and sugar) have to be "made up" somehow. Enough has been said about the hollowness of the calorie theory earlier.

In addition to diet reform, the patient could take the non-violent enema (even daily, if need be). The spinal bath, Pranayama, sun-bath, etc., can also be taken daily. The patient should be happy that he is building up his health the safe and sensible way. He should not give in to any kind of tension.

## Hypertension (High Blood Pressure)

High blood pressure in a condition which is largely due to the stress and strain of modern living; characterized by undue nervous tension and ingestion of unhygienic foods. So long as the underlying causes of this condition are not removed, there can be no radical cure.

Hygienic living is the answer. The sufferer needs to undertake a fast for a short period (of two or three days), which may be followed up by highly positive dieting for a few weeks--a diet of vegetables (raw and conservatively cooked) and fruits, not more than twice daily, in strict moderation. Avoidance of salt, spices and condiments has a positive and relieving effect in restoring normalcy.

Occasionally fasting for a day or two, at intervals during this period, could be undertaken. The observance of Vital Economy is very essential as this alone would provide the needed biological rest for the various organs and promote elimination of the toxic matter from within the body. Spinal baths, twice or even thrice a day, would be found useful, in as much as the nerves would be toned up. Non-violent Pranayama may be practised every morning for a few minutes. Sun baths would activate the skin. The non-violent enema may be taken, so long as it is found necessary.

With the change-over to hygienic habits, the symptoms that go along with the condition termed 'high blood pressure' would disappear and, once again, a healthy blood stream would surge forth along clean channels doing its allotted task. With the 'inner rhythm' restored, and knowing the way to keep up the 'rhythm', the erstwhile patient can continue to live healthfully, by becoming an adherent of Natural Hygiene.

## Gastric and Duodenal Ulcers

An ulcer in the stomach is termed gastric ulcer; if it is in the duodenum (the bit of intestine immediately after the stomach), it is called duodenal ulcer. Ulcers are caused by malfunctioning of the nervous and hormonal mechanisms regulating the secretory and motor functions of the gastro-enteric system, which, in turn, upsets the normal balance between the activity of the acidic factor and the protective abilities of the mucous membranes of the stomach and the duodenum.

So long as the digestive organs are in tone, there cannot be any ulcerations in the stomach or the duodenum. Only those who persistently commit serious dietetic errors and/or enervate themselves in various ways, including emotional strain, can lose the tone of the stomach and duodenal lining to such an extent that it is possible for the hydrochloric acid to act upon the stomach or the duodenal walls resulting in the formation of ulcers.

It is not only the strongly acidic gastric juice that can act on the atonic stomach (or duodenum) walls thus; the acids which form in the stomach as a result of persistent indigestion also exert a very similar influence on them in such circumstances.

A radical cure is possible only when Natural Hygiene is adopted by the patient in *toto.*

The real difficulty in dealing with a peptic ulcer patient is that while he cannot cure himself without giving the digestive system the needed physiological rest through fasting, he finds it well nigh impossible — especially during the acute phase — to do so, as it would cause the affected surfaces to be irritated by the acidic gastric juice. The solution does not, however, lie, as the medicos think, in compelling the patient to eat small and frequent meals and suck antacid tablets continuously.

If extreme caution is exercised during this phase, the disease will not turn out to be 'treacherous'; no haemorrhage or peritonitis will occur.

The first object should be to help the patient in overcoming the extreme pain in the stomach (or the duodenum), the gnawing discomforts with the accompanying depression and misery. This can be achieved by adopting the following dietetic programme:

177

| 7 to 7.30 a.m. | – Either tender coconut water or juice of ashgourd (mixed with a small quantity of juice of solanum nigrum). No seasoning. |
| 10.30 or 11 a.m. | – Fresh (raw) juice of ashgourd, snakegourd, carrot, carrot leaves or raw cabbage leaves (juice of the outer green leaves preferred). No seasoning. |
| 4 to 4.30 p.m. | – Four ounces of raw juice, as in the morning, or soup prepared from ripe bananas (without the pulp) or tender coconut water. No seasoning. |
| 8 or 8.30 a.m. | – Vegetable soup made from green vegetables (only the soup must be taken and not the vegetables) without salt, condiments or spices. |

Adoption of the above dietetic programme would give the least trouble to the stomach and the duodenum, so that healing would go on unimpeded, quickly. The juice or soups, suggested are highly alkaline and would relieve the burning sensation within. Unlike the artificial antacids, which would tax the liver and kidneys, these highly alkaline juices and soups would benefit the system.

The programme should be continued, until perceptible relief is felt. It should be possible to have quite a lot of relief through this programme within a week or ten days.

Along with the dietetic regimen outlined above, the non-violent enema may be taken once daily. Spinal baths may be taken daily.

A sun bath followed by a spinal bath would be very useful in toning up the nervous system. Either a simple wet pack (or a stimulating wet pack) over the abdomen may be had twice or thrice daily. daily.

When the excruciating pain in the gastric or duodenal region has been overcome to a great extent, the patient can proceed confidently to the second phase of the treatment. The diet, during this phase, might consist of a moderate quantity of conservatively cooked vegetables with grated coconut, twice daily. Early in the morning and again in the afternoon, raw vegetable juices could be had. The non-violent enema, baths, etc., are to be continued as during the first phase. The patient should, of course, scrupulously avoid too hot and too cold foods. White sugar and confectionery are taboo. The programme may last two to four weeks.

By the end of the sixth or seventh week, the patient would have sufficiently improved; ulcers would have healed by this time. Henceforward, the patient could, by following the principles of Natural Hygiene, keep himself healthy. He may fast occasionally for short periods, so that he can maintain his health at a high level.

## Amoebiasis

Amoebiasis is a term which covers a wide range of diseases of the gastro-intestinal tract, with dysentery as its commonest manifestation. The symptoms may vary from a mild 'stomach upset' to a fatal rupture of an 'amoebic' liver abscess. A person having any of the following symptoms may be 'diagnosed' as suffering from amoebiasis.

i)   Recurrent episodes of diarrhoea, bowels opening approximately 6 to 12 times daily. (The stools may be blood-stained and may also have mucus along with them. There may be little or no abdominal discomfort. In certain cases, there could also be fever.)

ii)  Occasional loose motions, along with widespread lethargy, depression, joint pains, dehydration, lack of initiative, weakness, "gas trouble," tiredness, nausea, an earthy appearance of skin, tenesmus (a frequent urge to defaecate), an exaggerated gastro-colic reflux (an urge for bowel movement soon after taking food).

iii) Rectal bleeding.

iv)  Repeated belching and abdominal symptoms of discomfort, bloatedness, etc.

v)   A slight dietary indiscretion followed by diarrhoea.

vi)  Peptic ulcer or a non-ulcer type of dyspepsia with a feeling of heaviness after intake of meals.

vii) Chronic constipation or diarrhoea with or without blood or mucus.

viii)Liver enlargement and tenderness (pain over the liver region occasionally referred to the shoulder too), without fever, rigors and malaise, nausea and anorexia.

ix)  Rupturing of the liver abscess into the chest giving rise to pulmonary infarction or pericarditis.

x) Ulceration of the colon with the liability to haemorrhage or perforation.

xi) Development of a chronic inflammatory mass in the colon (known as amoeboma).

xii) Development of a toxic megacolon (amoebic colitis), with the liability to haemorrhage or perforation.

Of the symptoms indicated above, those which appear to be very complicated are, in reality, the result of suppressing the minor ones through repeated drug treatment.

Instead of attributing a simple case of dysentery or diarrhoea to wrong habits of living, medical men look for the *cause* in a germ, parasite or protozoon. A case is diagnosed as one of amoebic dysentery if the patient has, in his gut, the protozoon *entamoeba histolytica*. Having found the amoeba there they hold it to be the villain of the piece, capable of causing untold harm to mankind.

Instead of looking for a scapegoat in the protozoon *entamoeba histolytica,* let the sufferer understand that the minor symptoms he has — in the earlier stages, the symptoms are but minor ones — are all due to his committing the twin errors in dieting, viz, (i) wrong choice of foods and (ii) wrong modes of eating. Let him not take to any amoebicides and broad-spectrum antibiotics and worsen his condition. Let him try to understand what kinds of mistakes he commits in eating and let him reform himself.

More or less the same treatment as suggested earlier for dyspepsia can be followed by the patient.

## Haematuria

Haematuria (discharge of blood in the urine) may be a painful or painless condition. An occasional discharge of blood in the urine can be dismissed as harmless. If in an otherwise healthy individual, it occurs after an exceptionally strenuous manual job or exercise, he must undertake a fast for two or three days (on tender coconut water or raw vegetable juices), take complete rest and have a spinal bath or the cooling (or stimulating) abdominal wet pack twice or thrice in the day. In two or three days, he would become normal.

False haematuria is a condition wherein the 'redness' of the urine is not due to the discharge of blood in it but due to food (or drugs) containing pigment. The excretion of the pigments present in beet-root, senna, as also in some dyes used in confectionery, etc., may make the blood 'red'. Some 'proprietary' purgatives contain substances which turn red in alkaline urine. If anyone has taken any of such things and 'redness' appears in the urine let not the condition be mistaken for haematuria.

Haematuria is an unique early warning system for urinary tract disease affecting the kidneys, ureters, the urinary bladder and the urethra. Any one or more of these parts may be diseased or inflamed. Or, there may be-one or more stones in the kidney(s) or the urinary bladder. Or, there could be a tumour in the kidney, bladder or the prostate gland. The kidney or the bladder might be tubercular or cancerous.

Haematuria also occurs in certain types of fevers like malaria, in purpura, scurvy, syphilis, leukaemia, haemophilia, etc. It may also be induced by drugs such as salicylates or anticoagulants.

As the causes of haematuria vary, it would be necessary to study the case history of each patient carefully. A study of the duration, frequency and severity of the complaint, as also any other symptom (like pain in the loin region or the supra pubic region) should give a clue as to where the trouble has originated. It should be obvious that in certain cases of haematuria, having no background of degeneracy, the condition could be radically cured fairly quickly, whereas in other cases with a destructive disease in the background (e.g.. tumour, cancer, tuberculosis, etc.) it may, depending on circumstances, not be easily curable, for there might be little vital power left in the body and its structural integrity might have broken down.

## Urinary Disorders

The programme suggested earlier for dyspepsia may be followed by patients of urinary disorders with great benefit.

## Heart Diseases

The heart falters and fails in numerous cases in the modern world not because of old age, but because of the fact that their "owners" had subjected them to continual strain and stress physically and emotionally. The constant drugging that they might have indulged in to "treat this disease or that" would have weakened the organism to such an extent that ultimately the heart too got attected.

The increased incidence of heart disease in modern days is due to:

a) The strain and stress of modern life;

b) The continual intake of devitaminised and demineralis foods;

c) The intake of too much fats, especially saturated fats;

d) The consumption of drugs and of the so-called stimulants, cc fee, tea, cocoa, etc., as a regular routine;

e) Worry and similar negative emotions; and

f) Use of tobacco in any form.

Once the causative factors of heart diseases are understood, any sensible individual would be able to maintain his heart health.

## Angina

In the condition termed angina pectoris (angina, in short), a sudden intense pain is experienced off and on in the chest region, accompanied by feelings of suffocation. If the patient takes rest for a little while, he would feel better. But if the same lifestyle is continued, angina may be experienced again and again. Let no drug treatment be taken for this condition, for if this is done, the patient will become a confirmed heart patient; the disease will progress.

Let the cause of angina be understood clearly. Due to wrong, unhygienic, habits of living, a condition known as arteriosclerosis (hardening of the arteries) might develop. When some of the coronary arteries (the arteries which supply pure blood to the heart muscles) get hardened, or clogged, blood supply to the muscles of the heart is affected. In this condition known as coronary sclerosis, pain or discomfort is felt in the region of the heart. The pain may be mild in most cases and this is what is called angina. In certain cases, there may also be a slight inflammation of the heart muscles.

Let not anyone be misled by the medical nomenclature of different symptoms affecting the heart. Many of these names instil fear in the people, mainly because of the so-called incurability and supposed fatal nature of the disease. The following measures will be helpful to the readers in understanding how by adopting simple Natural Hygienic methods, health can be restored not only in cases of angina but in other cardiac ailments too.

Positive diet, with occasional approaches to fasting, the sun bath, the spinal bath, the non-violent Pranayama and the non-violent enema — these would be the chief features of a daily programme to be followed by the patient for a period of four to six weeks, or sometimes more. Stimulants and sedatives will have to be completely given up. This would restore the tone of the digestive system, the heart and the lungs. The "de-silted" arteries would now joyfully discharge the vital duty that Nature has cast upon them. The arteriosclerosis, the coronary sclerosis and angina pectoris would have become a thing of the past and would not recur, if the hygienic sins, which previously caused them, are not repeated.

If, however, angina is neglected or medically treated, the patient's bloodstream becomes more and more toxin-laden, leading to clot formation (thrombosis) in some coronary artery. This condition is termed *coronary thrombosis*.

When such a clot in formed is one of the main coronary arteries, the situation is bad indeed. The circulatory network from that point onwards must go without its blood supply and the cells and tissues in the affected area die *(infarction* and *anaemic necrosis)*. Despair not, even in such cases. Nature does repair the situation. Immediately after the coronary attack, Life starts a tremendous activity to bypass the block and re-route the blood so that the affected area may once again get the much-needed oxygen and nutrition through the medium of the blood. The new supply is created by the growth of small branches from the surrounding arteries into the starved areas. Unless this area is large, the process of building a detour around the block is surprisingly efficient, and the area heals.

The Great Architect, Life, sometimes forms a series of tunnels through the very clot itself to keep the blood flowing.

While a crisis is thus overcome and fatality avoided by the extraordinary job that Life Power does immediately following a heart attack, the patient could carry on only as an invalid or a semi-invalid, at least for some time. The further process of healing that takes place is, has to be, slow. In fact, this healing process could be considerably hampered if the patient were to take to drugging and conventional modes of dieting.

To heal is Nature's job. The process of healing will take place at a fairly quick pace if the work of the heart is reduced to·a very low level by keeping the body and the mind at rest as completely as possible.

To prevent the possibility of formation of further clots in the coronary arteries, the atherosclerotic condition has to be radically cured by following Natural Hygiene.

The patient having an acute attack of coronary thrombosis needs absolute rest, physical and mental. If the injury to the heart is great, that is, if a large portion of the heart muscle is deprived of blood supply, the attack proves fatal. But, as explained earlier, in quite a good number of cases, Life takes immediate steps to restore the blood supply at least partially, and if the patient survives the first hour or so of the acute attack, recovery is possible. The room where the patient rests is not to be crowded and there should be ample ventilation. The patient is not to be moved from one place to another. In fact, for the first few days, no movement is desirable. Fasting is recommended for a period of three or four days, or even some more. During this period, very small quantities of ashgourd juice, tender coconut water, fruit juice or banana stem juice may be given twice or thrice a day.

After the first week, certain water cure applications may be applied. As the patient is in need of absolute rest even at this stage and as there should be the least possible movement on his part, the attendant should be careful in giving water cure treatment. Cooling (or stimulating) abdominal wet packs may be given; if not inconvenient, the non-violent enema may be administered.

When a marked improvement is observed — and this can be seen well within one week if the above instructions are followed--the patient is to be given at least for a period of two or three weeks thereafter, a diet of only raw and conservatively cooked vegetables and fruits. A spinal bath or two, the sun bath and non-violent enema could form part of the daily programme. If tender coconut water is available locally, it can be taken twice or thrice daily. Now the actual "de-silting" process is on and hence at this stage or a little thereafter, the healing crisis may appear. If the healing crisis comes about, well and good, that is a sure indication of progress towards health. A short fast of two or three days during the healing crisis should improve the health considerably.

After the fourth week, the patient may be permitted to include a small quantity of cereals (unrefined) in the daily diet, which should still be predominantly positive. It would be wise to eschew foods "rich" in protein and fat altogether, for quite some time more. (In fact, it may not even be advisable to take such "rich" foods even after full recovery).

At this stage, the patient may be able to go out for short walks. Walking barefoot on grassy lawns or on an uneven surface like an unploughed field (clean and free from thorns, etc.) would be advisable. Pranayama should be done according to capacity for a few minutes daily. Enema may be taken non-violently, as and when needed.

The programme outlined above is intended to achieve a high level of health and if followed long enough non-violently, with due regard to the principles of Vital Economy and positive dieting, a radical cure could be had in three to six months' time in most cases. In no case is there any likelihood of recurrence of coronary thrombosis.

At this stage, it is necessary to explain some other heart diseases, e.g., pericarditis, myocarditis, endocarditis, etc.

The heart is surrounded by a serous membrane called the pericardium. There are two layers of it. The layer adhering to the heart is known as the visceral pericardium; the other, which surrounds the heart like a loose sac, is called the parietal pericardium. Serous fluid occupies the place between the two layers. It protects the heart from friction and at the same time renders its work much easier.

The inner lining of the heart is called the endocardium. The valves are simply thickened portions of this membrane. The middle muscular layer is composed of a network of muscular fibres. This is known as myocardium.

The inflammation of the pericardium is known as pericarditis. As usual, medicos attribute this and the associated condition (known as rheumatic heart or rheumatic pericarditis) to a "complication of infections such as rheumatic fever". In the later section on Rheumatic Fever, we have explained in detail how this view is wrong. It is the suppression of rheumatic fever that leads to the development of rheumatic heart disease, as pointed out therein.

The inflammation of the endocardium, specially of the portion covering the valves, is known as endocarditis. This also called valvular heart disease. The common symptoms are shortness of breath, fever, weak and irregular and rapid heart-beats, cardiac pain, headache and dizziness. In certain cases, the toes and fingers, especially the portions beneath the nails, turn rather bluish.

Inflammation of the myocardium is termed myocarditis. This is often accompanied by hypertrophy and dilatation of the heart (due fundamentally to the strain of greatly increased work and degeneration of the heart which, in turn, is occasioned by insufficient coronary circulation). There may be a dull pain over the affected region.

The condition known as cardiac enlargement (hypertrophy of the heart) is always the result of the severe strain the heart is subjected to over a long period of time.

A highly toxic condition of the system, which is often the result of persistent dietetic errors, including violation of Vital Economy, may lead to any chronic disorder such as arteriosclerosis, hypertension or severe anaemia. In such cases, the heart has to cope with an extra load of work. Dilatation of the heart often follows the hypertrophic condition.

None of the conditions known as pericarditis, endocarditis, myocarditis, rheumatic heart disease, valvular heart disease or hypertrophy with dilatation of heart can be diagnosed by medicos until the symptoms denoting the particular condition have developed to an extent where they can be clinically found out. Diagnosing in such a state is nothing but naming the symptom-complex. It will not shed any light on the causative factors of the disease.

None of these conditions appear as a bolt from the blue. By hygienic living, it would be possible to prevent an onset of these painful conditions It is not only the lack of proper nutrition but also the strain to which the heart is subjected for long periods that results in the so-called breakdown.

Long before the onset of such painful conditions, the so-called breakdown, the patient goes through a number of acute diseases, which are, in reality, the efforts of Life to eliminate the toxaemia. If these efforts are not suppressed, there is no reason why one should develop a heart disease.

The question may be asked how Nature Cure could help patients who have already developed any of the diseases named above. Where there is any kind of inflammation (as in pericarditis, endocarditis, myocarditis, valvular heart disease etc.), the first step should be to reduce the strain on the heart, to the greatest extent possible. This can be done by internal and external rest.

The heart strain may, in quite a number of cases, be due to psychological causes. The patient may be lacking a basic philosophy of life and consequently, may feel upset over every little event that happens in daily life. These upsets may strain the heart to a great extent. If this is so a particular case, the patient should be educated properly by a person with a spiritual background. This itself may ease the strain to a very considerable extent and pave the way for a radical cure of the disease, over a shorter period of time.

Having had repeated disappointments in the past, the heart patient might consider his condition as utterly hopeless and incurable, condemned to die' soon. He might have developed utter frustration and the 'will to die'. It is, therefore, necessary that the basic philosophy of Natural Hygiene should be explained to the patient (so far as conditions would permit) and the patient should be enabled to develop an optimistic attitude and the 'will to live'.

The room where the patient rests should not be a crowded one; there should be ample ventilation. The only way of giving the needed biological rest is by fasting; hence, fasting is recommended during the so-called critical stage. During this period, very small quantities of coconut water, fruit juice or herbal juice may, with advantage, be given twice or thrice a day. Cold water (or, if preferred, tepid water) in achamana doses may be given once every two or three hours. Enema may be given non-violently, once daily. A cooling wet bandage or stimulating wet bandage may be applied over the affected region, twice or thrice every day, for about 45 minutes each time. The former is found useful in cases where the heart action is very fast and the latter when the heart action is very slow.

No synthetic foods ought to be given. The author would specially warn against the use of synthetic glucose. Commercial glucose is poison. Please keep it away from the patient, if you want him to recover.

When a marked improvement in the condition of the patient is observed — and this can be seen soon enough if the above instructions have been sincerely followed — he may be given a diet of raw salads or conservatively cooked vegetables and fruits, in very moderate rations, twice a day. A mild sun bath followed by a spinal bath may be given daily. The non-violent enema may be taken, as needed. As and when healing crises are experienced, generally for two or three days at a time, the patient should undertake short fasts. Water cure and other methods may be followed.

## Rheumatic Fever

As pointed out in the introductory remarks in the chapter on Acute Disease civilisation and the medical profession have so corrupted the sources of life today that most children are born with a great inheritance of disease, with weakness and organic defects of vital and other organs, which makes purely acute diseases exceedingly rare. It was pointed out therein that most acute diseases of today have a background of chronic ill health, which greatly complicates the problem of health recovery. Rheumatic fever is one of them.

Rheumatic fever is said to be common among children. People are told through brief press notes off and on that if this fever is not medically diagnosed in time and treated, the patients are likely to develop rheumatic heart disease (RHD) later.

In rheumatic fever, fever is no doubt a symptom; apart from this, painful swelling is observed in the joints all over the body. There may be rashes on the trunk and the limbs and even nodules near the joints. As the fever persists, in quite some cases, delirium, convulsions and coma may also be experienced by the patient.

Rheumatic fever is also called acute articular rheumatism. Another name therefore is inflammatory rheumatism.

Before developing rheumatic fever, the patient should have had serious indigestion and constipation and, perhaps, even tonsillitis. If, in these conditions, symptomatic treatments were resorted to, he would have developed rheumatic fever later. If, however, the earlier purely acute conditions were attended to naturally, or prevented sensibly by hygienic care, the onset of rheumatic fever could have been avoided.

As observed in the section on Feverishness in the last chapter, before the onset of any type of fever, the patient feels feverish for two or three days. This period of 'feverishness' should *not* be neglected. The patient should follow the instructions given under that section to clear the body of as much of foreign matter as possible; if this is done, either the onset of the fever itself is prevented or even if fever develops, the symptoms thereof would be mild. With further hygienic treatment (as given in the last chapter), this mild fever could be radically cured. If, however, the rheumatic fever condition is neglected or medically suppressed, the pericardium of the heart might be affected, the muscle might become inflamed and the condition known as rheumatic heart or rheumatic pericarditis might develop. Even the heart valves may become crippled because of inflammation of the endocardium.

Dr J.H. Tilden, M.D., says in his *Criticisms of the Practice of Medicine:* "The most formidable complication in rheumatic fever is the heart involvement, but I am not disposed to believe that the fever has much to do with the heart complications as the prevailing treatment. Years ago, when I gave drugs with the superstitious idea of curing this disease, I succeeded in establishing a heart involvement in every case. Since I gave up the use of drugs I have seen but little rheumatic heart disease of a serious character, except when consulted by those who have been medicated and 'properly' nursed (that is, overfed)."

Dr Maclyn McCarthy, M.D., Chairman, Council on Rheumatic Fever and Congenital Heart Disease, American Heart Association, admits that when it comes to the question of diagnosing a patient having rheumatic fever, the physician "is on a perilously shaky ground". He says there are no well-understood diagnostic tests for rheumatic fever. He adds that not a single symptom is specific for this disease alone.

Rheumatic fever, diagnosis of which is "most difficult" even according to medical experts, is supposed to be caused by different kinds of haemolytic streptococci. When this so-called "strep" infection takes place, rheumatic fever follows. As there are different kinds of "streps", there may be different infections at different times and rheumatic fever may repeat itself. While the first attack may be mild, successive attacks may cause substantial damage to the heart. These are ideas of the allopathic school, the school of despair which holds that everyone must suffer.

Does this school, which asserts that rheumatic fever is the result of haemloytic streptococcal infection, know the exact relationship between rheumatic fever and the preceding haemolytic streptococcal infection? Does this school know how rheumatic fever can be prevented?

The answer to these questions is in the negative.

Without knowing anything about the real causative factors and under the supposition that streptococcal infections lead to rheumatic fever, the allopathic school prescribes sulpha drugs, penicillin, ACTH, cortisone, etc., "for their great value in controlling the symptoms of the disease".

If some or all of these poisons are used in dealing with rheumatic fever, the heart structure may be extensively altered or damaged. The scars that may be caused in the heart muscles by the use of these drugs will make the heart lose some of its pumping force. If the valves become scarred, they may fail in their function and heart-health will suffer considerably.

Rheumatic fever could be prevented by hygienic living. Even if a person suffers from it, normalcy could be restored by Natural Hygiene; the instructions given in the previous chapter on treatment of fevers should be borne in mind by the patient.

## Rheumatism

Rheumatism is a disease marked by inflammation of the connective tissue structure of the body, especially the muscles and joints and by pain in those parts. There are several 'types' of rheumatism, some of which are even termed arthritis.

Whether it is termed osteo-arthritis, fibrositis or rheumatoid arthritis the patient should give up all types of drugs and take to hygienic living, in its most comprehensive sense.

The line of treatment suggested for dyspepsia, if followed, will help the patient in radically curing himself of rheumatism (or other diseases of joints).

## Hints on Treating Chronic Disease

The intelligent reader will have seen from what has been said in the chapter that, in spite of the difference in name and symptoms — which are only apparent — all these kinds of ill health are really only the outgrowths of a background of dyspepsia and are curable by removing that background.

The patient must proceed as if his particular symptoms did not exist and without attaching any value to the allopathic label given to his 'disease'. If, in spite of the above dictum, we have at places given the 'different' names (and sub-groups) of 'different diseases' in the preceding and succeeding pages, it is only to remove the fear from the readers' minds. Once the meaning of the 'technical jargon' is understood and once the patient understands that he has only to rebuild health, brick by brick, the fear will be off the mind.

Most patients wish, to get into a sanatorium for treatment for at least a month or two, because of serious handicaps in their own places, due to the hostility of relations and friends who are firm believers in allopathy and are convinced that one must be a lunatic to take to Nature Cure even after becoming a medical failure. As a rule men running sanatoriums are not themselves well versed in the Art of Non-violence in healing. Most of them believe that one particular author is the sole authority on the subject, and that those who do not accept him are unworthy of consideration. The so-called authority may be unaware that there is a principle called Non-violence, which is of fundamental importance in practice. The reader knows that this is the principle of sanity in our hygienic practice and that it can be set at naught in great many ways, as shown before. Non-violence requires recognition of the right of the patient to have a say in what treatment is to be given to him. If one calling himself a Nature Cureist treats his patients little better than cattle, he is, in our opinon, not a Nature Cureist at all. The patient, if treated with due respect as one capable of judging for himself what would suit him, at least after necessary explanations are given to him, can correct the dogmatism of the 'doctor'. In Sarma's Nature Cure sanatorium at Ganeshnagar, Pundukkottai, the patients where possible, are asked to read *Practical Nature Cure*. Their doubts and difficulties are cleared so that they become co-partners in framing the programmes for their cure. Another point is that it would be violence to prescribe a routine treatment for all patients, without regard to their idiosyncrasies, peculiarities or personal likes and dislikes. Father Kneipp, a very sane healer in his day, told us to 'individualise in treatment', a maxim that seems to have almost died with him for in practically all Nature Cure sanatoriums as a rule this is not done. Prescribing baths or fasts or anything else according to a routine without regard to the patient's personal needs and limitations would result in Violence to some of them at least. These

191

measures have to be adjusted in each case to suit the patient, and often it would be needful to consult him and make a decision with his assistance.

There are likely to occur *ups and downs* in the apparent health of the patient. These should not be taken at their face value for what appears to be a 'down' is not really a down, but a concomitant of a spell of vigorous curative elimination. The truth is that this elimination does not proceed at a uniform rate of speed all the time, like the movement of the hands of a clock. For some time it proceeds vigorously, when it slows down or is suspended for a period and thereafter the process is recommended; thus it goes on, somewhat irregularly, until there is a return of positive health, at which the patient will remain steady for a considerable time, if he follows a sufficiently healthful regime. During these suspensions the patient feels well and even thinks his cure is complete, which is not true, because when the elimination starts again he may feel ill. This on the surface  But underneath there is a steady healthward progress. That is to say, though the final cure will come long after, the patient will be making some improvement, of which he will become aware at intervals. With this he must be content, and persevere calmly and faithfully till the cure is complete. Being a 'patient' he must not be impatient. No one can make bargains with Nature, because She is Divine.

During the progress of the cure, the patient is not unlikely to have what have been called 'Curative Crises', which are acute illness; these are proof that the encumbrances have become less and vitality has increased, because without these favourable changes acute crises cannot arise at all. Therefore, he must not be frightened or discouraged by their coming, but must welcome them.

The next point the patient must take note of the observance of Brahmacharya or sexual self-denial. The rule of self-restraint is not the same for the chronic as for the patient of acute disease. The author does not seek to lay down a uniform rule for *all* chronics, because their vitality and mentality vary greatly. He rather makes the patient responsible for his actions and expects him to steer a line of safety between the two extremes of abstinence and excessive indulgence, as stated before in the chapter on continence. But during the acute phases — the curative crises — he must be *strictly* continent, as he would have to be in a fever or other acute illness.

The chronic must, from time to time, deal with the varying states of his mind so that it will not put spokes in the wheel of progress — so that it would faithfully and enthusiastically cooperate in carrying out the curative programme. He must remember that this Science is based on the truth of Biology as taught here. He should be concerned with his own part in the conduct of the methods of cure, leaving to God what belongs to Him alone. He must not be elated, or depressed by the changing conditions, the ups and down mentioned before. He must remember that on the whole what Nature does is for the best.

If the patient's constitution is not good enough for continuous practice of Nature Cure methods, then it is permissible for him to suspend the treatment at intervals and resume it after each suspension with renewed zeal. What sort of programme he will follow during the suspensions is also a question the author would gladly leave to the patient, with the hint that it would not be proper for him to go to the other extreme and indulge himself recklessly, so as to undo the good effects earned by him by the practice of Hygiene. Let him follow the Middle Path.

Let not the patient forget the main theme of this book, that all disease is one, that chronic disease, whatever its medical label and its symptoms, is one, and hence requires only the restoration of health by the cure of the basic disease, dyspepsia. He must read the *whole* book and understand this central teaching and act upon it. It is not proper to search for the place where one's particular disease is dealt with and copy the treatment described there, because the disease is not the same in every case and varies from patient to patient It is also not right to feel disappointed if one's particular disease is not specifically named and dealt with. That would be an allopathic approach to disease. The patient must make up his mind to be his own doctor, at least in part to begin with, and master the science as a whole, before considering how to cure himself.

A useful caution is about rest and relaxation. On this subject there prevails a great deal of ignorance. Really, there is no rest, but only economy of Vital Power, saving it from waste in certain ways, so that it may be available for the urgent work of cure by elimination. Such saving is effected by a fast, or an approach to fasting or such practice of Vital Economy as is suitable and necessary. Allopaths who prescribe 'absolute' rest make it negatory by imposing unwanted rations of heavy negative food. What one needs to observe is the golden mean — the middle path — which means avoiding excess of work or exercise. Rest in bed may be necessary in such cases; but even in bed, it is not necessary to remain motionless like a log of wood.

Methods of treatment which are unpleasant to the patient must not be employed. Only those he finds pleasant should be made use of.

In drawing up a programme to be followed for a radical cure, the patient has a reliable guide in the knowledge of the Fivefold Food, given in Chapter 6. Of these five, the first, namely Ether, is obtained by Vital Economy, which embraces Brahmacharya, fasting and restraint in eating. Earth in represented by positive food. The other three are plain enough.

Let the patient remember that he can retain his mental poise through prayer. Let him also remember that prayer is *not* a superficial mechanical gramophone-like repetition of a verse, a formula, a *mantra* or the like. Prayer is not supplication, nor is it a plea or request. *Prayer is communion — communion with the One, who is the All.* With humility and sincerity, let the patient pray daily, repeat His Names. Let him combine his prayer with prayerful living, which Natural Hygiene is. Thus lived, the whole of life will be one of prayer. Every action done by the person will be based upon his understanding of the Law of Cause and Effect and the Great Law underlying it.

# TWENTY-FOUR

# Destructive Disease

This belongs to the third and last stage of disease progression. As diseases retain the chronic character of those of the middle stage, they are called *Chronic Destructive Diseases*. They have as their background the further impairment of the patient's bodily and mental constitution. Undeniably, this is due to the medical treatment continued during the two preceding stages. There is *no* third stage for those patients who get themselves *radically cured* of the second stage by the rational methods of Natural Hygiene.

Referring to cancer, which is admittedly a destructive disease, Dr A.S. McNeill, in his book *Cancer* has observed that *the disease is chiefly due to the general poisoning of the living tissues by the use of vaccines and serums*.

In his lecture at John Hopkins Medical School, Sir William Arbuthnot Lane, M.D., England's most famous abdominal surgeon, observed:

> "Gentlemen, I shall never die of cancer, for I am taking measures to prevent it. It is caused by poisons created in our bodies by the food we eat. What we should do then if we wish to avoid cancer, is to eat whole-wheat bread, raw fruits and vegetables and their juices. First, that we may be better nourished and, secondly, that we more easily eliminate waste products. We have been studying disease when we should have been studying diet and drainage. The world has been on the wrong track. The answer has been within ourselves all the time. Drain the body of its poisons, feed it properly, and the miracle is done. No one need have cancer who will take the trouble to avoid it."

It would be utter folly to hope that such destructive diseases could be prevented or cured by allopathic means. Since violent drugging and improper feeding have brought about this 'progress' from the chronic to the destructive stage, further treatment on the same lines can only lead to the release of the patient from these doctors by death. It must be remembered also that medical prophylaxes — vaccinations and inoculations — also contribute to the passage from the first stage through the second, to this, the third and last stage.

In some cases what begins as a simple acute disease, such as a simple fever, changes under medical care into a destructive disease, as in the case of the author's friend, at the end of which a fatal dropsy arose, of which he died. In another case a boy who was treated for 'typhoid' fever finally became a consumptive and died; the tendency to this disease had come to him from his father whose death was due to it. The patient might have been saved if his "typhoid" had been treated rationally. These cases show up the true nature of allopathy as a builder up of incurable disease, not of health.

The endless search for less dangerous remedies, to replace those that have been found too dangerous for use on patients, itself shows that "medicine" is not medicine. All these drugs have uniformly failed, as stated before. Among them is streptomycin, an antibiotic guaranteed to be a harmless, but effective "cure" of tuberculosis. It has since been proved more deadly than the disease itself; the patient dies because he is unable to eliminate this deadly poison. So are radium and deep X-ray for cancer. The third stage of disease being the last, there is no further stage to which the patient can be carried; there is only death waiting for him, if he does not return to Nature. Cure can come only by reversing the direction of the progress of disease, as explained before, and allopathy does not even know of it.

The hygienic cure of destructive disease as explained in this chapter, should be of help to the reader in taking to Natural Hygiene for the prevention and cure of such disease.

## Tuberculosis

Consumption is a term applied to a condition where there is a continuous wasting away of the body; this is generally used to denote the disease known as *phthisis* or *pulmonary tuberculosis*. Any part of the body can be affected by tuberculosis and when the lungs are affected, the condition is termed pulmonary tuberculosis.

Medicos, as is their usual practice, consider it to be an "infectious" disease. According to them, the infection is caused by tubercle bacilli and they recommend immunisation against it with BCG vaccine.

The medical approach to TB has been categorically condemned by Dr. David C Muthu, probably the greatest expert in pulmonary tuberculosis among the allopaths. He had abundant experience in the sanatorium treatment of consumptives. Later, he became an ardent admirer of Nature Cure. He was literally hated by the orthodox medicos for his outspoken condemnation of their methods. His book *Pulmonary Tuberculosis* was the outcome of an extensive study as well as his own personal experience; therein he has gathered together telling pronouncements from a great many authorities, supporting his own stand and refuting that of the orthodox medicos. He advocated a line of treatment which differs little from the naturotherapic method.

The bacteriological approach to consumption is all the more unreasonable, because in most cases consumption begins and proceeds on its course for quite a long time, without the supposed causative germ being present at all. Consumption gives the lie to the germ theory. It is a telling proof of the naturotherapic teaching that germs are products of disease and never its cause.

What the medicos use for 'massacreing' the tubercle bacilli (streptomycin etc.) are all agents of destruction. The more often they are used, the more inevitable is death, preceded by a long period of terrible suffering. Such suffering is needless.

Those who have been glibly "accepting" that the BCG vaccine would "protect" them may like to know the findings of a seven-and-a-half-year study recently conducted by the Indian Council of Medical Research (ICMR) with financial assistance from the World Health Organisation and the Centre for Disease Control of the U.S. Public Health Service.

The Rs. 35 crore trial, "the biggest in the history of tuberculosis prevention", was launched in 1968 and it involved the entire population of 209 villages of Chingleput district and the town 40 kilometres west of Madras in South India. During the three years from 1968 to 1971, some 200,000 persons older than one month were vaccinated with BCG. Another 80,000 were used as unvaccinated "controls". For the next seven and a half years both the vaccinated and the unvaccinated persons were followed up at regular intervals.

The Chingleput trial was a "double-blind" study — to root out any bias that might creep into the assessment. Nobody working on the project knew which group was the vaccinated one and which the control one. They only knew some code numbers. The key to the code was with the ICMR.

At the end of 1978 when the results were analysed, it was found that the incidence of new cases of tuberculosis was surprisingly higher (though statistically insignficant) among the BCG-vaccinated group. After considering various reasons for this "surprising" finding, the project authorities concluded that "BCG did not show any protection against this becilliary disease."

So much for the Chingleput study. Now what are the risks and side-effects of BCG vaccination? The Morbidity and Mortality Weekly Report (for the week ended June 1, 1979), published by the U.S. Department of Health, Education and Welfare, observed that full, lasting protection from BCG vaccination could not be assured. The report also listed the risks and side-effects of BCG vaccination in the following terms:

"BCG vaccine has been associated with adverse reactions including severe or prolonged ulceration at the vaccination site, lymphadenitis and — very rarely — osteomyelitis, lupoid reactions, disseminated BCG infection, and death. Available data on adverse reactions do not necessarily pertain to the vaccines currently licensed in the U.S.A. and the reported frequency of complications has varied greatly, depending in part on the extent of the surveillance effort, from 1% to 10% depending on the vaccine, the dosage, and the age of the vaccinees. Osteomyelitis has been reported to occur in 1 per 1,00,000 vaccinees, although limited information indicates that *with newborns it may be higher.* Disseminated BCG infection and death are very rare (1-10 per 10,000,000 vaccinees) and occur almost exclusively in children with impaired immune responses."

Besides administering drugs, medicos also feed the patients wrongly. Their view is that, since consumption is a "wasting" disease, it can be "countered" only by feeding the patient, using the "most nourishing" foods, containing the maximum of protein.

starch, sugar and fat. The patient is induced to take such foods — egg, meat, milk and the like — in addition to the regular meals consisting of cereals and grams or pulses, with *some* vegetables. At first the patient is able to assimilate at least a part of this food, puts on weight, and is said to be "on the road to recovery". But, in a real case of consumption, the gain in weight is only temporary. It is lost again, when Life gets exhausted by the repeated demands on its powers of assimilation. If a patient is in an allopathic sanatorium, he is discharged at this stage, after which he goes home, where he dies in a few months. For this the "wicked tubercle bacilli" are blamed. Really, it is the medical profession that should be blamed. The food that is given is not only too heavy in quantity but it is also *negative* — highly deficient in the essences that are needed for aiding the elimination of foreign matter. Less food, taken less often, but consisting almost entirely of positive items, is what is needed for making a cure possible.

Nature Cure treatment of not only pulmonary tuberculosis but of other types of tuberculosis as well should be on the following lines.

In the first phase of the treatment, lasting for two to four weeks, the patient should take the non-violent enema daily. In the mornings, he should also take a sun bath followed by a stimulating wet pack (or clay pack). The stimulating wet pack (or clay pack) could be repeated in the afternoon and late in the evening. The patient could be allowed to live, as much as possible, in the open air, or in a very well-ventilated place. During this period, he should be on an approach to fasting.

Some definite improvement in the patient's health level may be seen at the end of the first phase. Thereafter, for about four to six weeks, he could be allowed to take raw salads and cooked vegetables twice a day, with either tender coconut water or Sattvic herbal juices in the morning and in the afternoon. Instead of abdominal wet packs, the spinal bath could be taken during this phase. The enema and sun bath are to be continued.

At the end of the second phase, it is quite likely that there will be a healing crisis, which should be treated as acute disease.

In the third phase of the treatment, the individual could be allowed to take a little cereal at night, with raw salads and conservatively cooked vegetables. The rest of the diet programme must be the same as in the second phase. Spinal baths, sun baths and enema could be continued daily. At this stage also, there may be some healing crises.

By following this programme, the patient can recover his health to a great extent in six to twelve months' time. Therafter, he should follow the Law of Vital Economy in his daily life to improve his health progressively.

## Cancer

Cancer was rare till nearly the end of the 19th century. In the present century, and especially during the past two or three decades, its incidence has been increasing. Recently, the World Health Organsiation warned that soon a "cancer epidemic" might engulf the Third World countries.

It is accepted by everyone that cancer is caused by cigarette smoking. There are various other cancer-producing substances, carcinogens as they are called, in the modern world, viz., pesticides, insecticides, diesel fumes, chemical pollutants in the air, etc.

Cancer, being a destructive disease can be developed by a person only if he has been assiduously prepared himself for it by indulging in unhygienic living habits day in and day out, consuming stimulants. sedatives, traquillisers, etc., and repeatedly suppressing acute and chronic diseases by drugs, etc.

No cell in the body will grow abnormally so long as it is healthy. It is the unhealthy cell, the extremely unhealthy cell — which can come into being *only* in a person violating the Law of Life in ever so many respects — that can play the role of cancer cell, acting as a focus for drawing all types of poisons towards it to grow abnormally and ultimately develop into a tumour.

A tumour is a neoplasm (abnormal new growth of tissue) — a mass of new tissue which persists and grows independently of its surrounding structures and which has no physiological use. Obviously, it can grow only in a person who is leading a reckless life, violating all Laws of Life and not in a healthy individual.

There are various 'types of tumours, e.g., adenoma, lipoma. haematoma, carcinoma, chondroma, paraganglioma, epithileoma, fibroma, sarcoma, folloiculoma, hyloma, myxoma, etc. but these terms only indicate either the location where the tumour is growing and/or its nature and nothing more. All types of tumours are just foreign matter. rather serious toxic matter, unwanted by the body and likely to hinder, or even actually hindering normal physiological activities.

Tumours are generally sought to be divided into two categories — benign tumours and malignant tumours. The former are considered to be 'innocent' while the latter are termed 'serious. To determine whether a tumour is a 'benign' one or a malignant one, a test known as 'biopsy' is done. Biopsy is a process in which a small piece of the concerned tissue is taken out and examined microscopically to detect the presence of abnormal cells.

Now, is biopsy necessary or desirable? If a biopsy is conducted, will it lead to any complications? In our view, biopsy is not desirable. Our question is a fundamental one. What for is biopsy done? Obviously, to find out whether the tumour is a benign or malignant one. Suppose after biopsy it is found that the tumour is a benign one, is it worth keeping inside the body? *What is the need for doing biopsy when it is conceded that both benign and malignant tumors are unwanted growths, having no physiological use?* As will be pointed out a little later, there is a sensible, natural, drugless way to get rid of the tumour — whether benign or malignant — and the sooner the patient adopts it the better it will be for him.

Even medicos agree that biopsy is an accelerator of cancer. John H. Tobe, in his book *How to Prevent and Gain Remission from Cancer,* refers to an extract from *JM's Nutritional Review* (Vol. 22), where one woman quotes her doctor as saying:

> "The only conclusive way to establish whether or not malignant tissue is present is by biopsy. However, biopsy requires cutting into the tumour which may result in releasing cancer cells throughout the body. For that reason we do not take a biopsy or conduct any surgical procedure. Nor do we treat with radiation because much good tissue is destroyed along with the cancerous cells and side-effects can, in some cases, be very damaging to the health of the body...."

The poisons inside the tumour — there is nothing else inside it — are locked up, as it were, inside a thick membrane covering it all over. When, during a biopsy, the thick membrane over it is cut, *you have literally opened the Pandora's box!* Now, there would be a free flow of the poisons from within the tumour to the rest of the body, whereas in the earlier condition prior to the biopsy, encased as the tumour was inside a thick membrane, such outflow of poisons would not have been possible.

*Biopsy can even turn a benign tumour into a malignant one before long. And satellite tumours can also be formed after the biopsy.*

So, biopsy is neither necessary nor desirable, and it can lead to further complications.

Now, what leads to the formation of a tumour inside the body? John H. Tobe in his book mentioned above says:

"I will list here what I believe to be the most common causes of cancer in order of their importance:

1. Chemical additives in food.
2. Refined and fragmented food.
3. Smoking.
4. A heavy protein diet.
5. Excessive use of dairy products.
6. All commercial oils and fats (refined) (especially when heated and reheated).
7. *Diethylstilbesterol.
8. Hormones (contraceptive pills and medicines).
9. Hydrogenated oil as found in many foods.
10. Sugar in any form, including molasses.
11. Nitrates or nitrites added to food.
12. Monosodium glutamate used in food and tobacco.
13. Saccharin and other forms of artificial sweeteners.
14. Biopsies and other forms of surgery.
15. Pollutants, occupational and environmental.
16. X-rays and radium exposures.
17. Cosmetics, detergents and soaps.
18. Water, cholorinated and fluroidated, or otherwise contaminated.
19. Aluminium.

"All of the above either destroy, prevent or interfere with the body's normal cellular regenerative process... and this, in my opinion, is cancer."

We have come across numerous cases of leukaemia (blood cancer) even in fairly young children. In practically every case, it was found that before the birth of the child, the mother had been exposed to repeated X-radiation.

It has also been observed that an unhealthy state of mind habouring greed, lust, avarice, jealousy over the years can also cause cancer.

What to do if a person has already developed such a tumour? Without going in for biopsy, even if the existence of such a tumour is only suspected within the body, let the patient start living hygienically. It has been seen in numerous cases that adoption of an approach to fasting or even the adoption of progressive fasting has led to the 'autolysis' of the tumour. The patient regains his/her health before long, but, again, we repeat let this be done before opening the Pandora's box, before biopsy.

As, in Nature Cure we "do not fight the disease with poisons" but aim at building up the health level of the patient suffering from cancer in tune with the Laws of life, we recommend health culture programme suggested earlier for the tubercular patient. This programme will enable the patient to improve his health considerably. The perversions in the body chemistry (which really had been the cause of his developing a tumour or cancer) having been removed by his hygienic living, he can feel normal in every sense of the term, in six to twelve months' time. Wisdom decrees that he should stay cured by sticking to the principles of Nature Cure.

## Helpful Hints

Destructive disease being a chronic disease with a fatal tendency, the hints given for the latter are equally applicable in the treatment of the former. But because these diseases belong to the third and last stage of the disease progression, there must be greater restriction of the diet. Also, there must be more stringent observance of Nonviolence in every possible way, since the least violence will prove fatal to life. Long fasts are not to be thought of in the beginning and for a considerable time, until the general health improves. Negative foods must be completely excluded until definite improvement is established, and thereafter they must be used sparingly. There is no room in these cases for even one substantial meal in a day though in some cases limited rations of solid food may be given cautiously. For here the underlying dyspepsia is far more advanced, and the nervous system far more weakened than during the previous stage. A patient who takes two substantial meals a day, suffering from one of these conditions, is practically certain to die from failure of vital power. Also hungerless eating is dangerous to life; if hunger cannot be revived by repeated short fasts, or by a close approach to fasting, it would mean that the patient is fated to die.

Immersion baths of a long duration, in comfortably warm water, would do good to the patient. These may be concluded with moderately cold baths or simply with baths at blood heat level kept up long enough to normalise the circulation. To the water of the immersion bath may be added juices of mild, Sattvic herbs. Sufficient precaution against chills must be taken if the weather be too cold for comfort. In the immersion bath the patient may remain as long as he finds it pleasant. If the weather is not sufficiently warm he would do well to remain in bed, well wrapped up for 10 to 15 minutes, or until his skin function is fully restored. The milder methods of sun bathing, water cure and exercise should be used in preference to the more strenuous ones. Also, there must be the fullest use of pure, cool, or even cold air in breathing. To ensure the best results the patient should lie on a cot in the shade of a tree during the warmer part of the day, except when basking or taking a sunbath. He must see to it that his bodily warmth is maintained almost all the time, especially when the weather is colder than he can tolerate. In the latter case he must make sufficient use of warm clothing and woollen blankets or quilts, but without depriving himself of access to light and air to the needed extent. An important caution is not to overdo the treatment. The middle path is the safest as well as the most profitable one. This caution applies to exercise also. On the other hand, absolute rest in bed, as advised by allopaths, may be harmful. An undisturbed mental state should be maintained.

Destructive diseases by their very nature involve wasting of the human cells and tissues. It takes quite some years to cure them radically. The patient must accept the fact that despite his best efforts he cannot attain 100% health. A certain degree of health is lost for ever, necessitating some loss of active life. This necessitates a rescheduling of the work and other activities of the patient

# TWENTY-FIVE

# Who Can Benefit the Most from Nature Cure?

There are many people who think that Nature Cure is very slow in producing results and therefore it cannot be of any practical utility to those leading a busy life. Their argument is that if an executive — or the busier social worker or yogi — were to have a severe headache, fever, high blood pressure or some such complaint and if he were to keep away from medication of every type, he would be frequently 'compelled' to cancel his engagements at very short notice, causing inconvenience to others. They contend that the busy executives, etc., are 'compelled' to take to medication or resort to the use of stimulants, etc., only to see that their commitments are fulfilled on time, even if they happen to be unhealthy or suffering physically.

Such arguments, which appear to have a lot of force behind them, are advanced by people who have no clear conception of the Laws of Life. Let us go deeper into this subject.

Nature Cure is not slow. It may look as if drugs of different types give immediate symptomatic relief to the sufferers, perhaps even enabling them to get up and move about, "attending" to their various engagements. But the questions for serious consideration are: 1) Is it desirable or safe to seek symptomatic relief, without improving one's level of health? 2) Are not the drugs taken into the system injurious in the long run? Answers to both these questions have been given in the earlier chapters and they need not be repeated here. If the busy executives are so much duty conscious, they owe it to themselves and to the nation that they should all the time maintain their health at a high level, by living in tune with the Laws of

Nature. They should clearly understand that it would not be possible for them to discharge their duties effectively without having good health and that drug-takers can never enjoy such health at any time. The same applies to the social worker, the politician, the yogi and the sannyasin.

When drugs cannot cure and when Nature alone can, there is no meaning in the busy ones saying that Nature Cure is slow.

## Patients Having Acute Diseases

It has been seen in practice that in cases of acute complaints, Nature Cure methods, applied non-violently, restore health sometimes within a few hours. Cure does not take much time, as is feared by those who have never practised these methods.

## For Chronics

As for chronic and degenerative conditions, medicos admit that they are powerless. Natural healing has to its credit tens of thousands of radical cures of persons who were once sufferers from chronic and degenerative conditions. The cures came about within a reasonable period of time.

It does and it should take time to put a chronic or advanced chronic patient back to normal health. The restrictions imposed on him during the period of treatment are for his own benefit. If he is advised to live on vegetables, or even raw juices, if he is advised to give up drugs, stimulants and sedatives, it is not with a view to weakening him or to turning him into an ascetic.: *We do not advocate asceticism.*

When the patient loses weight, during the course of the Nature Cure treatment, many people around him start offering their 'condolences' to him. Poor souls! they mistake weight for health!

Often enough, after some recovery, the patient feels better, but then his old cravings and "tastes" return. And when we tell him *not* to indulge in the perversions of the past, he feels sorry. He does not carry on the further programme cheerfully or with understanding. In his anxiety to recover soon, he starts consulting other people, and sometimes even astrologers.

## Conviction Needed

Not a superficial adoption of Nature Cure methods at the physical level but a strong conviction in the Basic Truth underlying the Science of Nature Cure is needed to effect a radical cure within a short time. Persons who lack this conviction and are carried away by the whims and fancies of the so-called 'well-wishers' around them, suffer much. *The iron in the will is more important than the iron in the blood.*

While all patients who take to Nature Cure want to benefit the most from it, it is seen that some benefit very quickly, some others take a long time to benefit, and a few do not benefit at all. One question that is often asked of us: Why are not *uniform* results achieved in every case?

## Two Categories of Patients

Of the patients that turn to Nature Cure, there are two categories: 1) Those who are *not interested* in the Philosophy of Nature Cure and whose mind is 'itching' to return to their old ways of living as soon as they regain some health through Nature Cure; and 2) Those who are mentally, and even spiritually, ready to receive the knowledge enshrined in the Science of the Life Natural, and adopt its way of Life all through.

*The first category of patients would benefit the least.* Every time they revert to their environmental ways of living, they enervate themselves more and more. On every subsequent occasion when they switch back to Nature Cure for a short while their Vital Power will be less than on the previous occasion and their Vital response to Nature Cure methods will be progressively less. Such patients bring disrepute to the Nature Cure movement.

Of the second category of patients, who form a minority, there are two sub-divisions; (i) the strong and (ii) the not so strong.

Realising their personal responsibility, the strong ones take to a changed life-style, in harmony with Nature's Laws, totally and happily. Understanding that their changed life-style is normal living, they overcome all obstacles and opposition (posed by their relatives and friends) and go steadily towards the Goal of Health, never looking back. *They benefit not only quickly but the most.*

The not-so-strong are 'intellectually' convinced of the rightness of, and the advantages to be gained by, living in tune with Nature's Laws; they find it rather difficult to break away from years of conventional living and to change their whole way of life. Such persons start the Nature Cure treatment full of hope and enthusiasm but soon 'find' that their new way is not as easy as they had imagined it to be. They find their life beset with difficulties and temptations of all sorts. They find it difficult to acquire a taste for the simple, natural, whole foods recommended for adoption by health seekers, in the Science of Nature Cure. They find it very uncomfortable to face a healing crisis. As their own conviction is not a strong one, they find that their difficulties are increased by the environment, home influence and occupational problems. Often they express their desire to avoid "inconvenience and annoyance or even active opposition, in home and the social circles".

Such patients carry on with the Nature Cure methods much better than patients of the first category. If, with a little effort on their own part and with some effort put in by the Nature Cure adviser they begin to discover new and positive pleasure and progress which more than compensate them for the 'sacrifices' they have to make, they can benefit far better. Let them realise that a fuller, healthier and happier life lies ahead, where they could experience the joy of living, day after day.

# TWENTY-SIX

# Why Only Basic Nature Cure

The question is sometime raised whether "drugless" systems other than those not included in the sixfold system of Nature Cure dealt with in the preceding pages of this book may or may not be considered as integral parts of Nature Cure. The answer is that there are no other branches of Nature Cure besides. Mental Healing, Fasting Cure, Air Cure (air baths and Pranayama), Sun Cure, Water Cure and Positive Diet.

The methods of treatment the questioner may have in mind are Chromopathy, Osteopathy, Electrotherapy, Magnetotherapy, etc. Some people think that Homeopathy may also be considered as a branch of Nature Cure. These systems of treatment are based on the maintenance of the distinction between patient and doctor, because in practising them, one cannot be one's own doctor. These systems are highly technical and difficult to master. It also happens that in many of them doctors disagree regarding diagnosis and the proper method of treatment in particular cases.

In Nature Cure are included only those methods which can be employed by the patient himself on himself as his own doctor after a thorough study and a few trials. It is therefore the only universal system of Cure. The others are outside the sixfold system. It may be said that they are drugless methods and therefore may be legitimate aids in Nature Cure. This depends upon the degree to which they respect the principle of Non-violence.

## Deep X-Ray and Ultra-violet Therapies

It is claimed by some that deep X-ray and ultra-violet therapies are good, because these too are drugless. Being violent and harmful to the patient in the long run, whatever their "short-term benefits" might be, these methods should not be employed by any Nature Cureist.

## Osteopathy

We were told by an European patient who has had experience of osteopathy that this treatment should be had from a thoroughly competent operator. Such persons are however few, because the practice requires the pre-existence of a natural skill which is not easy to acquire. We were also told by the same person that the spinal bath produced the same effect as the osteopathic treatment. From this we may conclude that for those who take the spinal bath, osteopathy is not necessary.

We also learn from Dr Lindlahr that the benefits we can obtain from osteopathy come of their own accord to the follower of Nature Cure in course of time.

## Chromopathy

The natural way of applying the Colour Cure is to pass sun's rays through green leaves. Such rays are useful in the treatment of eye defects and in sun baths. The rays are of universal value and dispense with the requirement of diagonsis for discovering what particular colour a patient having a particular complaint might need. What will the chromopath do if the patient has a number of complaints, each "requiring" a different colour of the sun?

The professional Nature Cureist who practices chromopathy as a means of earning money may be able to show "spectacular results" But the treatment aims at 'relief' of particular symptoms and so cannot be relied upon for a redical cure.

## Homeopathy

About homeopathy it is enough to say that it has only served as a halfway house between the systems of Violence and Non-violence. Its so-called philosophy falls far short of the true philosophy of Nature Cure. Its founder, Dr Hahnemann, believed that "Nature is a poor healer". He thought that she needs to be helped by means of his minute dose of drugs which he called 'similars'. The hygienic system that Basic Nature Cure is come into existence because some of its pioneers, who were hopelessly sick, failed to get a radical cure, not only by allopathy by also by homeopathy.

## Acupuncture

As for acupuncture, it has of late become a craze and even many allopaths in the west have started taking to it. Allopaths seem to have adopted it as they consider it a "potentially cheap and safe form of treatment for relieving some types of pain". Even for this restricted purpose of providing relief from pain, there is a different view. In the *Journal of the American Medical Association* (1975: 232: 1133) it has been pointed out that acupuncture is no more effective than the placebo in the relief of chronic pain! We shall not bother here about whether acupuncture can afford the much-needed relief from pain to patients and/or whether the system can even 'cure' diseases. Our fundamental objection to it is that it is a highly technical system and cannot be mastered by everyone. The art of acupuncture depends on knowing precisely which point to stimulate in a given disease. It sounds as simple as knowing which keys to press on a typewriter; in fact, however, a considerable knowledge of the human anatomy and physiology is needed before acupuncture can be practised satisfactorily. If an inexperienced person practises acupunture on a patient, the latter's condition may well get worse! As a sane and safe way of obtaining relief from pain acupuncture is clearly ruled out. It also involves violence to the human organism.

## Magnetotherapy

Magnetotherapy too is violent and the relief it induces in the patient is a symptomatic one. It cannot improve the health level of the patient, as it clearly overlocks the Law of Cause and Effect.

## Electrotherapy & Reflexotherapy

The same objection would hold good in regard to electrotherapy and reflexotherapy.

## Auto-Urine Therapy

What is known as 'auto-urine therapy' is bandied about as Nature Cure by many. Urine is an excretion of the human body containing waste products. To consider it as 'Natural' medicine' is illogical, to use the mildest of terms. To say that the term 'living waters' or 'water of life' found in some Christian scriptures refers to urine and to recommend the drinking of one's own urine on the strength of the 'correctness' of such an interpretation, is again wrong ethically as no scripture would permit the intake of dirt and filth.

## Yoga

A word in passing, about Yoga. If the term 'Yoga' means *simple asanas* or the sane and time-tested principles enunciated in Gyana Yoga, Raja Yoga, Karma Yoga or Bhakti Yoga, we would have no objection to its practice. Any person well or ill may do these asanas, non-violently and well within his capacity or undertake any other type of Yoga, provided he has understood its principles laid down in the Yogic scriptures. But when, in the name of Yoga, violent exercises and *Kriyas,* such as *jala neti, sutra neti, kunjal* etc. are taught, we have to point out that such methods can have no place in Basic Nature Cure.

## Law of Force Vs. Force of Law

The various drugless systems referred to above appear to be mostly concerned with giving immediate symptomatic relief to patients, ignoring the Law of Cause and Effect and the Law of Dual Effects. We could say that it is through the Law of Force that the practitioners of these systems seek to provide relief to their patients. The Law of Force is the law of the jungle. Any system that tries to work against the Law of Cause and Effect and the Law of Dual Effects cannot help the living organism to become better and holier in mind. We, the Natural Hygienists, believe in the Force of Law. Anyone who wants to maintain his health or improve it, has to live in tune with the Laws of Life, which are unchangeable, immutable, inviolable. Basic Nature Cure, or Natural Hygiene, has codified these Laws of Life, so that people could easily understand them and follow them in their daily lives.

## Definition of Basic Nature Cure

The reader might want to know what the term Basic Nature Cure precisely connotes. Here it is defined:

Basic Nature Cure or Natural Hygiene is that branch of the Science of Life which deals with the care of the Organism in a State of Dis-ease or Disease. It recognises that there is a LAW OF HEALTH which is the LAW OF CURE and that by OBEDIENCE TO THIS LAW, BOTH HEALTH AND HEALING ARE OBTAINED. It includes all HYGIENIC MEASURES such as proper dieting, fasting, rest and relaxation, exercise (active, corrective and recreational), Pranayama, sun-bathing and hydro-therapy, which form part of the fivefold food medicine.

212

There is no place in this science for drugs of any kind or for electrical, mechanical or other applications or so-called aids which ultimately impair or endanger health. Non-violence to the human organism is accepted as basic principle governing the application of all Nature Cure measures advocated herein."

So, let no one consider acupuncture, acupressure, electrotherapy, magnetotherapy, etc., as parts of Nature Cure.

The supreme excellence of the system known as Basic Nature Cure or Natural Hygiene lies in the fact that herein we do not seek to cure disease by direct attack, but by raising the patient's health level. That this is the proper policy to follow will be evident to the reader who has studied the book with due attention. Here, in this system, we advocate Self-reliance. *You should become your own doctor and not rely upon others.*

Let the Science of Basic Nature Cure be studied in depth by every health-seeker, by at least one member in every family, and let everyone become health-conscious.

Let the Truth embodied in the succeeding chapter on 'THE LIGHT WITHIN be remembered all the time by every health seeker.'

Let none be misled by vested interests! Let Truth prevail!

# TWENTY-SEVEN

# The Light Within

Whence did we get the understanding which is the life and soul of this unique science? Whence shall we get further light on its dark areas whereby it will become more perfect?

The author can say with a clear conscience that what he learnt from external sources — from books and periodicals — was very little. Fresh light was thrown on the problems that arose from time to time from that mysterious source, the Light Within, of which we are told in the *Bhagvad Gita* and the *Vedantas*. Later, the author found that nearly the same knowledge had also come to seekers of hygienic truth elsewhere. He has the impression that the latter obtained it from the self-same Source, whatever they might call it.

For those not familiar with the wisdom of the *Gita* and the *Vedantas* the author would mention the name of a western interpreter of this wisdom, Emerson, who gave it out in his inspired essay on *The Over-Soul*. A study of this profound writing will be an eye-opener to those who are not satisfied with the twilight of wisdom which is all they have had so far. The essay should be read slowly and patiently many times until the truths revealed in it are clearly understood. The reader will obtain confirmation of what is said here on this point, namely, that the Guiding Principle of Life and Mind is this Over-Soul (Paramatma), spoken of in Vedantic Philosophy as the Self. This is the Light Within, to whose guidance we must unreservedly submit ourselves, because what we consider as ourselves is not really different from Him. It is not demanded of every follower to accept this teaching. What we say is that He that has this understanding, is in a better mental condition to follow the Natural Way more faithfully and successfully. The Oversoul is the ultimate source of all right knowledge. The more thoroughly the mind becomes receptive to this Source, the more accurately it (the mind) understands the principles of this Science. The mind becomes free from all outside authority. That this freedom is absolutely necessary will be seen from the fact that these "authorities" contradict one another.

## Self Reliance

Freedom from all external support is the secret of true success in life, as taught by the first of all law givers, Manu who said: "All dependence on others is misery, dependence on one self alone is happiness." Herein we should remember the explanation given by Bhagavan Ramana Maharshi, that true self-reliance is the same as reliance on God, who is the Oversoul spoken of by Emerson. It is not proper for the follower to allow himself to be exploited by self-styled authorities who, being human, are almost certain to be ignorant on points that are too subtle for them to understand. We have said already that nearly all these "authorities" are unaware of the need for Non-violence in the practice of this Divine Science. The true teacher is one who seeks to liberate the pupil from dependence on others by showing him that this true source of knowledge and guidance is within.

Reliance on books should be for a time, not for ever, because they are only sign-posts on the road to Truth. Books impart to the reader only as much of Truth as the authors have realised themselves. Few are the authors who grow wiser with time and are able to write better books. Most of them are held fast in the maze of their own inconclusive interpretations of life's experiences. The facts observed in the course of their experiences may be true, but the reader must verify them by his own experience and then interpret them, in his own way, subject to guidance from within.

## Revelations From Within

The revelations from within are progressive. No one should assume that he has learned everything and that he has no need to hearken to the Inner Voice any more. He who does so may be said to be suffering from mental rheumatism, if not something worse. The follower should keep his mind always open to new truths coming to him from any source from without, or from within; he must ever be ready at short notice to march forward to a new and better knowledge through experiments on such lines as may be indicated by his own Inner Guide. As taught by Shri Ramakrishna Paramahamsa, his motto must ever be: "Keep going forward always, make not your permanent Home anywhere on the Way.

# Instructions for Preparing the Spinal Bath Tub

For the benefit of the readers who wish to procure a spinal bath tub in their place itself, the method of fabricating the tub (adult size) is given hereunder.

Adult Size

Draw the above diagram on a white cardboard with instructions given below.

| | | | |
|---|---|---|---|
| A — B | | A — C | |
| | = 48 inches | | = 36 inches |
| C — D | | B — D | |

A B C D is a rectangular galvanized iron sheet of 4 ft. × 3 ft. in size of 22 gauge.

Mark from B at a distance of 12″ E along AB and H along BD. Similarly, mark at a distance of 12″ from D,G along BD and F along CD.

Similarly, from C mark at a distance of 12″ J along AC and from A at a distance of 12 I along AC.

Mark from A at a distance of 15″ along AB and from C at the same distance Y along CD.

Join XY, EF, IH and JG. The resulting rectangle, QRST, is the base of the tub. Mark at a distance of 6″ from IG, and similarly P from J, M from E, K from H,L from G, and N from F.

Mark U at a distance of 11½″ from X similarly, Mark V from Y.

Join UQ PS,NT, LT, KR, and MR, OQ and PS are equal in length.

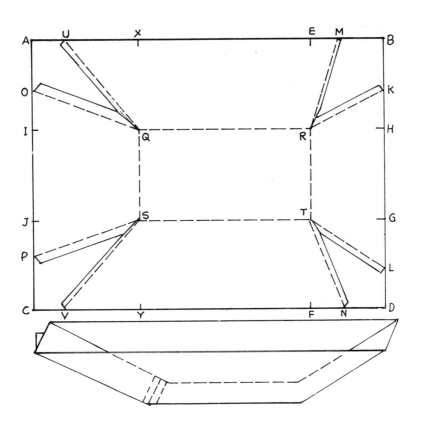

Join UQ and SV

Parallel to QO, SP, RK, and TL and ¾″ apart from them draw lines as shown in the top figure.

Similarly parallel to VS, UQ, MR and TN and ½″ apart from them draw lines as shown in the top figure.

Study the diagram well with the help of the instructions given above. Do not cut the model before making the diagram on the galvanized iron sheet as explained above. Cut along straight lines, fold along dotted lines after making light creases with the end of the scissors, join the flaps by pasting them and you will find the model complete.

The top figure gives the plan. The bottom figure represents the perspective view of the tub. Note the side AC is more sloping than the side BD. Side AC is the headside and BD is the leg side.

An iron rod 5/16″ in round section is fixed all round the edge, PO, UM. KL, and NV The rod must be one single piece starting and finishing at a point between M and E.

Two pairs of legs are provided by fixing with rivets a flat bar ½″ × 2″ at a distance of 1″ inwards one from QS and the other from RT. The edges of the flat bar are turned down as shown for support on the ground.

Two handles are provided, one between I and J and the other between H and G.

Read, and re-read the instructions several times until you are able to understand the drawing.

# INDEX